REASONS TO KILL

Rebels in Eden: Mass Political Violence in the United States

Left Turn: Origins of the Next American Revolution

Alchemists of Revolution: Terrorism in the Modern World

Comrade Valentine: The True Story of Azef the Spy

*When Jesus Became God: The Struggle to Define Christianity
During the Last Days of Rome*

*Aristotle's Children: How Christians, Muslims, and Jews Rediscovered Ancient
Wisdom and Illuminated the Middle Ages*

*Thus Saith the Lord: The Revolutionary Moral Vision of
Isaiah and Jeremiah*

REASONS
to KILL

Why Americans Choose War

————

RICHARD E. RUBENSTEIN

Bloomsbury Press

New York   Berlin   London

Lyrics from "The Ballad of High Noon" reprinted with permission of Patti Washington Music and Catharine Hinen Music/Universal Music.

Published by Bloomsbury Press, New York

All papers used by Bloomsbury Press are natural, recyclable products made from wood grown in well-managed forests. The manufacturing processes conform to the environmental regulations of the country of origin.

LIBRARY OF CONGRESS CATALOGING-IN-PUBLICATION DATA

Rubenstein, Richard E.
Reasons to kill / Richard E. Rubenstein.—1st U.S. ed.
p. cm.
Includes bibliographical references and index.
ISBN-13: 978-1-60819-026-3 (alk. paper)
ISBN-10: 1-60819-026-9 (alk. paper)
1. United States—History, Military.   2. War—Moral and ethical aspects—United States.   3. United States—Military policy—Moral and ethical aspects.   4. War and society—United States.   5. Strategic culture—United States.   6. Deception—United States.   I. Title.
E181.R829 200
355.00973—dc22
2010010031

First U.S. Edition 2010

1 3 5 7 9 10 8 6 4 2

Interior design by Rachel Reiss
Typeset by Westchester Book Group
Printed in the United States of America by Worldcolor Fairfield

For Buzz and Alice Palmer

War contains so much folly, as well as wickedness, that much is to be hoped from the progress of reason; and if any thing is to be hoped, every thing ought to be tried.

—JAMES MADISON

CONTENTS

PREFACE

On September 13, 2001, two days after al-Qaeda's assaults on the World Trade Center and the Pentagon, I found myself unexpectedly at the center of a local media storm.

The previous day, a producer at the local NBC-TV channel in Washington, D.C., had asked me to appear on the *Morning News* program to talk about the 9/11 attacks. Since I had been writing about terrorism since the 1980s and was thinking about al-Qaeda and the meaning of the attacks, I quickly agreed. I presented myself at the station at 6:30 A.M., wondering how many people would be watching Channel 4 so early in the morning.

The anchor introduced me as an expert on political violence and conflict resolution. Then he asked, in a tone both baffled and angry, what kind of people could have performed such senseless, cowardly acts. I took a deep breath and answered. The slaughter of thousands of innocent people was obviously an unforgivable atrocity. But describing terrorist acts as senseless or cowardly didn't help us to understand them or deal with them intelligently. The al-Qaeda attacks were motivated not just by malice and fanaticism, I said, but also by opposition to U.S. policies in Iraq, Saudi Arabia, and Israel/Palestine. Usama bin Laden had made that clear in his public statements. We certainly needed to bring the perpetrators to justice, but we also needed to think about why our policies in the Muslim nations were generating so much hatred and anger.

The whole interview took two minutes at most. I left the studio wishing that there had been more time to discuss the issues but happy enough with the content and tone of my remarks. By the time I arrived at my office half an hour later, the telephone was ringing nonstop. One caller was my boss: Alan Merten, the president of George Mason University. "Rich, I want you to know that your job is safe, even though twenty people have called in the last fifteen minutes to demand your head. Some even threatened to withdraw their children from classes or to cancel donations to the university."

"What did you tell them?" I asked.

"I told them that a professor's duty is to tell the truth as he sees it, and a university's duty is to give him the chance to tell it. But what the hell did you say on television?"

I thanked Dr. Merten for standing up for me and gave him a brief report. One cause of the mini-firestorm, we agreed, was that most people were still reeling from the traumatic events of 9/11. Before they could think about the causes or implications of the tragedy, they needed to recover from their shock, mourn their losses, and vent their anger. I had probably spoken too soon about issues most people were not yet ready to consider.

Even now, however, this is not an easy subject to discuss. Many people still perceive the terrorists who perpetrated the attacks as devils, which removes them from the universe of historical causes and effects. Satanic figures do evil because they *are* evil, period. Talking about *why* they do what they do not only seems senseless but also exposes the speaker to the charge of "sympathy for the devil."

During the years after the 9/11 attacks, as the United States became embroiled in war first in Afghanistan and then in Iraq, I found myself repeating in various ways what I had said on that news program. There were serious reasons, in addition to fanaticism and malice, that many people abroad hated and feared the United States.

But the arguments, slogans, and images used to gain our consent to war avoided identifying these reasons or considering their implications for American policies and activities abroad. Unable to look squarely at our relationships with other people, unwilling to calculate the consequences of our military adventures, we seemed to be acting almost as mindlessly as the terrorists we criticized.

What impelled me to begin this book, finally, was George W. Bush's invasion of Iraq in 2003. As the drumbeat for war grew louder in the run-up to the invasion, I found myself wondering why so many Americans, including most of Bush's critics, would willingly accept his administration's assertions that Saddam Hussein was in league with al-Qaeda and that he possessed weapons of mass destruction, which he was planning to use against us. Even if these charges were true (which I strongly doubted), why assume that invading and occupying Iraq was the best possible response? The UN Security Council had declined to authorize an American invasion. Why not require proof that war was the only answer before putting one's own family, friends, relatives, and countrymen in harm's way?

For me, the situation was déjà vu with a vengeance. Thirteen years earlier, when Saddam Hussein sent his armed forces into Kuwait, I chaired a discussion, broadcast on C-SPAN, on "Alternatives to War in the Gulf."[1] (As director of a conflict resolution program, I knew that many experts in my field believed that there *were* peaceful and honorable alternatives to war.) The panelists argued strongly that a U.S.-led war in the Persian Gulf would only set the stage for a future Iraq War. They agreed that Saddam could be pressured to withdraw from Kuwait without great difficulty, and that negotiations facilitated by trusted Muslim leaders could then be used to resolve the ongoing disputes between the two nations. Conflict resolution processes could also help mitigate the internal conflicts that were causing so much suffering inside Iraq. If these problems were not dealt with peacefully, they warned, the Persian Gulf would remain a hotbed of conflict and a magnet for continuing foreign intervention.

The war ordered by the first President Bush a few months later destroyed Saddam Hussein's army, crippled Iraq's infrastructure, and impoverished the Iraqi people, all without solving any of the underlying social problems that wracked that nation and the Gulf region. Now, more than a decade after the American victory, history seemed to be repeating itself. A new President Bush and his advisers informed us that Saddam was an Evil Enemy out to destabilize the region and to harm Americans. They asserted that we had a sacred right to defend ourselves against him and a moral duty to liberate his oppressed subjects; that his defeat would set a chaotic region on the road to democratic government and civil order; that U.S. interests in Iraqi oil had nothing to do with the matter; and that there was no way to achieve our objectives other than an American-led war and postwar reconstruction.

It struck me that these arguments and images were a good deal older than the Persian Gulf War—older, indeed, than the wars in Vietnam and Korea—and that they had a peculiar resonance for citizens of the world's oldest and most powerful democracy. Similar appeals had been used to convince people to support America's wars against Mexico and Spain, as well as U.S. participation in two world wars. Of course, the ghastly trauma of September 11, 2001, had something to do with the fear coursing through the country in 2003. Fear inclined many Americans to look to the authorities for protection and reliable information, and, perhaps, to seek an enemy that they *could* destroy. But that did not explain why we were so often moved to fight by arguments about self-defense, Evil Enemies, and moral obligations. I began reading to discover how these appeals had been framed in earlier times in order to discover the sources of their continuing persuasive power.

And so, here we are. As this book goes to press, American troops have been fighting abroad for the longest continuous stretch in their history—almost a decade, or longer, if one starts with the Persian Gulf War and the campaign of military and economic sanctions that followed it. To many of us, making war now seems a normal and permanent activity, even though its outrageous costs, financial, physical, psychological, and spiritual, are inflicting acute damage upon us and upon future generations. Clear thinking about military intervention is now an urgent necessity. Few tasks could be more important than to examine the rhetorical and philosophical strategies that move us to fight, explore their sources in our national culture, and consider how to make better choices when presented with reasons to take others' lives and risk our own.

Despite the striking increase in the number and duration of American wars during the past half century, only a few books have thus far responded to this challenge. Historians and social scientists still discuss the "causes of war" in individual conflicts mainly by analyzing the motives of influential policymakers. Sometimes they describe the propaganda techniques used to secure mass approval of particular wars. What they seldom do is explore the patterns of persuasion that appear and reappear in American history, and explain the reasons for their effectiveness. As a result, each time a new U.S. military intervention is proposed, we deal with the arguments used to justify collective violence as if we have never encountered them before.

This book is not the definitive answer to the question of why we so often choose war. It is an incitement to think more independently about common justifications for collective violence. I do not argue here that there is no such thing as a just war. On the contrary, I think that there are situations, although rare, when Americans may be compelled to shed their own blood and the blood of others. My fondest wish, however, is that this book and others like it will strengthen the healthy skepticism that has traditionally been such a strong component of the American character. The next time our leaders inform us that we must fight for freedom, national security, or world order; the next time they insist that there is no other way to secure our interests and defend our values than mechanized violence; the next time they try to define patriotism as a willingness to choose war, let our response be "I'm from Missouri, show me!"

I

WHY WE CHOOSE WAR

———

In 1831, when Andrew Jackson was campaigning in his first term as president and the American West ended at the Rocky Mountains, a liberal French aristocrat named Alexis de Tocqueville came to see for himself what the new society was all about. He ended his tour by composing an astonishing book called *Democracy in America*, still one of the most vivid and revealing analyses of American culture ever written. Despite the profound changes we have undergone since then, we can still recognize ourselves in his portrait, like the sixth-grader's face one recognizes as one's own in an old school yearbook.

Open de Tocqueville's book and there we are: democratic, conformist, litigious, moralistic, suspicious of government, hardworking, and jealous of wealth and privilege while craving it for ourselves. One dramatic difference, though, is immediately apparent. We seem to have lost our distaste for war. De Tocqueville described the Americans he encountered as "fond of peace, which is favorable to industry and allows every man to pursue his own little undertakings to their completion."[1] He understood, of course, that settlers along the nation's frontiers were often embroiled in conflicts with the native inhabitants they called Indians, and that the young republic had fought a war against England in 1812–15. But what impressed him most strongly was the general disinclination of America's "new men" to engage in foreign wars, and the absence among them, except for a handful of professional soldiers, of any cult of military power and glory. This was a natural consequence, he thought, of the new nation's lack of military tradition, its social egalitarianism (at least among white males), and its passion for business. Perpetual warfare was one of the social diseases of the Old World. The New World, at least in this respect, seemed far healthier.

One wonders what de Tocqueville would make of us today. In the years since *Democracy in America* appeared, the United States has fought ten major wars, conducted eighteen extended campaigns against Native American nations, and intervened abroad militarily more than twenty-five times. If one adds minor interventions, covert actions, assassinations, joint military actions, and proxy wars, these numbers explode, amounting to more than 150 seriously violent episodes since World War II.[2] No other modern nation has a more bellicose record—and our pace is accelerating. Since 1950, the United States has spent more than twenty years at war, with military operations in Korea, Indochina, Iraq, and Afghanistan killing more than a hundred thousand Americans, wounding at least five times that number, and consuming several million foreign lives. We have been fighting continuously since 2001 with no end to the violence in sight.

The question that most wants answering is not why America's leaders go to war but why we follow them into battle. Influential policymakers have many reasons for proposing to use force, ranging from economic interests to geopolitical ambitions, security concerns, ideological and moral commitments, and even efforts to win the next election. (Congressman Abraham Lincoln of Illinois famously called America's war with Mexico "a war of conquest fought to catch votes.")[3] Analysts across a broad political spectrum agree that the United States has become a global empire, and that maintaining this status in order to fulfill various imperial roles (lawgiver, police officer, development agency, etc.) is now a major motive for military intervention.[4] A voluminous literature discusses why powerful politicians and interest groups advocate war. By contrast, comparatively little has been said about the reasons ordinary citizens so often agree to fight, when it is they who pay the lion's share of the human and financial costs.[5]

Among the features of our history often overlooked is this interesting fact: from the War of 1812 to Mr. Bush's invasion of Iraq, virtually every proposed war has generated very strong opposition, sometimes amounting to a majority of citizens.[6] For reasons not well understood, this opposition generally weakens or disappears in the run-up to combat or in the war's early stages. (Occasionally, it reappears later on.) Why is this so? Do most Americans consent to make war because of patriotic sentiment or out of a habit of obedience? Do they make decisions like this rationally, or are other factors involved— for example, fear of nonconformity, paranoia about foreign enemies, or a taste for violence? In one sense, of course, the answer is "all of the above." One can find people who back wars for all sorts of reasons in a society as vast and diverse as ours. My studies convince me, though, that the reasons most likely to persuade otherwise reluctant Americans to get on the military bandwagon are those that appeal primarily to their religious or moral sensibilities. We agree to put ourselves and others in harm's way because we are convinced that the sacrifice is *justified*, not just because we have been stampeded into okaying war by devious leaders, scaremongering propagandists, or our own blood lust.

Most of this book is devoted to an exploration of the moral justifications that play a decisive role in popular decision making about matters of war and peace. Nevertheless, it is useful to begin with two common explanations for why we fight, each of which contains an important piece of the truth while obscuring or distorting the larger picture. The first of these, which I call the *innocent dupe hypothesis*, emphasizes the extent to which Americans are misled in making decisions by false or exaggerated messages disseminated by political leaders and uncritical news media. *Are* we often misled in deciding to go to war? Definitely! But this alone is not an adequate explanation of why

Americans choose to fight. The second explanation, the *frontier killer hypothesis*, traces our propensity to approve of warmaking back to the heritage of colonial settlement and continental expansion. Does this cultural heritage still play a role in our thinking? Again, the answer is "Yes, but . . ." We do continue to reproduce narratives and images derived from the white settlers' frontier experience—but American attitudes toward violence and nonviolence cannot be explained merely by invoking the spirit of Davy Crockett. Our thinking is more complex and interesting than that.

Although neither of these approaches teaches us enough about justifications for war in America, there is much to learn from each of them. We start with the innocent dupe hypothesis, as embodied by Herman Melville's fictional hero Billy Budd.

The Billy Budd Syndrome and the Record of Official Deception

The hero of Melville's famous novella *Billy Budd* is a sailor so innocent and trusting that he is unable to recognize the evil in other people. When a malicious ship's officer accuses him unjustly of treason, shock and anger strike Billy dumb. Unable to defend himself verbally, he lashes out with his fist and strikes his accuser dead. "I did not mean to kill him," Billy tells the captain. "Could I have used my tongue I would not have struck him. But he foully lied to my face and in presence of my Captain, and I had to say something, and I could only say it with a blow, God help me!"[7]

To some observers, we are a nation of Billy Budds, naïvely convinced of our own purity, uncomfortable with diplomatic speech, overly trusting of authority, and easily moved to violence by the discovery of maleficent enemies. According to these critics, all that is needed to get gullible Americans to fight is strong propaganda stating that war is required to defend the nation against vicious aggressors who cannot be dealt with in any other way. Blinded by uncritical trust in authority and conditioned to accept the assertions and promises of commercial advertising, we are said to be easy prey for manipulative politicians and biased news reports. As one recent study puts it, "Americans will always buy a war if it is skillfully sold to them."[8] Some analysts explain this apparent gullibility by emphasizing the government's power to shape public opinion in an age of news monopolies and high-tech information control. Others emphasize our Billy Budd–like inability to recognize the selfish private interests hiding behind appeals to the "national interest." All rely on the considerable evidence of manipulation of the public by politicians and interest groups using the news media to deliver pro-war messages.

Are we innocent dupes? To some extent, certainly, especially if one adds the notion of insecurity to that of innocence. Most of us are not so unworldly as Billy Budd, who was unable to recognize the malice in other people. On the contrary, we worry a lot about the bad intentions of others, and this worry makes us vulnerable to manipulation by leaders who exploit popular fears. For this reason, Americans have often been influenced, and sometimes taken in entirely, by official lies and misstatements. "Fool me once, shame on you," goes an old saying famously garbled by President George W. Bush, "fool me twice, shame on me." Yet we have gone to war many times for reasons that turned out to be dubious or deceptive. Mr. Bush's charges that Saddam Hussein was in league with al-Qaeda terrorists and that he possessed weapons of mass destruction were the latest in a long line of false accusations used to whip up popular enthusiasm for military action. Even if misleading tactics of this sort are *not* sufficient to explain our willingness to fight, it is important to keep in mind the colorful and appalling record of official misrepresentation.

A few brief examples will make this clear:

United States vs. Mexico, 1846–48. George W. Bush might have taken lessons in obfuscation from President James K. Polk, a Tennessee Democrat and an apostle of American expansionism. In 1846, Polk appeared before a joint session of Congress to declare that

"Mexico has passed the boundary of the United States, has invaded our territory and shed American blood upon the American soil . . . War exists, and, notwithstanding all our efforts to avoid it, exists by the act of Mexico herself."[9] To paraphrase Mary McCarthy, every word of this statement was a half-truth at best, including "and" and "the." Polk himself had goaded Mexico into attacking U.S. troops by sending them into disputed territory that an international court would probably have awarded to Mexico. For this reason, Congressman Abraham Lincoln of Illinois famously demanded that Polk indicate the exact "spot" where American blood was shed.[10]

Lincoln and other Whig dissidents insisted that the Mexican expedition was a war of conquest provoked by Mexico's refusal to sell the entire Southwest, including California, to the United States for pennies per acre. Polk's vaunted efforts to avoid war consisted of sending one diplomatic mission to Mexico City; predictably, the presidential envoy, Louisiana congressman John Slidell, failed to convince the Mexicans to part with one third of their entire territory. An anti-war movement including John Quincy Adams, Ralph Waldo Emerson, and Henry David Thoreau noisily denounced the conflict as an immoral land grab masterminded by southern slaveholders. But the anti-war forces remained a minority, and the ensuing struggle consumed more than thirteen thousand American lives, most of them lost to disease—the highest casualty rate suffered in any of America's foreign wars. Mexican losses, probably amounting to ten times that number, were never counted. As a result of the war, the United States acquired a vast western domain, paying less than half the previously offered price. As many critics had feared, however, these acquisitions reopened the question of whether new states should be slave or free states, leading in little more than a decade to the Civil War and its six hundred thousand dead. Looking back in his memoirs, ex-president Ulysses S. Grant, who had fought in Mexico as a young officer, called the Mexican War "one of the most unjust ever waged by a stronger against a weaker nation."[11]

United States vs. Spain, 1898. Fifty years later, public support for a war against Spain surged when an enormous explosion sank the visiting battleship USS *Maine* in Havana Harbor. More than five tons of gunpowder—ammunition for the warship's big guns—had gone up in a blinding instant, sending the forward third of the ship, where most of the crew slept, to the bottom of the harbor. Two hundred fifty-eight American sailors were killed outright; eight more would shortly die of their wounds. The next day, the bellicose assistant secretary of the navy, Teddy Roosevelt, declared, "The *Maine* was sunk by an act of dirty treachery on the part of the Spaniards."[12] The great newspapers—the sole source of mass information in a pre-electronic age—agreed. At first tentatively, then with increasing confidence, they published articles and editorials naming Cuba's Spanish overlords as the evildoers who had sunk the American ship.

In March 1898, a U.S. Navy board of inquiry operating with the primitive equipment of the day concluded that the culprit was a naval mine that had exploded under the vessel's hull. A few weeks later, Congress declared war against Spain. As American fighters stormed Cuban beaches and sank Spanish warships from Santiago to Manila Bay, the cry heard everywhere was "Remember the *Maine*! To hell with Spain!" Yet there was no evidence, then or later, of Spanish involvement in the tragedy. For months before the battleship went down, a new government in Madrid had been maneuvering frantically to avoid a war over Cuba.[13] If a naval mine *was* the cause of the explosion, the most likely suspects were rogue Spanish officers opposed to the peace negotiations or Cuban rebels attempting to involve America more deeply in their independence struggle. But no suspects were ever discovered, and it is highly unlikely that any mine sank the battleship. In 1976, a team of investigators assembled by U.S. Admiral Hyman Rickover concluded that a slow-burning fire in the vessel's stores of soft coal had ignited the gunpowder magazine and destroyed the ship. The immediate *casus belli* of America's "splendid little war" against Spain was a bum rap.[14]

United States vs. Germany (1917–18). In 1915, with a war of unprecedented destructiveness ravaging Europe, American readers were

shocked by lurid news reports of German soldiers raping nuns, killing babies, severing people's hands, and engaging in other shameful
atrocities in occupied Belgium. These stories were used to generate
an image of the Germans as bloodthirsty "Huns" and to induce the
public to abandon neutrality and support the British side in the
Great War. Although the Germans, like most occupying forces, had
undoubtedly committed violent acts against civilians, the worst of
these tales had been fabricated by British intelligence and passed
along by pro-British officials and newspapers in the United States.[15]
By this time, the Royal Navy had cut the transatlantic cables con-
necting Germany with the United States so that the British alone
would dictate what news of the war reached American shores.

One year later, Woodrow Wilson was reelected president as a
peace candidate; his campaign slogan was "He kept us out of war."
A few months later, Wilson decided to take America into the war.
Some of his reasons for doing so, like his belief that an Allied victory
would make the world "safe for democracy," he made public. Others,
such as the enormous debts owed by Britain and France to Wall
Street banks, were spoken of only behind closed doors.[16] To convert
the American people to his newfound cause, Wilson and his Committee on Public Information relied on the Belgian atrocity stories
and equally spurious accusations throwing the blame for the war exclusively upon Germany. The CPI whipped up public outrage against
the German campaign of submarine warfare targeting ships carrying goods or munitions to Allied ports but refused to publicize the
British blockade of Germany, which was causing starvation and disease throughout Central Europe. President Wilson's double standard
so dismayed Secretary of State William Jennings Bryan that Bryan
resigned his office in protest.[17]

United States vs. Germany (1941–45). World War I and its after-
math left most Americans sorely disillusioned and in no mood to
undertake another international crusade. As a result, even Franklin
D. Roosevelt, the master persuader, felt compelled to rely on deception to help mobilize a reluctant nation for combat against the fas-

*Pershing's Crusaders, 1918. U.S. Signal Corps poster distrib-
uted by the Committee on Public Information. General John
J. Pershing, commander of the American Expeditionary Forces
in World War I, sits on his charger, flanked by U.S. soldiers
and the spirits of medieval Christian crusaders. (Source:
University of North Texas Digital Library, Posters Collection.)*

cist powers. During his campaign for a third term in 1940, FDR
promised peace, as Wilson had done in 1916: "I have said this before,
but I shall say it again, and again, and again. Your boys are not
going to be sent into any foreign wars."[18] Less than one year later, in
his Navy Day speech in Annapolis, he revealed the existence of

"a secret map made in Germany by Hitler's government, by the planners of the new world order. It is a map of South America and part of Central America, as Hitler proposes to reorganize it." According to him, the map, which incorporated Latin America into the Third Reich as five new nations, revealed Germany's "design not only against South America but against the United States as well." The document was a forgery—apparently not a very good one—provided by British intelligence.[19] Commenting more generally on the way FDR gradually overcame America's anti-war sentiment prior to World War II, one sympathetic historian concluded that "he repeatedly deceived the American people during the period before Pearl Harbor . . . He was like a physician who must tell the patient lies for the patient's own good."[20]

United States vs. Vietnam (1964–73). Evidently, President Lyndon B. Johnson also thought it was "for the patient's own good" that Americans believe that the North Vietnamese had attacked two U.S. destroyers in the Gulf of Tonkin in August 1964. In fact, the Tonkin Gulf Incident was a deception that made Roosevelt's "secret map" look like a college prank.

By the summer of 1964, with a Communist-led rebellion against the government of South Vietnam rapidly gaining ground, the Johnson administration was seeking a way to justify large-scale U.S. intervention in Vietnam. Earlier that summer, South Vietnamese coastal raiders operating with CIA support had begun covertly knocking out "radar sites, fuel storage facilities, utilities, roads and bridges" in North Vietnam.[21] Simultaneously, American warships like the destroyers USS *Maddox* and USS *C. Turner Joy* were ordered to patrol the Gulf of Tonkin inside the twelve-mile limit claimed by Hanoi. On the night of August 2, after a particularly damaging South Vietnamese raid, three North Vietnamese PT boats came out looking for the perpetrators and discovered the *Maddox*, which seemed to be providing them cover. Torpedoes fired at the destroyer by the North Vietnamese missed their target. Fire from the *Maddox*'s guns damaged one PT boat, killing several crewmen, and the North Vietnamese vessels fled.

Probably in order to keep the coastal raids secret, none of these events was publicly reported. Two nights later, with a heavy storm roiling the gulf's waters, a nervous sonar operator aboard one of the two destroyers thought that he detected approaching torpedoes. The sky lit up as both U.S. ships fired their guns and launched torpedoes at an invisible enemy. The captain of the *Maddox* later attributed the report of an enemy attack to "freak weather effects and an overeager sonar man."[22] President Johnson, in private, was less gentle. "Hell," he fumed, "those dumb, stupid sailors were just shooting at flying fish."[23] That insight did not prevent the president from accusing the North Vietnamese of mounting an unprovoked attack on the destroyers and using the fictitious assault to convince Congress to write him a blank check: a joint resolution authorizing him to "take all necessary measures to repel any armed attack against the forces of the United States and to prevent further aggression."[24] Within one year, he had used this authority to send 180,000 U.S. troops to fight in Vietnam. By 1968, when Johnson decided not to run for re-election, more than half a million men and women were bogged down in a bloody war.

Since the end of the Vietnam War, the record of official misstatements has lengthened, culminating in the false charges against Saddam Hussein's regime that helped convince most Americans to support the U.S. invasion of Iraq in 2003.[25] Even so, the notion that they accept such accusations out of sheer gullibility or faith in the government seems unconvincing, especially considering the normal tendency of Americans to distrust political and commercial "sales pitches." (Consider, for example, their continued widespread skepticism about global climate change.)[26] In the case of the Iraq War, a dread of malevolent Islamism provoked by the 2001 al-Qaeda attacks surely played a key role in popular thinking, even though Saddam Hussein was no Islamist. To speak more generally, it seems clear that while erroneous or misleading charges may help to sell Americans on war, they are seldom the decisive factors inducing us to fight. Small stories such as "the Spanish sank the *Maine*," "the Communists attacked our destroyers," or "Saddam Hussein is stockpiling weapons of mass destruction" are each part of a bigger narrative about our relationship with some alleged enemy. We don't ordinarily buy into a war because we are deceived by the small stories; we allow ourselves to be deceived by accepting the broader rationale for war.

Why did most Americans support the war against Mexico? Clearly, not just because they believed President Polk's allegations, but because many favored transcontinental expansion and most considered a war against Catholic, autocratic Mexico justified. Similarly, the sinking of the *Maine* would not have had the galvanizing effect it had were it not for intense popular sympathy for Cuba's independence struggle and hatred of the cruel "Dons." Certainly, Lyndon Johnson's Tonkin Gulf Incident was a phony. Nevertheless, most Americans took the bait because they loathed Communism, believed in supporting South Vietnam against a North Vietnamese takeover, and feared the fall of other "dominos" predicted by Cold War ideologues.[27] George W. Bush's accusations against Saddam Hussein were equally specious. But Americans traumatized by the 9/11 terrorist attacks were fearful of hostile Muslims, frustrated by their own inability to find and punish al-Qaeda, and in need of a morale-restoring victory. The larger story they told themselves was the tale of an untamed globe full of wild places ("failed" or "failing" states) harboring malicious enemies of the United States, and therefore in need of forcible pacification.

Deceptive propaganda aside, something deeper in our culture was at work in all these cases, inclining Americans to respond favorably to stories that portrayed them as innocent victims of foreign aggression, God-sent liberators of the oppressed, or the indispensible guarantors of a civilized world order. How to describe this underlying stratum of ideas, attitudes, and images about America and other communities? If we are not a nation of Billy Budds, what are we?

Some commentators have answered by standing the innocent dupe approach on its head. According to them, we are a nation of frontier warriors.

NOT BILLY BUDD BUT DAVY CROCKETT?
THE FRONTIER WARRIOR HYPOTHESIS

Rather than portray Americans as naïve victims of propaganda, some scholars picture us as "natural-born killers" conditioned since frontier days to pursue our interests violently, wield destructive weapons, admire military heroes, and devalue alien lives.[28] From this perspective, Davy Crockett, who fought the Indians, won election to Congress, and died defending the Alamo against General Santa Anna, is a more relevant role model than Billy Budd. Our most powerful cultural narrative, according to this analysis, is the story of White Settlers vs. Indians. Especially when contemplating war against non-Western people, Americans unknowingly reenact a drama in which they are cast as the brave, outnumbered defenders of civilized values, circling the wagons and using their technological superiority to hold off hordes of fanatical savages. As author Robert D. Kaplan puts it, " 'Welcome to Injun Country' was the refrain I heard from troops from Colombia to the Philippines, including Afghanistan and Iraq . . . The War on Terrorism was really about taming the frontier."[29] John Brown, a U.S. Foreign Service officer who resigned his office to protest the Iraq War, carries the analogy even further:

> The methods employed by the U.S. in [the War on Terrorism] and the Indian wars are similar in many respects: using superior technology to overwhelm the "primitive" enemy; adapting insurgency tactics, even the most brutal ones, used by the opposing side when necessary; and collaborating with "the enemy of my enemy" in certain situations (that is, setting one tribe against another). What are considered normal rules of war have frequently been irrelevant for Americans in both conflicts, given their certainty that their

enemies are evil and uncivilized. The use of torture is also a feature
of these two conflicts.[30]

Clearly, some stories ingrained in a nation's culture can achieve
the status of popular myths.[31] Images of the enemy as a dangerously
uncivilized, nonwhite Other have long been deployed as part of
efforts to persuade Americans to fight.[32] Even where an enemy is
technologically advanced, the old symbols resonate. Although the
Germans were as white and Westernized as most Americans, and
German-Americans were the nation's largest single ethnic group,
posters and cartoons during World War I presented them as dark-
skinned savages. The Japanese of World War II were pictured as
loathsome yellow animals or insects.[33] And who can forget the actor
Slim Pickens waving his ten-gallon hat, shouting "Wahoo!" and riding the H-bomb cowboy-style toward its Russian target at the end
of Stanley Kubrick's *Dr. Strangelove or: How I Learned to Stop Wor-
rying and Love the Bomb*?

This being said, the frontier warrior hypothesis is no more satisfactory an answer to the question of why we choose war than the
idea of the innocent dupe. Americans are neither naïve simpletons
easily deceived by manipulative leaders nor obsessive killers compelled to reenact some violent primal scene. The role of Davy Crockett is an aspect of America's cultural heritage, not its "essence." The
Settlers vs. Indians drama represents one choice of story among a
rich variety of stories, not a cultural destiny. Even that narrative
provides us with alternative roles, one of which (realized by Boston
Tea Party revolutionaries in the 1770s and some anti-war activists in
the 1960s) is to identify with the Natives. If the nation is an "imagined community," as political theorist Benedict Anderson maintains, this means that there is more than one way to imagine it.[34]

Harvard professor Stephen Peter Rosen, a celebrator of America's
martial spirit, reveals the multiplicity of national traditions when he
argues that "the United States had two near-simultaneous found-

ings, one by Scots-Irish people ready to fight when challenged, and one by Puritans ready to use force when legally authorized." Rosen thinks that the Scots-Irish were "born fighting," an ethnic heritage reinforced by their frontier experience in both Britain and the United States, while the New England Puritans were ready to make war when their preachers declared that the cause was just. In his view, "the experiences of the Frontier and the Revolution mingled the distinct but mutually reinforcing predispositions of these two groups, producing an American national culture united in the idea that being an American citizen meant being ready to fight and die in its wars."[35]

Well . . . not really. There *is* a warrior culture in the United States with roots in the Appalachian frontier tradition that still supplies recruits to the U.S. armed forces. But it is a minority strain—a subculture—in a much richer and more conflicted mix. American society was never as united in its devotion to military duty as Rosen implies. Rather than functioning as a "reinforcing predisposition," the Puritan insistence on fighting morally defensible wars has clashed more often than not with the frontier warrior spirit. Puritanism's heirs like Abraham Lincoln denounced the Mexican-American War as unnecessary and unjust, while frontier heroes like Andrew Jackson vehemently supported it. In 1865, the neo-Puritans marched to the tune of "The Battle Hymn of the Republic" to defend the Union and end slavery, while neo-frontiersmen fought to defend the South's independence and honor against "the guv'ment." Much later, opponents of the Vietnam War often sounded like (and, in some cases, were) New England preachers, while war hawks like President Johnson spoke in Jacksonian tones about the need to demonstrate manly toughness, stand up to bullies, and defend the nation's honor. Perhaps the Scots-Irish were born to fight (although I have my doubts about this sort of stereotype), but the Puritans were trained to moralize— a different kettle of fish altogether.

In any case, these clashing cultural strains are only two traditions

among many that can be drawn on by Americans confronting
choices of war or peace. Focusing exclusively on these two relegates
other historical narratives to the dustbin, even though they present
alternative frameworks for public discussion and have sometimes
played important roles in our decision making. One example is the
pacifist tradition, originally associated with the Society of Friends
and other peace churches, which carved out a "conscientious objec-
tor" exception to the conscription laws, gained substantial public support after World War I, and later influenced the movement against
the Vietnam War. Another is the leftist anti-war perspective originally formulated by labor leaders like Eugene V. Debs, further developed by the New Left, civil rights, and Black Power activists of
the 1960s, and currently expressed by members of Congress like Representatives Dennis Kucinich (D-Ohio) and Barbara Lee (D-Calif.).
And a third is the conservative/libertarian viewpoint associated with
such figures as Senator Robert A. Taft, political analyst Patrick J. Buchanan, and presidential candidate Representative Ron Paul (R-Tex.).[36]
Despite their diversity, all these approaches deny that American citi-
zenship means being willing to fight on command. All preach skepticism of pro-war claims and narratives. And all remain lively currents
in American political discourse.

In addition to these traditions rooted in U.S. history, furthermore, one needs to pay attention to *new* social and political developments that affect public decisions about matters of war and peace. It
is clearly a mistake to assume that a nation's cultural development is
determined once and for all by the events of its original "founding."
Rather, our character as a people is continually transformed by changing circumstances. A dramatic recent example is the rise of what
some analysts have dubbed the "new American militarism"—the
worshipful admiration of a high-tech, professionalized fighting force
supported by a powerful military-industrial complex and engaging
in continuous armed activities abroad.[37] Arguing that the new militarism represents a modern version of the frontier warrior ethos is a
bit like maintaining that the computer is nothing but an updated

abacus. There are continuities, of course. But it is the changes that are most striking.

The new system emerged shortly after World War II, when President Harry S. Truman announced his Truman Doctrine legitimizing U.S. intervention anywhere freedom seemed to be threatened by totalitarianism. In order to halt the spread of Communism and establish American supremacy over the USSR, China, and their allies, America's Cold War leaders reinstituted conscription, raised military spending well above World War II levels, and vastly increased spending on weapons systems research and development. In addition, they established military bases in scores of nations and engaged in two hot wars, as well as dozens of covert actions and proxy wars around the globe. Moreover, when the Cold War ended, leaving America the sole surviving superpower, George H. W. Bush, Bill Clinton, and George W. Bush upped the ante, *increasing* military spending in order to create an all-volunteer, fully technologized, integrated fighting force capable of intervening anywhere in the world, and committing it to action in the Middle East, the Balkans, and Central Asia. These latter developments were accompanied by a new, post–Cold War ideology emphasizing America's duty to maintain world order, and its right to conduct preemptive and preventive wars in order to nip potential aggression or other bad behavior in the bud.

Whatever cultural determinists may imagine, all this has very little to do with how the West was won. Can one imagine Davy Crockett piloting drone aircraft over Pakistan from a computer terminal in Langley, Virginia, or negotiating cost-plus contracts with Northrop Grumman? Of course, the armed services make use of old symbols and narratives when it suits them to do so. The wildly romantic, "chivalric" film commercials produced by U.S. Marine Corps recruiters provide a vivid example. To be sure, there are some parallels between U.S. intervention in places like Afghanistan and fighting Indians in the North American wilderness. But this is because of the asymmetric nature of this sort of conflict, not because Americans are the captives of fixed cultural patterns. The British fought similar wars in Afghanistan, India, and East Africa, and the French in North Africa and Southeast Asia, not as an expression of some frontier heritage but because, like American leaders today, they were trying to maintain a global empire against dogged local resistance. One can be thankful, in any case, that a nation's culture does not stand still or repeat itself endlessly. Just as a new militarism transformed the earlier American warrior spirit, new forms of peace advocacy, negotiation, and problem solving have begun to appear as a response to the current crisis in U.S. foreign policy. A bit later, we will have more to say about these hopeful developments.

Finally, theories of innate American aggressiveness collide with an uncomfortable fact of history: the prevalence of opposition to proposed wars by large numbers of citizens from 1812 to the present. Were we a nation of irascible fighters waiting impatiently for a chance to attack some designated enemy, one would expect enthusiastic approval when military campaigns are first suggested, as well as when they are prosecuted. But the record belies these expectations. At times, anti-war sentiment is so strong and so widespread that leaders shy away from proposing armed intervention, even though they might otherwise do so.[38] Even when war is proposed, however, as noted earlier, its advocates must ordinarily overcome substantial popular opposition to clear the way for combat.[39] True, these mobilizations are seldom effective to prevent determined leaders from making war. In most cases, although not all, the initial opposition to war decreases in the course of debate or when actual hostilities begin, remains low in the early stages of conflict, and rises again if the war is not brought to a relatively quick and successful conclusion.[40] But our initial tendency to oppose wars is crucial. Since Americans are neither clueless Billy Budds nor violent Davy Cocketts, pro-war advocates must bring out the heavy guns of persuasion to gain their support for military action. How those rhetorical weapons are loaded—which ideas and images are most potent in persuading us to fight—is the issue that will drive our inquiry from this point forward.

Rationes Belli: Our Reasons for Choosing War

To develop a fuller understanding of why Americans choose war, it helps to examine the arguments that pro-war advocates advance most often, and most effectively, in their efforts to convert reluctant citizens to their cause. I will state the key rationales for war here in shorthand form, with a brief comment on each one. Later, we will talk about them in greater depth and detail.

1. Self-defense: (So and so) has attacked us. We have a sacred right and collective duty to defend ourselves.

Since the eighteenth century, Americans have considered the right to defend one's life, liberty, and property not just a matter of narrow self-interest but a natural or moral right. Extended from the individual to the collective level, the "self" entitled to defense is generally understood to include both the American people *and* their most cherished institutions and values. Combined with other rationales, self-defense has therefore been used to justify every U.S. war, including some that would seem to have little to do with protecting Americans or U.S. territory. The most recent expression of this principle is the doctrine of national security, which defines a broad range of physical, psychological, political, and economic risks, foreign and domestic, as intolerable threats to the nation's safety and integrity.

2. Evil Enemy: (So and so) is an evil aggressor whom we must either appease or defeat; there is no other option.

Although American images of the enemy have changed over time, they frequently involve a classical Christian conception of evil as malicious wrongdoing, or pure hatred of the Good. This sort of evil exists outside the realm of history and is by definition nonnegotiable. If Islamist terrorists "hate our freedoms," as President George W. Bush told Congress in October 2001, it makes little sense to consider their beliefs historically conditioned or subject to change. The mass media often play a major role in convincing the public that a nation or leader previously considered a mere competitor or violent thug is evil in the satanic sense. A classic example is the transformation of the

German kaiser into "the Beast of Berlin" during the early years of World War I. A second is the transformation of our former ally Saddam Hussein into "the Beast of Baghdad."

3. Unacceptable Consequences of Appeasement: If we do not fight, the nation will be weakened, humiliated, and dishonored.

While usually expressed in terms of "realistic" geopolitical interests, this rationale for war often masks deep anxieties about America's national identity, potency, and prestige. The frontier warrior hypothesis has some relevance to how we define national honor; for us, the concept has long mixed virtuous behavior (for example, keeping one's word) with a touchy macho sensitivity to perceived insults, an exaggerated fear of public humiliation, and a need to defend our reputation for courage on the battlefield. Today, the issue of national honor appears most frequently in connection with proposals to *terminate* wars that have come to seem unjust, unwinnable, or not worth fighting. Very often, the opponents of termination equate a withdrawal of U.S. forces with dishonor and a damaging loss of prestige.

4. Patriotic Duty: We have a moral duty to fight wars when our government asks us to make this sacrifice.

Patriotism is not a peculiarly American sentiment, but the American version is known around the world for its intensity, ubiquity, and strong military coloration. Forged in the fires of the Civil War, this principle of our civil religion took its modern form during the struggles over national identity coinciding with the peak years of European immigration (1890–1920) and the debate over U.S. entry into World War I. Successive versions of the patriotic myth have celebrated the American nation as a coherent, unified community superior to other nations and entitled to advance its unique values and interests by force. Since the end of the Cold War, however, the doctrine has tended to fragment, generating internal conflict rather than increasing national unity. We will describe this "crisis of patriotism" a bit later.

5. Humanitarian Duty: We have a moral duty to rescue oppressed

people when they are helpless to resist atrocious violations of their hu-
man rights.

Humanitarian duty was presented as a justification for war as early
as the colonial period, when wars against Native Americans were
explained as necessary to rescue them from heathenism and rule by
savage chieftains. Applied to southern slaves, this "missionary" rationale also played a role in developing northern support for the
Civil War. But its first important modern use was in the war of
1898–1902 to liberate Cuba, Puerto Rico, and the Philippines from
Spanish oppression. Humanitarian goals were important in convincing Americans to participate in both world wars and were offered as secondary but significant reasons to fight in Korea, Vietnam,
Iraq, and Afghanistan. Given the large number of human rights crises
currently troubling global society, as well as the difficulty of separating humanitarian from self-interested motives, the question of when
the United States should intervene on behalf of oppressed peoples
continues to generate intense debate.

6. Unique Virtue: We have a moral right to make war because we are
disinterested liberators and peacemakers, not selfish imperialists.

A key idea underlying several rationales for war is the assumption
of unique virtue, which originated in the concept of Americans as
a New World people especially blessed by God and charged with a
duty to avoid repeating Old World patterns of violent domination.
Since World War II ended, every U.S. president has assured the international community that we are not interested in territorial acquisitions, economic privileges, or military hegemony. Yet the United
States has become the world's leading superpower, with dependent
allies on every continent, hundreds of military bases in other nations, and combat forces in action from the Middle East to Central
Asia. Does this make us a nation of hypocrites, as some critics maintain? Is it a sign of divine favor or a fulfillment of America's mission?
Or is there a better way to understand the relationship between
power, nationhood, and morality? Those advocating war in America
have often emphasized our moral duty to lead an armed crusade

for freedom, democracy, or world order around the globe. The Bush administration's vision of the Iraq War as part of a crusade for democracy in the Middle East revealed that this rationale was by no means obsolete. Especially since the 2001 al-Qaeda attacks on the United States, it has been modified and expanded by positing world order, rather than freedom or democracy, as a noble and valid goal of military intervention. This justification, which has come to the fore in the case of the current war in Afghanistan, poses special problems both for war advocates and for their opponents.

7. *War as a Last Resort: There is no peaceful alternative to war, either because the enemy has refused to negotiate in good faith or because "you can't negotiate with those people."*

Virtually every argument for an American war concludes by alleging the inefficacy or immorality of peaceful alternatives to armed conflict. While the United States has tried to find a nonviolent way to resolve the dispute, officials say, the hostile party has refused to negotiate seriously and/or cannot be trusted to keep its word. The nightmare figure haunting this sort of discourse is Adolf Hitler pulling the wool over Prime Minister Neville Chamberlain's eyes at Munich—an image that makes talking peace seem a dangerous expression of weakness, cowardice, or naïveté. In reality, the U.S. government has refused to negotiate, engaged in peremptory negotiations, or broken talks off prematurely more often than its adversaries. Ironically, it has also used negotiation and dialogue to settle a number of potentially violent conflicts, such as the Cuban Missile Crisis, while characterizing the results as victories achieved through threats of force alone. An underlying symbolic theme is that threatening to fight is masculine and courageous, while talking peace is feminine and weak.

A striking feature of all these justifications for war is their strong moral and ideological content. Americans will seldom consent to fight unless they have first been persuaded that the cause is morally compelling. To put this negatively, our people are generally unwilling to put family and friends in danger merely to increase some industry's profits or to preserve U.S. hegemony in some far-off region. Knowing this, and, perhaps, seeking to avoid uncomfortable questions about the distribution of war's benefits and burdens, those who advocate military action almost always put their case in moral or religious terms. Oil is never cited as an official reason for intervening in the Middle East, any more than economic interests were cited as a reason to conquer the Philippines. As one analyst puts it, "Even skeptics about the influence of morality on national security policies admit that idealistic rhetoric is often needed to convince a moralistic public to support realpolitik policies."[41]

Is this formulation accurate? Do national leaders use high-flown moral principles to persuade the public to consent to wars fought for narrower, less admirable reasons? To some extent, the answer is yes. In 1990, for example, after the Iraqi armed forces had invaded Kuwait, the first President Bush dispatched several hundred thousand troops to Saudi Arabia. Five months later, he ordered air and ground attacks to expel Iraqi troops from Kuwait. The official reasons for fighting were to liberate the Kuwaitis and defend international law, but in the run-up to Operation Desert Storm, former Defense Department official Lawrence Korb spoke with rare candor about U.S. material interests in the region. What if Saddam Hussein had invaded a poor agrarian country instead of the world's sixth largest source of oil? "If Kuwait grew carrots," Korb remarked breezily, "we wouldn't give a damn."[42] Insiders understood that the larger purpose of the war was to secure U.S. economic and geopolitical interests in the region (as defined by Bush and his colleagues) by degrading Iraq's military capability, halting that country's modernization, and eliminating Saddam Hussein as a major player in regional politics.[43]

So, were the noble justifications offered for the Persian Gulf War mere window dressing designed to conceal less noble economic and geopolitical interests? Are such ideological and moral appeals nothing more than efforts to sucker the citizenry into backing wars advocated by policymaking elites? In my opinion, this overstates the case. Elites do have their own reasons for making war, but there is

considerable evidence that they, too, are more likely to advocate military action when they believe that the cause is just and the war necessary.[44] Many analysts of the Iraq War have noted, for example, that
President George W. Bush was strongly motivated by the principles
enunciated by his neo-conservative advisers. He and Vice President
Dick Cheney clearly believed their own public statements justifying
the war on grounds of self-defense, humanitarian concerns, and transformation of the region in accordance with American values of democracy, human rights, civic order, and material progress. Had they
not been committed to these ideas, their policies would probably have
resembled those of the elder President Bush, who had refused to extend the Persian Gulf War of 1990–91 to encompass the goals of regime change in Iraq or regional transformation.

Conversely, when hawks cannot convince other policymakers and
the public that there is a strong moral case for fighting, the chances
of armed intervention decrease sharply. This helps explain what happened (or didn't happen) in the mid-1950s, after the French army in
Vietnam was defeated by Communist/nationalist insurgents. Some
U.S. leaders strongly favored intervening to keep Indochina from
falling to the Communists. Others, supported by a war-weary public
(the Korean War had recently ended), insisted that the French had
been defeated because their cause—the maintenance of their Southeast Asian empire—was unjust. American intervention in Vietnam
had to wait until most policymakers were convinced that a war to
defend the South Vietnamese regime could be justified as part of a
global crusade for democracy and freedom. Then they could attempt to persuade the public, in Lyndon Johnson's words, that "if
freedom is to survive in any American home town it must be pre-
served in such places as South Viet Nam."[45]

To put this in slightly different terms, war is ordinarily sold to the
American public as warranted, if not required, by the principles of
this nation's civil religion. Civil religion, as the sociologist Robert N.
Bellah explained, is a rough system of attitudes, beliefs, and behaviors that overlaps, but is not identical with, those of organized

religions and supplies an ethical dimension to national identity.[46] According to anthropologist Michael V. Angrosino,

> American civil religion is an institutionalized set of beliefs about the nation, including a faith in a transcendent deity who will protect and guide the United States as long as its people and government abide by his laws. The virtues of liberty, justice, charity, and personal integrity are all pillars of this religion and lend a moral dimension to its public decision-making processes quite different from the realpolitik that presumably underlies the calculations of states not equally favored by divine providence.[47]

Our particular brand of civil religion is often said to include the belief in America as a chosen nation with a mandate to spread the blessings of democracy, Christianity, capitalism, scientific thinking, political freedom, and civilized order throughout the world.[48] But the idea that exercising this beneficent influence means making war in foreign lands is a modern twist—in fact, a 180 degree turn—in the development of earlier doctrine. In colonial times, many white settlers considered themselves chosen in the Hebrew sense. God had covenanted with them and had led them out of the fleshpots of Europe to the American Promised Land, a wilderness in which they flourished, against the odds, by doing God's will.[49] The Puritans believed that their activities had cosmic religious significance, but while their divine mission justified taking the land and fighting the Native Americans, it was not a rationale for foreign military adventures. America would exercise worldwide influence by the force of moral example—by being the "cittie upon a hill" of which John Winthrop spoke—rather than by taking up arms to conquer or liberate foreigners (an impossible notion in any case for those whose hands were full trying to survive). Principles of the civil religion played an important role in justifying both the American Revolution and the Civil War, but it was only with World War I, portrayed by fervent Protestant clergy as a "war for righteousness," that they were used to mobilize support for an international moral crusade.[50] This militant missionary spirit was drawn upon again to fuel enthusiasm for World War II and the Cold War, as well as for Mr. Bush's campaign to depose Saddam Hussein and "liberate" Iraq.

It is important to recognize, though, that civil religion is *not* a systematic theology or a single creed to which everyone subscribes. There are numerous conflicting versions of America's moral mission, ranging from the USA Church Militant doctrines of some conservatives to the radically anti-imperial beliefs of the Rev. Jim Wallis or of Bellah himself.[51] Disagreements extend from the definition of American values (*Is* there anything "sacred" about capitalism? *Does* democracy require multiparty elections?) to the appropriate methods of defending them and the rightness or wrongness of trying to export them. Moreover, between the extremes of neo-conservative and ultra-liberal civil religion, there are other expressions of the national faith, some of them masquerading as pure common sense.

In its current intervention in Afghanistan, for example, President Barack Obama's administration has avoided the fervent crusading rhetoric that accompanied the Iraq War. Like other self-declared foreign policy realists, the president and his advisers prefer to speak in seemingly value-free terms about the need to protect America against terrorist attacks by pacifying the untamed areas of the world that might otherwise give our enemies refuge. The question is whether this rationale is as coolly rational as it sounds, or whether it is a less emotional way of affirming America's world-civilizing mission. As we know, al-Qaeda's leaders have already abandoned Afghanistan for Pakistan. Must we establish a stable Afghan society ruled by faithful American allies and enduring a sustained U.S. military presence to prevent their return? And, if they move to Somalia or Ingushetia, must we pacify/occupy those societies, too? The pragmatic, knowledgeable tone of current U.S. commanders in Afghanistan is virtually identical to that employed in the 1960s by talented technocrats like Robert McNamara and McGeorge Bundy to explain why the United States needed to pacify Vietnam, win Vietnamese "hearts and minds," and "Vietnamize" that war.[52] We will have more to say in the next chapter about the concepts of self-defense used to justify America's wars, including the Afghan War. For now, it is worth noting that exponents of the civil religion need not be pulpit-pounding fundamentalists to commit the nation to lengthy military campaigns in the name of Goodness and Order.

Clearly, the American civil religion is a good deal less coherent than that of any ordinary church. Even so, its existence helps to explain why it is so difficult to mobilize Americans to fight for mere wealth, status, or power. For us, the only reasons that legitimate war are those that reflect generally accepted moral principles, including the right of self-defense, the duty to rescue the oppressed, and the unavailability of nonviolent remedies. The more material, self-interested, or simply neurotic reasons for fighting tend to be tabooed or repressed. And, like other repressed ideas and feelings, these darker motives tend to return to consciousness when the immediate crisis is past. This is when we discover, as if for the first time, that some people were actually making money, accumulating power, or getting psychological kicks from war while thousands, even millions, of others were being killed and maimed. Although periods of postwar disillusionment seem to follow virtually every American war (the great exception is World War II), the "lessons" learned during such periods are quickly forgotten when civil-religious duty calls again.

It is essential to examine the reasons for war sanctified by civil religion not in order to debunk them, or to show that they are mere veils for uglier motives, but because they are the products of deeply felt, widely held ethical aspirations. These principles and longings, so highly valued that many people will kill and die to realize them, represent America at its best, even while they have often been invoked to justify U.S. violence at its worst. The misuse of this civil religion for purposes of conducting unjust and unnecessary wars is every bit as obnoxious as al-Qaeda's misuse of Islamic beliefs for the same purpose. To recognize the existence and potency of such principles is also to recognize the possibility that we, too, can become jihadists fixated on violence as a panacea—participants in a perpetual war that we have convinced ourselves is just.

There *are* such things as just wars, in my view, but they are rare. Let us look further at the arguments and images that have persuaded so many of us that they are common.

2

THE TRANSFORMATION OF SELF-DEFENSE

Of all the reasons used to mobilize people for war, the most common claim, the one with the strongest visceral appeal, is self-defense. Although religion may command turning the other cheek, the modern world considers it a sacred right to protect oneself against assault. As a rule, resorting to violence to get one's way is condemned as aggression, while responding violently to aggression is considered permissible, if not mandatory. This is surely the American understanding as well. From the Indian Wars of the colonial era to current struggles in Iraq, Afghanistan, and Pakistan, virtually every war fought by Americans has been presented to the public as a legitimate exercise of the nation's natural right to defend itself against wrongful attack. Yet there is something very odd about many of these claims.

Self-defense originally referred to an individual's right to fight back when personally attacked. Applied to the nation, the phrase still has the commonsense meaning suggested by the U.S. Constitution's grant of power to Congress to call out the militia to "suppress Insurrections and repel Invasions." When someone at home or abroad threatens to deprive Americans forcibly of life, liberty, or property, they have the right to defend themselves, forcibly if necessary. But most invocations of the right to self-defense are not about this sort of threat. In the two and one-third centuries since independence was declared, there have been only three overt attacks on American soil: the British assaults on Washington, D.C., and New Orleans during the War of 1812; the Japanese bombing of the fleet at Pearl Harbor, Hawaii (then a U.S. possession) on December 7, 1941; and al-Qaeda's attacks of September 11, 2001, on the World Trade Center and the Pentagon. One major civil insurrection, which began with the Confederate bombardment of South Carolina's Fort Sumter, was suppressed at enormous cost. All the other claims of self-defense have involved something more than direct attacks on the American people.

What is this something more? In some cases assertions that America was under attack proved mistaken, tendentious, or fraudulent. The Mexican "invasion" of 1846 was provoked, the Tonkin Gulf Incident of 1964 was fictitious, and the imminent threat allegedly posed by Iraq in 2003 was based on faulty or misinterpreted intelligence. But what of World War I, in which more than a hundred thousand Americans died to help England and France defeat Germany and Austria? Was that a war of self-defense? What about the Korean War, Operation Desert Storm in the Persian Gulf, and the current war against the Taliban in Afghanistan? For that matter, what about the wars in Vietnam and Iraq after misleading U.S. accusations were exposed? In all these cases, self-defense (or its more recent equivalent, "national security") was given some broader meaning: a designation of threats that many Americans considered real, even if they were not under direct attack. To make sense of this, it may help to consider three stages in the metamorphosis of self-defense doctrine, each of which represents a further expansion of the original commonsense notion.[1]

First stage: defense of the domestic system. The "self" requiring defense (or "nation" needing security) includes not only the American people and their territory but also the domestic institutions, cultural values, and self-images that they hold dear. The source of the threat

is an enemy considered alien and dangerous but not necessarily diabolical or unusually powerful. The serious damage that people fear
is expected to materialize in the near-term future. And the costs of
averting this damage are relatively moderate. Examples of this sort
of self-defense are the War of 1812 and the First Seminole War (we
will describe the latter in a moment).

Second stage: *defense of universalized values and national independence.* Here the national self expands to include American values
expressed in the form of universal principles (for example, democracy). The spatial frame expands to include the world stage, and the
time frame lengthens to include the medium-term future. The
enemy considered the source of these threats is now pictured as
deeply evil and powerful enough to threaten America's autonomy,
and the costs of defeating it are high. Examples are the American
Civil War and the two world wars.

Third stage: *defense of superpower interests.* The self or nation expands to include U.S. geopolitical interests and representatives on
every continent of the globe. American/Western values are felt to be
under attack, as are the bodies of our troops, diplomats, development
workers, business representatives, and others. The enemy, still considered evil, now consists of numerous rebels against the U.S. empire
and its local allies. The time frame encompasses both immediate
threats and those that may take decades to materialize, and the costs
of combating them are virtually incalculable. Examples are the Vietnam War and subsequent U.S. interventions in Iraq and Afghanistan.

Let's consider each of these metamorphoses more carefully. A
little-known piece of American history illustrates the first stage: the
story of Andrew Jackson and the First Seminole War.

DEFENDING THE DOMESTIC SYSTEM:
THE FIRST SEMINOLE WAR

In January 1818, General Andrew Jackson was enduring a restless
semi-retirement at his home in Tennessee when he received a welcome

message from President James Monroe's secretary of war, John C. Calhoun. Jackson was ordered to muster an army, march it some four hundred miles south, and set about punishing the Seminole Indians, who were reported to be raiding American settlements along the frontier separating Georgia and Alabama from Spanish-owned Florida. A party of U.S. troops dispatched to Florida a few months earlier to put a stop to these depredations had been massacred, and there were rumors that the Indians were being armed by British agents, who were still plotting against America despite their recent defeat in the War of 1812.[2] The administration understood that Jackson would have to invade West Florida to carry out his orders. There could be no question of asking Congress to declare war against Spain, a nation with which the United States was at peace. Nevertheless, since the Spanish government seemed incapable of controlling the Seminole evildoers, Jackson was authorized to cross the international border to vindicate America's sacred right of self-defense.

Andrew Jackson had already won national glory as a fighter against both the Indians and the British. In 1814, he annihilated nine hundred rebellious Creeks at the Battle of Horseshoe Bend in Alabama. He then forced the tribes—including those who had fought on his side—to cede enormous tracts of land to the United States without compensation, after which many of them moved across the border to join their Seminole kinsmen in Spanish Florida. The following year, Jackson's triumph over British invaders at the Battle of New Orleans cemented his status as a national hero. With the Creeks defeated, the War of 1812 over, and the United States at peace with Spain, the only remaining "enemies" that might threaten Americans settling the Deep South were hostile Indian tribes based in Florida, especially if they were incited by British agents to attack white settlements.

But did such a threat really exist? The official story of innocent Americans under attack concealed a more complex and ambiguous tale. Long a Spanish possession, Florida was occupied by the British from 1763 until the end of the American Revolution. When the British withdrew, the territory reverted to Spain, and Spanish settlers flooded in. But so did another type of immigrant: slaves escaping from white homes and plantations in the Lower South. The Seminoles welcomed them as allies, and the newcomers' numbers were small enough to permit their integration into the Seminole community. The Indians did not treat the immigrants as social equals but as tenant farmers, a respectable role that permitted the "Black Seminoles" to settle in their own communities, raise families, acquire property of their own, and learn to fight. As one historian writes, "They wore the Indian garb and were hunters and fishermen as well as tillers of the soil and stock raisers; the men all carried arms, went into battle under their own captains, and were on terms of familiar intimacy with their so-called masters."[3]

It is not hard to understand why this situation seemed so threatening to white southerners. To Jackson and Calhoun as well as their white constituents, the escaped slaves and their families were property, no less stolen for being self-stolen, and the Seminoles were aiding and abetting the theft. Worse yet, the Black Seminoles' very existence was an insult and a provocation to racist Dixie. By living like free men and women just across the border, they violated a central taboo of southern society and struck at the myth of black unfitness for freedom. By carrying weapons, they advertised their military competence and (in the view of whites) implicitly encouraged other slaves to rebel.

As early as 1812, Georgia volunteers calling themselves Patriots, later aided by Tennessee militiamen, began raiding Seminole towns and farmsteads in Florida to secure the slaves' return and punish their hosts. The Indian raids of which Secretary of War Calhoun complained were almost certainly reprisals for these repeated episodes of killing, looting, burning, and kidnapping by southern invaders in Spanish territory. The last straw, so far as Andrew Jackson was concerned, was the creation of the "Negro Fort." Reports spread of a fort in West Florida originally built by the British but now manned by black fighters under whose protection escapees could live and work in dignity.[4] The cure for this unhealthy situation, according to Jackson, was obvious: the United States should annex the entire territory. In 1816, he demanded that the Spanish governor of West Florida seize the Negro Fort and kill or imprison its defenders. When the governor demurred, the enraged Tennessean ordered his own officers to cross the border and destroy the fort themselves. One of them quickly did so by firing a "hot shot" from his riverboat gunship (a cannonball heated to red hot in the cook's galley) that landed in the fort's powder magazine, leveling the structure and killing more than three hundred defenders.

Although a setback to the Black Seminoles, this blow did not end the threat posed by their existence or Jackson's determination to eliminate it. When finally given the go-ahead from Washington, he invaded West Florida with five thousand troops, destroyed the major Seminole and Black Seminole villages along the Suwanee River, and court-martialed and executed two British subjects who were alleged to have "stirred up" the Indians.[5] Then he turned his attention to the Spanish. After falsely informing the War Department that he was returning to Tennessee for reasons of health, Jackson marched on Pensacola, the capital of West Florida, where he arrested the Spanish governor, raised the American flag over the city, and appointed one of his officers to administer the territory. These unauthorized adventures provoked a brief storm of protest in Congress, but resolutions to censure the Hero of New Orleans for executing two British troublemakers and putting the Spanish in their place fell far short of passage. When his congressional enemies charged that Jackson had acted without authorization in seizing West Florida, Representative John Rhea (R-Tenn.), replied that, officially sanctioned or not, they were "authorized by the supreme law of nature and of nations, the law of self-defense."[6]

Meanwhile, Jackson found that he had acquired a surprising ally in the person of John Quincy Adams, Monroe's ambitious secretary of state, who had already begun negotiating with the Spanish ambassador for the cession of Florida. Jackson's "indiscretion," which exposed Spain's inability to defend Florida against U.S. aggression, was made to order for a hard bargainer like Adams. He followed the diplomat's code: first apologize for the hothead's action, then take advantage of the weakness that it revealed. Adams's motive was *not* to protect the slave system, which he despised. He wanted to absorb Florida because he was a passionate nationalist who dreamed of creating a great continental empire, as well as a "global republican" who believed in spreading American-style democracy to the ends of the earth. He therefore offered to assume $5 million worth of Spanish debts if Spain would cede all of Florida to the United States and recognize U.S. claims to lands extending north of Spanish territory to the Pacific Ocean. The Spanish ambassador had little choice but to agree. Executed in 1819, the Adams-Onis Treaty has justly been called "the first determined step in the creation of an American global empire."[7]

Was this self-defense . . . or a territorial power grab? At first glance, it appears that America's true war aims were concealed behind the rhetoric of self-preservation. If there were Seminole and Black Seminole raids across the border, they were provoked by the aggressive activities of the white Patriots. It also seems clear that the threats perceived by Jackson and the settlers as most dangerous—the attraction of life among the Black Seminoles for southern slaves, and the activities of foreign agents in support of Native Americans—were wildly exaggerated. The number of slaves finding refuge in Florida did not amount to more than one thousand or so out of a total slave population of about two million. Even at the height of anti-slavery agitation and the creation of the Underground Railroad system, slave escapes were more an irritation than a threat to southern society. The British threat to American interests in the region was even more overblown. There was no evidence that the hapless Britishers executed by Jackson were anything more than lone adventurers, or that any European power had an interest in acquiring Florida.

The alleged defender in the First Seminole War was therefore the aggressor, and the result was a significant expansion of U.S. territory and influence. Even so, I would argue that the claim of self-defense was *not* a deliberate fiction. Andrew Jackson and the white settlers of the South did not invade Florida out of sheer lust for land or love of battle: in fact, there was little settler interest in Florida's wild, swampy land. The territory was considered a wilderness breeding all sorts of deviant behaviors. The Seminoles befriended escaped slaves and refused to play the role of "good" (i.e., obedient) Indians. Escaped slaves acting like free whites committed unspeakable violations of the southern caste system. Foreigners befriended the natives, mixing with them socially (and, if rumors were to be believed, sexually). And a weak Spanish colonial government allowed this dangerous disorder free rein. Jackson and his constituents felt menaced and outraged by a situation that they repeatedly described as disorderly, lawless, immoral, and intolerably chaotic. *That* is what they and many other Americans considered an intolerable threat—not the raids, but the chaos.

In this situation, there were two meanings of the claim of self-defense. The first was not so much territorial as psycho-political and moral. What the Seminoles and Black Seminoles threatened was, above all, the *idea* of America, as men like Jackson conceived of it—a national image epitomized by the free, independent, self-reliant white man, combining democratic commitments (to the community of white men) and material ambitions with a passion—or mania—for personal discipline, "civilized" behavior, and social order. Especially west of the older coastal settlements, white American society was barely more civilized, if at all, than the Native American and African American societies it looked down on.[8] Many Americans feared internal disorder both as individuals unable to master their passions (compare the synonym for brothel: "disorderly house") and as participants in social systems, such as the slave system, that were constantly incubating personal transgressions and violence. It is not far-fetched to conclude that the anger and revulsion expressed by bellicose patriots like Jackson often involved a projection of anxieties originating *inside* the boundaries of the self/nation onto the "savage" regions not yet under personal and political control.

These apparent threats were magnified and given a nationalist expression when such regions were weakly governed, raising the possibility that some power hostile to the United States might take advantage of the situation to expand its own empire or sphere of influence. Ironically, weak government—"a tolerable anarchy," in Jedediah Purdy's words—was a value greatly cherished by most Americans until relatively recent times. But, as Purdy notes, there was always a struggle in American thinking between the love of freedom and independence and a sense that individuals driven by competitive instincts and sinful desires required strong controls to keep them from misbehaving.[9] John Quincy Adams (a New England Puritan at heart) viewed any uncontrolled territory on the continent as an irresistible temptation to takeover by forces hostile to the United States and its democratic values. He cared about Florida because if America failed to absorb it, somebody else might do so.

According to analyst John Lewis Gaddis, Adams's takeover of that territory established the basis for the modern doctrine of preemptive wars to take control of "failed states":

The modern term "failed state" did not appear in Adams's note [to Spain], but he surely had that idea in mind when he insisted that power vacuums were dangerous and that the United States should therefore fill them.

"Concerns about 'failed' or 'derelict' states," Gaddis adds,

are nothing new in the history of United States foreign relations, nor are strategies of preemption in dealing with them. So when President George W. Bush warned . . . that Americans must "be ready for preemptive action when necessary to defend our liberty

and to defend our lives," he was echoing an old tradition rather
than establishing a new one."[10]

Perhaps. But the leap from J. Q. Adams to G. W. Bush is more
dizzying than this scholar seems prepared to admit. When asked to
intervene on the side of freedom fighters then seeking independence
and democracy in Europe and Latin America, Adams replied,
"America goes not abroad, in search of monsters to destroy." If she
were to become involved in foreign wars, even in a just cause, "the
fundamental maxims of her policy would insensibly change from
liberty to force." America might then become "the dictatress of the
world," said Adams, but "she would be no longer the ruler of her
own spirit."[11] Still, Gaddis has a point. To put it less approvingly
than he does, the fear of "power vacuums" remains an enduring motive for expanding self-defense doctrine to legitimize expansionist
wars. If we cannot be safe without occupying every failed or failing
state from Afghanistan to Indonesia, we must make up our minds
to be a global empire permanently at war.

The story of the Seminole War suggests several key questions that
wary Americans will want to raise when told that a war is needed to
defend their nation. First, *what is it, exactly, that we are defending?*
Are American lives, liberties, and territory in danger, or is there a
threat to some more complex idea or manifestation of the nation?
Another way to phrase this is to ask what really frightens us. In the
case of Islamist terrorists, for example, the answer may seem obvious: another 9/11 attack. But Andrew Jackson would have said, "Another Seminole raid." It may be that what makes us feel insecure is
not only the possibility of another terrorist act but the realization
that millions of people abroad resent our activities in their countries
and wish us ill, or the feeling that the "magic" that seemed to protect us in the past has vanished. Further attacks are certainly to be
feared, but terrorism may also act as a fear magnet, attracting and
focusing all sorts of other anxieties and concerns.

Second, *whom, exactly, are we defending against?* Does the threat emanate from the individuals or group that attacked us, or does it also include their allies and sympathizers, those who give them sanctuary, and, perhaps, those who remain neutral rather than springing to our defense? If we defend against the "maximum enemy," we risk alienating potential friends and spreading the conflict to new groups and locales. The question of our adversaries' intentions is a critical piece of this inquiry. They may be out to dominate or hurt us, or, like the Black Seminoles, they may only want us to leave them alone. In the latter case, if we insist upon confronting them violently, we may be acting as aggressors rather than defenders.

Third, *is the method of self-defense rational* in the sense that it makes us more secure, or does it generate more serious threats to our people? To John Quincy Adams, Florida must have seemed a "slam dunk." But when similar reasoning was extended to justify the seizure of the Southwest and California (i.e., if we didn't take California from Mexico, somebody else would), this fed sectional antagonisms that culminated in an unimaginably destructive civil war.[12] A relevant issue, of course, is whether or not there are effective nonviolent methods of dealing with the perceived threat. The assumption that a violent attack merits a violent response *may* be rational, but in some cases a thirst for revenge actually increases the dangers of further, more damaging attacks.

Finally, *what are the relevant costs?* Where self-defense is concerned, people are not inclined to base decisions to fight or not to fight on cost-benefit calculations. If the threat is serious and imminent, we prepare to "bear any burden, pay any price," as President John F. Kennedy said. But raising the issue of costs—which are physical, psychological, and spiritual, as well as financial—forces us to revisit the questions of seriousness and imminence, as well as that of effectiveness. It compels us to face the hidden damage to our own people and our long-term relationships caused by seemingly endless struggles like the current War on Terrorism. And it invites us to consider whether there might be less conventional but more effective ways of satisfying our basic need for security.

Defending Universal Values: The Two World Wars

The doctrine of self-defense took a dramatic turn in connection with the two world wars, when the United States sent vast numbers of military and civilian personnel abroad to fight against the Central Powers (Germany, Austria-Hungary, Turkey, and Bulgaria) in World War I and the Axis Powers (primarily Germany, Japan, and Italy) in World War II. Precisely because these struggles were so distant and involved so many foreign nations, it was natural for Americans to ask, "What has this got to do with us?" An isolationist tradition dating back to George Washington's Farewell Address had long counseled against entangling the nation in European politics. The reluctance of most Americans to take sides in other people's quarrels, especially when intervening meant killing and dying far from home, made proposals to send U.S. troops abroad massively unpopular. In 1916, Woodrow Wilson was reelected president as a peace candidate pledged to maintain U.S. neutrality, while Franklin Roosevelt won a third term in 1940 promising American parents not to send their boys into a foreign war. After their reelections, both candidates would explain that the wars they had sought to avoid were unavoidable struggles justified by principles of self-defense.

In the hands of liberal idealists like Wilson and Roosevelt, self-defense took on two new meanings. The first identified certain universal principles, such as democracy, human rights, and "civilized" morality, of which the United States was said to be the chief exemplar and defender. An attack on those values could therefore be said to be an attack on the United States, even if there was no immediate danger to our domestic institutions. This redefinition, which blurred the line between self-defense and moral crusading, had a special appeal to white, middle-class, Protestant Americans who identified culturally with England at the time of World War I.[13] But many recent immigrants, industrial workers, struggling farmers, nonwhites, and others not yet enjoying the full benefits of democracy at home considered this far too abstract a reason to kill and die in a foreign land. Therefore, the doctrine was supplemented by portraying one party to the conflict as an evil aggressor driven by its very nature to aspire to world domination. This way, it was not just American principles that were in danger but also American independence. If the German kaiser, for example, was embarked upon a plan of world conquest, an attack upon the United States, even if not imminent, was inevitable. And, if inevitable, it would be better to confront the danger now than to wait until the enemy grew stronger.

In the case of World War I, this argument was not an easy one to prove. Before 1914, Europe's Great Powers competed intensely for military supremacy, national prestige, spheres of economic influence, and colonial possessions. They constructed a system of military alliances so complex and interlocked that almost any violent incident could precipitate a chain reaction of mobilizations and invasions.[14] President Wilson himself had characterized the war as a struggle without heroes or villains and had called on Americans to remain "impartial in thought as well as in action."[15] Wilson adhered to his own principles at first by refusing to respond violently even when a German U-boat sank the British luxury liner *Lusitania*, killing more than 1,900 people, 128 of them American civilians. "There is such a thing as a man being too proud to fight," he said in a speech at Philadelphia. "There is such a thing as a nation being so right that it does not need to convince others by force that it is right."[16]

Most Americans agreed. In the chaos then engulfing Europe, who could tell the sinners from the saints? By 1915, with men dying by the millions in the trenches of France, the warring parties had become increasingly desperate. One sign of desperation was the increasing use of poison gas on both sides. Another was the British decision to mine the North Sea and to prevent anyone from shipping goods of any sort, including foodstuffs and other necessities, to German or Balkan ports. Winston Churchill, then First Lord of the Admiralty, frankly admitted that the purpose of the blockade was to "starve the whole population—men, women, and children, old and young, wounded and sound, into submission."[17] A third was the

Destroy This Mad Brute, *1917. World War I U.S. Army
recruitment poster showing German soldier as a beast and
rapist. Note the club labeled "kultur" (German for "culture")
and the self-defense rationale for WWI, namely if the war
was not fought to a finish in Europe, it would eventually reach
the soil of the United States. (Source: Harry Ransom Center,
University of Texas at Austin Collection.)*

German campaign of submarine warfare against ships carrying
goods of any kind to England or France, even if the carrier flew a
neutral flag. After the *Lusitania* went down, the Germans pledged
to avoid sinking passenger ships; a little while later, they also stopped

attacking neutral merchant vessels. Secretary of State William Jennings Bryan then asked Wilson to condemn both the German U-boat campaign *and* the British blockade of essential civilian goods. When the president refused, Bryan resigned his office, and Wilson replaced him with a pro-British diplomat, Robert Lansing.

Now the U.S. government began to move in earnest toward intervening on the Allied side. The business community had made Britain its largest foreign customer, and Wall Street had invested billions in loans to the Allies. By the time the president began his second term, this investment looked increasingly shaky. Mutinies had broken out among the French troops, and the Russian army, which had been fighting on the Allied side, was dissolving—the first herald of the revolution that would soon take Russia out of the war altogether. The British begged Wilson to intervene, arguing that even a late intervention could save the Allies from the necessity of making peace with Germany, as well as propel the United States into the position of postwar arbiter and global leader. Wilson was inclined to agree, especially when the Germans took two steps that could be presented as a *casus belli*—an immediate reason for war. In February 1917, with starvation stalking Central Europe, they resumed submarine warfare against any ships carrying goods to England or France and sank six American merchant vessels. And in March, their foreign minister, Arthur Zimmermann, sent a letter offering the Mexican government an alliance in case the United States declared war on Germany and holding out the possibility of a return of some of the territory taken in the Mexican-American War if the Central Powers were victorious.[18] The British intercepted the telegram and blew the whistle on Herr Zimmermann.

A few weeks later, Wilson went to Congress to request a declaration of war against Germany. He mentioned the Zimmermann telegram and accused the Germans of sponsoring a campaign of spying and sabotage against U.S. industry, but the bulk of his speech was devoted to the submarine warfare campaign. The dominant concept of self-defense for Wilson was the defense of American values, expressed in the form of universal legal and ethical principles. "The present German submarine warfare against commerce is a warfare against mankind," he told Congress. America would not defend herself because U.S. ships had been sunk—that would be ignoble and self-interested—but because we were the champions of legal and human rights. America's quarrel was not with Germany's people, Wilson insisted, but with its cruel and autocratic government, which had imposed a war upon them without their consent. "The world must be made safe for democracy," he declared memorably. Since a self-governing people would never consent to an elitist war, the road to democracy was also the road to a league of nations and world peace.[19] The fight against Germany (Wilson never mentioned fighting for the Allies) was the first step down this golden road.

The noble tone struck by Wilson's speech created two sorts of problems for the president and his supporters. Americans who opposed entering the war—still a substantial percentage of citizens—considered it mere propaganda, no less partisan for being high-flown. Not only did Wilson continue to ignore the British blockade, he also blamed the war solely on a few Prussian autocrats and militarists. But war credits had been voted with virtually no dissent by the German parliament, whose largest party, the Social Democrats, was also the largest working-class party in Europe. At its inception, the war was equally popular in England and France, allies who went unmentioned in Wilson's address, perhaps because these fellow democrats were imperialists far more powerful on a global scale than the Germans, and because their ally, czarist Russia, was one of the most autocratic nations on earth. To turn the European struggle into a fight between democracy and autocracy was something of a stretch, to put it mildly.

But Wilson's approach bothered the pro-war forces as well. By claiming that the German people had been misled by their rulers, he undermined efforts to portray the ordinary German soldier as a war-loving Hun. More important, his abstract references to autocracy did not help to convert the kaiser from the slightly ridiculous blusterer familiar to American newspaper and magazine readers as "Kaiser Bill" into a monster bent on world domination. The transformation of Wilhelm II into the "Beast of Berlin" was begun by administration spokesmen like Robert Lansing and finished by the newspapers—in particular by the cartoonists and poster artists who had a field day portraying him as the devil incarnate.

In a speech given a few months after war was declared, Lansing directly addressed the doubters who wondered why Americans should be "fighting other people's battles." "This is no war to establish an abstract principle of right," he declared—although that is precisely what Wilson had said it was. "It is a war in which the future of the United States is at stake." How so? Because of "the evil purposes of the rulers of Germany." The aim of German policy, said the secretary of state, was world conquest. The kaiser wanted to rule "a world empire greater than that of Greece or Rome or the caliphs" as an absolute monarch. Therefore—this was the punch line—even though he had not yet attacked the United States, he would inevitably do so in the relatively near future:

> Imagine Germany victor in Europe because the United States remained neutral. Who then, think you, would be the next victim of those who are seeking to be masters of the whole earth? Would not this country with its enormous wealth arouse the cupidity of an impoverished though triumphant Germany? Would not this democracy be the only obstacle between the autocratic rulers of Germany and their supreme ambition? Do you think that they would withhold their hand from so rich a prize?

Of course, if this threat of German attack was the clear and almost-present danger that Lansing said it was, it would make no sense to delay the inevitable confrontation. In words whose equivalents we have heard many times since, the secretary argued, in effect, for a preemptive strike against future aggression:

Let me then ask you, would it be easier or wiser for this country single-handed to resist a German Empire, flushed with victory and with great armies and navies at its command, than to unite with the brave opponents of that Empire in ending now and for all time this menace to our future?[20]

One wants to be fair to Mr. Lansing, but this was sheer fantasy. At the end of history's most destructive war, nobody, Germany least of all, would be in a position to threaten the United States. In 1918, France and England, "flushed with victory," were so exhausted by casualties, debts, and demoralization that they could do little but try, with increasing difficulty, to cling to their existing possessions— and Germany had suffered even more than they. Hindsight is even crueler to the argument for American intervention, for if we had remained neutral, the Allied and Central Powers would probably have been compelled to make a relatively equal "peace without victors" instead of imposing a punitive and humiliating settlement upon Germany at Versailles. Even with a fair peace, Europeans would have had difficulty keeping their balance when the Great Depression struck in the 1920s. But it seems clear that the vengeful terms ending "the war to end all wars" set the stage for a German Redeemer and seeded the massive conflict that followed.

Clearly, expanding the concept of self-defense is a risky business. The threats to America's core values and security interests are rarely as serious, imminent, or implacable as war advocates assert—and even "good" wars have incalculable consequences. This does not mean that arguments based on self-defense are always specious. In his influential Fireside Chat radio broadcasts, Franklin D. Roosevelt adapted both elements of Wilson's doctrine to make a case for military "preparedness" against Nazi Germany and Imperial Japan in the years before Pearl Harbor. Roosevelt's argument was based partly on U.S. vulnerability to military attack and economic disruption in a world made smaller by economic and technological advances:

If Great Britain goes down, the Axis powers will control the con-
tinents of Europe, Asia, Africa, Australia, and the high seas—and
they will be in a position to bring enormous military and naval
resources against this hemisphere. It is no exaggeration to say that
all of us, in all the Americas, would be living at the point of a
gun—a gun loaded with explosive bullets, economic as well as
military.

But his most powerful card was the evil nature of regimes that
"have proclaimed, time and again, that all other races are their infe-
riors and therefore subject to their orders." Driven by their own elitist, violence-worshipping attitudes, FDR suggested, the victorious
Axis Powers would force others to imitate them just to survive:

We should enter upon a new and terrible era in which the whole
world, our hemisphere included, would be run by threats of brute
force. And to survive in such a world, we would have to convert
ourselves permanently into a militaristic power on the basis of
war economy.[21]

Like Woodrow Wilson, Roosevelt identified the national "self"
requiring defense with American values expressed as universals on
the global stage. In his formulation, however, the system to be defended was not just electoral democracy or even human rights; it
was the entire panoply of values enshrined in the New Deal. Roosevelt summarized these in broad terms as the "Four Freedoms": freedom of speech and of worship, freedom from want, and freedom from
fear. All, he argued, were in imminent danger of loss if the Axis
came to dominate Europe and Asia. The last two freedoms represented something new in American civil religion. Freedom from
want referred to people's right to economic security, while freedom
from fear meant eventual world disarmament and an effective
United Nations organization. As well as America's First Amendment

freedoms, *these* were the values directly menaced by fascism. In the event of a Nazi victory in Europe, Roosevelt warned,

> The American laborer would have to compete with slave labor in the rest of the world. Minimum wages, maximum hours? Nonsense: Wages and hours (would be) fixed by Hitler. The dignity and power and standard of living of the American worker and farmer would be gone. Trade unions would become historic(al) relics, and collective bargaining a joke.[22]

FDR's argument was better grounded than those of Wilson and Lansing, since, unlike Wilhelmine Germany, the Third Reich had occupied most of Western Europe and Imperial Japan much of East Asia. The Axis Powers therefore had a record that could be pointed to, including treaties breached, nations subjected to surprise attacks, parliamentary regimes subverted and overthrown, trade unions outlawed, political opponents imprisoned or murdered, and "inferior races" enslaved or massacred. One may still argue, as Patrick J. Buchanan and others have done, that it was not necessary to make war against the fascists, since they were not interested in attacking the United States. Left to their own devices, Buchanan maintains, the Nazis would have spent their energy fighting the Russians, and the Japanese the Chinese, since each nation aspired to become a great power dominant within its region, not a co-ruler of the entire earth.[23]

Most historians disagree with this assessment, but even if Buchanan is right about the Axis leaders' intentions, he misses a point that Roosevelt saw clearly. Germany and Japan were not second-rate industrial powers like Russia, formerly one of the world's poorest societies, now being driven toward modernization by Joseph Stalin's dictatorship, but with a very long way to go. They were economic powerhouses whose productive capacity, growing exponentially with each new conquest, gave their elitist ideologies an unprecedented capacity for realization on a global scale. Roosevelt's fundamental assumption was that the United States could not coexist peacefully with

We're Free to Choose . . . This Today or This Tomorrow, *1942.*
U.S. Army poster showing Nazism as a threat to the American system
of collective bargaining. (Source: University of North Texas
Digital Library, Posters Collection.)

such a dynamic and oppressive system without having to accommodate it, which, for America, would mean losing its own moral compass and political identity. Simplifying the matter, Vice President Henry Wallace declared, "This is a fight between a slave world and a free world." Director Frank Capra would use that Lincolnesque reference in the first film of his famous series *Why We Fight* to depict a world divided between the forces of darkness and the forces of light.[24]

At this point, the two sides of Wilsonian self-defense merged. The defense of universal values like the Four Freedoms fused with the need to prevent an Evil Enemy from dominating the world. The result was something close to a doctrine of American jihad: an obligatory crusade to rescue the world from aggressive, vicious adversaries and their false ideologies. Ironically, though, just as this crusade was triumphing in the ashes of Berlin and Hiroshima, the stage was set for a further metamorphosis of the idea of self-defense. For the United States was the only nation to emerge from World War II richer, stronger, more united, and more capable of exercising global power than before the war. America bestrode the world as a new colossus, the natural successor to the weakened European empires, ready at last to follow Henry Luce's advice to make the twentieth century "the American Century."[25] Its only competitor, as the period of Allied solidarity gave way to mutual suspicion and conflict, was the far less wealthy and dynamic Soviet Union.

What would it mean, under these circumstances, to preach a moral crusade against evil aggressors and false ideology? From 1947 on, U.S. leaders like Harry S. Truman and Dean Acheson called for a global struggle to defend the Free World against the threat of Communist subversion and takeover. They apparently believed that they were simply carrying on the Wilson-Roosevelt tradition of self-defense under the new circumstances of the Cold War. What they were actually doing, however, was reframing the concept to justify the defense of America's new imperial position. Deferring further discussion of the Cold War to our next chapter, let us zero in on the main elements of this new doctrine in the current War on Terrorism.[26]

DEFENDING AMERICAN SUPREMACY:
THE WAR ON TERRORISM

Recall the basic questions that one needs to ask about any claim of self-defense: What are we defending? Whom are we defending it against? Is the method of defense rational? What are the likely costs?

When it comes to recent U.S. attempts to put al-Qaeda out of operation, the answers to the first two questions, at least, are relatively clear. But from its inception the so-called War on Terrorism triggered by the attacks of September 11, 2001, was conducted against a much broader range of groups than al-Qaeda and its immediate supporters. By 2010, it had expanded to include massive military operations in Afghanistan and Iraq, targeted missile attacks in Pakistan and Yemen, and covert operations of various sorts from Lebanon to the Philippines in the Islamic world, as well as in non-Islamic nations like Colombia and Congo.

How could these diverse, largely unrelated activities be justified on grounds of self-defense, when so few terrorist or insurgent groups had attacked the United States or had any plans to do so? Al-Qaeda, which killed or wounded Americans in East Africa, in Yemen, and, of course, in the United States, was treated as the archetypal terrorist group, although it was clearly the exception rather than the rule. Iraqi insurgents and the Afghan Taliban fought against American troops who had invaded their nations, but their activities were limited to those homelands. The Pakistani Taliban and Lashkar-e-Taiba, the Somali al-Shabaab, the Filipino Abu Sayyaf, the Colombian FARC, and most other groups denominated as terrorist made war on their own governments and rival organizations but seldom attacked U.S. armed forces or American civilians. Some militant organizations gave each other practical assistance, but most did not, and when they did cooperate, this was usually a result, rather than a cause, of U.S. actions against them. In fact, only a handful of the forty-five groups worldwide listed by the State Department as terrorist organizations have been implicated in any sort of violence against Americans.[27]

What, then, made the War on Terrorism, not just on al-Qaeda, a war of self-defense? The answer lay in a further redefinition of the nation, which was now considered to encompass the entire United States presence abroad, including military and intelligence forces, civilian employees, private contractors, development workers, business representatives, journalists, and others—an establishment numbering several million people, and growing rapidly. The expansion of this "America abroad" began during the Cold War, when the United States pledged to go to the aid of any allied nation threatened by Communist takeover and established military bases, cultural and propaganda centers, and economic aid missions around the globe. The Soviet Union's collapse left the Americans without a Great Power competitor, but rather than withdraw from any of the positions occupied earlier, they proliferated military missions and multiplied alliances in a broad arc ranging from Eastern Europe and the Balkans through the Middle East to Central Asia, South Asia, and the Pacific. When this expansion provoked resistance, assaults on those representing the United States abroad were assimilated to attacks on the homeland. In addition, the right of self-defense was explicitly broadened to legitimize preemptive strikes against groups or nations said to pose a threat to U.S. global interests. Finally, the list of nations or groups considered unacceptably threatening was expanded to include those that refused to participate as our allies in the War on Terrorism. The result of these revisions was the development of a greatly expanded rationale for warfare against perceived enemies around the world.

The notion that defending the nation means defending its most recently occupied advance position marks a major innovation in self-defense doctrine. It means that attacks against American forces or civilian workers anywhere—regardless of their reasons (or lack of reasons) for being there—are considered deserving of a violent response. For example, suppose we invade Iraq on grounds of self-defense, believing wrongly that Saddam Hussein is in league with al-Qaeda and that he possesses chemical and bacteriological weapons. Suppose further that forces opposed to the U.S. presence in Iraq respond by attacking our troops. Counterattacks by our forces are then called self-defense on the sole ground that they have been attacked, without regard to the justice of the U.S. invasion or the legitimacy of the subsequent occupation.

In effect, this is what the well-intentioned but mindless slogan "Support the troops" means. Its implications are quite startling. For if the defense of any advance position can be justified simply because it is *our* position, we have a right to undertake new conquests in order to defend old ones. This is the classic logic of imperial expansion. (Julius Caesar used it to justify invading Britain, and Hitler to justify his attack on Poland.) The emotional appeal of "Support the troops," of course, has to do with the fact that they are our kinfolk, friends, neighbors, or countrymen. We want them to stay out of trouble and come home safe. But justifying their activities abroad on grounds of self-defense, no matter what they may be doing, involves a more complex and dubious sort of identification. Repeated expressions of gratitude to soldiers and civilians working in war zones for risking life and limb to "preserve our liberty" and "keep us safe" are one indication of this. It is considered bad taste, or worse, to ask whether these activities actually further the causes of liberty or national security, and whether they embody the values we cherish. But failing to ask these questions creates what might be called imperial circularity.

Imperial circularity: we are defending a forward position because our previous position came under attack; we were defending that position because a prior position was threatened; and so forth. This logic, which produces a continuous expansion of U.S. military commitments abroad, effectively erases the distinction between self-defense and aggression. It also erases the distinction between America conceived of as a nation and as an empire. Before the end of the Cold War, most American commentators insisted that the USSR, not the United States, was an "imperialist" power. But a growing scholarly consensus now supports the idea that the United States' wide-ranging economic, political, and military activities, taken as a whole, constitute a type of global empire.[28] The American military and civilian personnel serving abroad play the same role, essentially, that those serving in the British Colonial Service or imperial armies did in Queen Victoria's day. Many of the activities that they engage in, from offering "natives" the benefits of civilization to suppressing rebels, training local soldiers and police, and paying off cooperative local chiefs, are classic imperial activities. Especially since the 1990s, the conflation of this imperial vanguard with the nation has produced a radical redefinition of national security.

Coinciding with this redefinition, self-defense has been extended to justify preventive and retaliatory attacks against those who obstruct America's global expansion. Following the September 11 disaster, Congress voted 420–1 in the House and 98–0 in the Senate to give President Bush the power "to use all necessary and appropriate force against those nations, organizations, or persons he determines planned, authorized, committed, or aided the terrorist attacks that occurred on September 11, 2001, or harbored such organizations or persons, in order to prevent any future acts of international terrorism against the United States by such nations, organizations or persons."[29] Two days later, Bush announced, "Every nation in every region now has a decision to make. Either you are with us or you are with the terrorists."[30] After ordering the invasion of Iraq, the president made the expansion of doctrine more explicit. The right of self-defense, he asserted, justified attacks on "any person, organization or government that supports, protects or harbors terrorists," since all these were "complicit in the murder of the innocent and equally guilty of terrorist crimes."[31]

To many of those traumatized by the events of September 11 and thirsting to apprehend their perpetrators, this approach seemed nothing more than common sense. If the Taliban regime in Afghanistan would not hunt Usama bin Laden down and turn him over immediately to the Americans, it must be overthrown. End of discussion. Americans were not made aware that U.S. representatives had talked with Taliban leaders about bin Laden many times before September 11, nor were they asked to consider that the Afghan regime's declared readiness to hand him over or have him tried under Islamic law, if there was evidence that he organized the attacks, might be more than a ruse or stalling tactic.[32] In the rush to retaliate, no one informed the public that international law (which is considered part of American law) condemns attacks on those who merely tolerate wrongdoers or give them sanctuary, since such attacks escalate and spread the violence.[33] Nor was any serious consideration given to the likely consequences of overthrowing the Taliban regime. A few independent commentators warned that a war in Afghanistan would take innocent lives, saddle the United States with a new imperial domain to occupy or administer, and greatly multiply the number of anti-American insurgents, but their views were considered dangerously soft and were ignored.

From the perspective of self-defense, the rationality of U.S. strategy in the War on Terrorism remains open to question. The Obama administration came to power in 2009 with a mandate to liquidate America's war in Iraq and took steps to do so. But after six years of invasion, insurgency, counterinsurgency, and civil violence, the future of that nation, and, with it, the size of a continuing U.S. military presence there, remain uncertain. The situation in war-torn, impoverished Afghanistan is even murkier. There, after reviewing eight years of relatively fruitless struggle, the new regime in Washington committed itself to an infusion of thirty thousand additional troops roughly modeled after the 2007 troop surge in Iraq, but with a promise to begin withdrawing an unspecified number of soldiers in 2011. The purpose of the war, according to the president, was self-defense; that is, it was to prevent al-Qaeda from using Afghanistan as a base of operations. But only a handful of al-Qaeda fighters remain in Afghanistan. The rest have departed either for Pakistan or for other lands. They seem to have no great need to use Afghanistan as a base. Nevertheless, the official reason for the U.S. campaign in that country is to prevent them from returning, if the Taliban should retake power there.

Does this make sense? If the enemy in the Afghan War is really al-Qaeda, not the Taliban, why not agree to withdraw U.S. troops in exchange for an enforceable agreement to keep al-Qaeda from returning? (One can imagine many ways of enforcing such an agreement with the aid of neutral Muslim nations and international observers.) American intentions toward the Taliban have become cloudier with the passage of time. Statements by top U.S. officials suggested that the purpose of the 2010 troop surge was not to defeat that organization but to prevent it from winning the war, thus setting the stage for future negotiations on terms favorable to America and its local allies. A second announced goal was to establish functioning local and provincial governments that could challenge the insurgents' record of honest civil administration, and a third was to "Afghan-ize" the war by training and equipping competent Afghan army units and police. Despite the low-key tone adopted by administration officials in describing this program, however, it seemed as ambitious as any of the "nation-building" projects proposed by the administration of George W. Bush. As James Jay Carafano of the Heritage Foundation stated of President Obama's anti-terrorist policies in general, "I don't think it's even fair to call it Bush Lite. It's Bush. It's really, really hard to find a difference that's meaningful and not atmospheric."[34]

The prevailing uncertainty about the feasibility and likely costs of these activities, combined with the war's tendency to spread to new theaters, left the public in a state that one might call passive discontent. Public opinion polls early in 2010 continued to show a clear majority of Americans opposing the Afghan War, as well as approving of the withdrawal from Iraq. Most respondents supported the Obama troop surge but remained pessimistic overall about the likelihood of a successful outcome of the war.[35] Since 2005–6, when opinion turned massively against the Iraq War, the American public has displayed a marked lack of enthusiasm for U.S. military interventions. This shift marked the most significant increase in anti-war sentiment since the Vietnam War. On the other hand, public opposition has not reached a level of intensity sufficient to produce a large, militant mobilization à la the anti-Vietnam "Movement." Rather, those who disapprove of these interventions have expressed themselves mainly by participating in electoral politics.

The Democratic Party was the chief beneficiary of this discontent in the congressional elections of 2006 and the presidential election of 2008. To some extent, President Obama's presence in the White House, as well as his somewhat oracular statements on Afghanistan, seemed to have tempered public disapproval, temporarily at least, and kept it from spilling into the streets. The nation's continuing economic difficulties, which turned people's attention inward, may also have played a role, especially considering that the armed services and military-industrial corporations remained among the few reliable sources of employment for working-class and middle-class Americans. Nevertheless, there are reasons to believe that, as the War on Terrorism wears on inconclusively, questions heretofore suppressed will force themselves into public consciousness, and the debate will intensify.

One such question, heretofore taboo, concerns the validity of continuing U.S. efforts to defeat al-Qaeda and the Taliban by assassinating or capturing their leaders, representatives, and top field commanders. To raise doubts about the rationality of this policy may seem timorous, disloyal, or simply irrelevant to those who seek to kill or capture those adversaries. The tendency to equate self-defense with retaliation is quite strong. We often think of it in terms of a fistfight. Yet, as the philosopher David Rodin warns us, "it is extremely important to clearly distinguish self-defense from punishment."[36] Depending upon the circumstances, violent retaliation may actually *decrease* national security. One shudders to think what might have happened to both Russia and America if Premier Nikita Khrushchev had retaliated for the invasion of Soviet airspace by U-2 pilot Francis Gary Powers in 1960, or if President John F. Kennedy had retaliated with air strikes after Soviet missiles were discovered in Cuba two years later.

It is vital to try to think more clearly about what self-defense really means in the context of the War on Terrorism. "Kill the terrorists before they kill us" sounds like a rational policy, but it assumes, first, that those designated as terrorist enemies are united in their determination to kill or grievously harm us; second, that there is no better way to deal with them than by killing or disabling them; and, third, that killing or disabling some of them will reduce the overall danger to us. Each of these assumptions is questionable. For example, relations between the Taliban and al-Qaeda are reportedly severely strained, and have been for some time.[37] Targeting Taliban leaders for assassination, however, drives them into al-Qaeda's arms. Similarly, although President Obama stated in accepting his Nobel Peace Prize that "negotiations cannot convince al Qaeda's leaders to lay down their arms," there is no evidence that he has offered to talk with them.[38] Yet offering to talk with terrorist groups has often generated splits within their ranks, separating militants with serious political interests from those interested only in expressive acts of destruction.[39] We will have more to say about this in the final chapter of this book.

It is natural to want to kill those who attacked us and to punish those who provided them with sanctuary. But is this strategic self-defense, or is it revenge? The use of violence in self-defense may be an effective strategy if it succeeds in dismantling the leadership of a hostile group *without* generating an even greater surge of violent opposition. But if violence escalates as each side takes revenge on the other in the name of self-defense, the result can be a widening spiral that makes victory either impossible or worthless. During the Vietnam War, for example, the United States sponsored the Phoenix Program, a campaign of assassination aimed at killing suspected Communist leaders and cadres at the village level, as well as in the cities. The program killed an estimated thirty-five thousand Vietnamese without notably improving the security of the South Vietnamese regime. Its main result seems to have been to strengthen the rebels' will to fight.[40] When anti-insurgent violence generates increased recruitment of insurgents, this not only creates more serious threats, it also confronts authorities with the prospect of killing thousands or tens of thousands of opponents—a policy that almost always demoralizes, corrupts, and ruins those who implement it.

Near the end of Joseph Conrad's famous novella *Heart of Darkness*, the narrator discovers a report written by the European ivory hunter and "universal genius" Kurtz. Kurtz's essay began by outlining grandiose, altruistic schemes to benefit the Congo natives, but he had later gone back and "scrawled" at the end a phrase Conrad calls "luminous and terrifying, like a flash of lightning in a serene sky: 'Exterminate all the brutes!' "[41] America's wars of self-defense teach us that attempts to pacify and civilize the wild places that may give our enemies sanctuary often end in campaigns to exterminate insurgent "brutes." Particularly when what we are defending is an expanding empire, this sort of self-defense represents a form of self-destruction. We need to discover more effective and humane ways of dealing with genuine threats to American lives and values.

3

BEAT THE DEVIL:

HUMANITARIAN INTERVENTIONS AND

MORAL CRUSADES

Arguments for war based on self-defense suffer from one great weakness: they invite debate. Leaders may declare that the republic is in danger, but declarations alone do not convince the public that an alleged threat is serious enough to warrant a violent response, or that violence is the only way to respond. Expanding self-defense to justify virtually every U.S. military initiative thins the doctrine out, and skepticism increases when these initiatives fail to make us more secure. As a result, Americans often ask hard questions before agreeing to support "defensive" wars. How serious, really, is the danger to our nation? How do we know this? Is military action the best way to counter it? What other methods have been tried?

The Diabolization of Saddam Hussein

These were precisely the questions voiced in 2002, when high-ranking American officials began to promote a war aimed at overthrowing the regime of Saddam Hussein. From President George W. Bush down, administration spokespeople declared that the Iraqi dictator, although defeated and largely disarmed in the Persian Gulf War ten years earlier, still posed a grave and immediate danger to the United

States. Why? Because of his possession of weapons of mass destruction, and his alliance with the terrorists who had attacked New York
and Washington on September 11, 2001. "Simply stated, there is no
doubt that Saddam Hussein now has weapons of mass destruction,"
declared Vice President Dick Cheney in August 2002. A few weeks
later, testifying before Congress, Secretary of Defense Donald Rumsfeld was equally blunt: "No terrorist state poses a greater or more immediate threat to the security of our people and the stability of the
world than the regime of Saddam Hussein in Iraq."[1]

But did Saddam have nuclear, chemical, or biological weapons?
Was he in contact with al-Qaeda terrorists or others of that ilk? As
we know, the answer to both questions was no. With members of
Congress and religious figures, community leaders, and journalists
demanding evidence to support these charges, Bush administration
officials unlimbered an argument that, if true, would make factual
evidence irrelevant. Saddam Hussein was more than a thuggish nationalist hostile to U.S. interests in the Middle East, they declared.
He was also an Evil Enemy determined to cause maximum harm to
America and its people. Even if it turned out that he had no chemical weapons, nukes, or good buddies in al-Qaeda *at present*, he was
bound to obtain them sooner or later and to use them against us. As
National Security Adviser Condoleezza Rice put it, Saddam was "an
evil man who, left to his own devices, will wreak havoc again on his
own population, his neighbors and, if he gets weapons of mass destruction and the means to deliver them, all of us."[2]

Condi Rice was something of a newcomer to the campaign to
diabolize Saddam, but neo-conservatives had been talking this way
about him ever since George W. Bush took office. Bush knew that
Iraqi officials had reportedly plotted against the life of his father, the
former president, in 1993, and that President Bill Clinton had retaliated for this by dispatching cruise missiles to destroy Iraqi intelligence headquarters in Baghdad.[3] The story that the president and
his advisers told was of a tyrannical figure so satanic and depraved
that attacking innocent people was dictated by his very nature. One

month after the twin towers of the World Trade Center came crash-
ing down, *Wall Street Journal* opinion editor Max Boot opined:

> The debate about whether Hussein was implicated in the Septem-
> ber 11 attacks misses the point. Who cares if he was involved in
> this particular barbarity? He has been involved in so many bar-
> barities over the years—from gassing the Kurds to raping the
> Kuwaitis—that he has already earned himself a death sentence a
> thousand times over. But it is not just a matter of justice to de-
> pose Hussein. It is a matter of self defence: he is working to ac-
> quire weapons of mass destruction that he or his confederates will
> unleash against the US and its allies if given the chance.[4]

Richard Lowry of the *National Review* agreed: "It doesn't take care-
ful detective work to know that Saddam Hussein is a perpetual enemy
of the United States."[5] And Senator Zell Miller (D-Ga.) supplied the
motive for this eternal enmity: "We don't have to prove [Saddam]
was involved with Sept. 11 or with Al Qaeda. We know he hates the
United States."[6] This unchangeable fact—Saddam's unquenchable
will to destroy good people and institutions—was the reason that not
even painful sanctions could deter him from attempting to harm
Americans. According to National Security Adviser Rice, there was
therefore no alternative to a war aimed at ridding the world of him:

> The case for regime change is very strong. This is a regime that we
> know has twice tried and come closer than we thought at the
> time to acquiring nuclear weapons. He has used chemical weap-
> ons against his own people and against his neighbors, he has in-
> vaded his neighbors, he has killed thousands of his own people.
> He shoots at our planes, our airplanes, in the no-fly zones where
> we are trying to enforce U.N. security resolutions.[7]

These accusations were mostly true, but they involved several gro-
tesque omissions. The U.S. government backed Saddam in his rise

to absolute power in Iraq. When he invaded Iran and used chemical weapons against the Iranians and the Kurds, he was a trusted ally of the United States. Before invading his neighbor Kuwait, he seems to have been given the green light to do so by the American ambassador to Iraq. Since other U.S. enemies, including the Afghan Islamists, also began as U.S. clients, this revealing story is worth recounting briefly.

The Americans "discovered" Saddam in 1959, when the Eisenhower administration decided to try to get rid of the old Iraqi dictator, Abd al-Karim Qasim. Qasim wanted Iraq to leave the U.S.-supported Baghdad Pact organization and play a more neutral role in the Cold War—a position that earned him the equivalent of a CIA death sentence. Since Saddam was violently anti-Communist, the CIA funneled money and other aid to him and his Baath Party comrades, who thereupon attempted unsuccessfully to assassinate Qasim. Wounded in the attempt, the young militant escaped to Egypt, returning to Iraq a few years later with a law degree and an ambition to rule as Supreme Leader. When Qasim was finally overthrown, Saddam became chief of intelligence and pleased his U.S. sponsors by executing several thousand Iraqi Communists.[8] His most valuable contribution to the American cause, however, came in 1980, when, as Supreme Leader, he started the Iran-Iraq War.

The Ayatollah Ruhollah Khomeini's Islamic Republic was then the Evil Enemy par excellence. America's nightmare—ironic in the light of more recent events—was that Khomeini would extend his influence over Iraq by fomenting an uprising among that country's majority-Shia population. The United States' gratitude to Saddam for striking preemptively at Iran took the form of loans, grants, food credits, "dual use" military equipment, and high-tech battlefield information, which he used to make chemical warfare attacks against the Iranians and Kurdish dissidents. President Ronald Reagan's administration protested formally against the use of poison gas, but the opposition to Iraq's use of chemical weapons was purely rhetorical.[9] Reagan sent a trusted representative, future defense secretary Donald

Rumsfeld, to rap Saddam's knuckles—and promise him further aid and cooperation. Of course, this "friendship" had its limits. After 1984, when Iraq seemed to be getting too strong, the U.S. government covertly funneled military aid to its Iranian enemies via Israel—an activity exposed when Congress investigated the Iran-Contra scandal.[10]

What finally ended America's long dalliance with Saddam was the Iraqi dictator's decision to invade neighboring Kuwait in order to settle a series of long-standing disputes with that nation. The role played in this decision by U.S. Ambassador April Glaspie remains a subject of considerable controversy. It is known that she met with Saddam and his foreign minister, Tariq Aziz, on July 25, 1990, eight days before the invasion of Kuwait. She questioned them about Iraqi troop movements toward the Kuwait border, expressed the Bush administration's hope that there would be a peaceful settlement of the dispute, and then informed them that the United States had "no interest" in the matter.[11] Perhaps the hottest item in that dispute was a huge oil field on the Iraq-Kuwait border known as the Rumaillah field. The Kuwaitis were said to be "slant-drilling" into the field and taking the lion's share of the oil—an activity that infuriated the Iraqis, whose economy had been devastated by the war with Iran, while the Kuwaiti sheikhs were richer than ever. There is some evidence that the Americans would not have objected if Saddam had merely seized the oil field, but that they did not expect him to take the whole country.[12] Richard Haass, a top official of the Bush administration, states in his recent memoir that he did not expect Saddam to "invade Kuwait (much less occupy all of it)"—an odd way of admitting that he and others anticipated a limited incursion.[13] But Saddam did invade in force, and George H. W. Bush responded by initiating the most massive U.S. military intervention since the Vietnam War.

Interestingly, in making a case for a war to liberate Kuwait, the first Bush administration did *not* take the position that Saddam Hussein was evil incarnate. In the run-up to Operation Desert Storm, the American president labeled him an international lawbreaker and a menace to world peace but stopped short of attributing his actions to sheer malice, irredeemable moral corruption, or sadistic impulses. Only one accusation suggested evil in the theo-political sense. Calling Saddam "the Emir of cruelty," Bush repeated the unfounded charge that Iraqi troops occupying Kuwait had removed babies from hospital incubators and thrown people off dialysis machines in order to send this medical equipment back to Baghdad. But, in almost the same breath, he remarked, "Now I don't know how many of these tales can be authenticated."[14]

For Bush, a veteran of World War II, the alleged cruelty of Iraqi troops was beside the point. Saddam Hussein's real offense was to invade and occupy a defenseless nation in pursuit of his dreams of national wealth, glory, and regional power—behavior that evoked memories of the fascist aggression that provoked the war of 1939–45. In the president's view, the invasion clearly justified intervention in support of Kuwait's independence, the principles of international law, and the current balance of power in the Middle East.[15] Although Bush did not say as much, Iraq's attempt to become the region's leading oil producer, contrary to American wishes, was clearly another motive for war. But these rationales did not justify carrying the fight to Baghdad in order to overthrow Saddam Hussein's government and put a new regime in power. If the elder Bush had truly believed that Saddam was Hitler reincarnated, he would have had no choice but to invade and occupy Iraq. That he did not do this reveals his true assessment of the Iraqi dictator as a violent nationalist who needed to be restrained, not a satanic figure requiring annihilation. It would be sufficient to weaken him and his nation to the point that they would not be able to play an important role in regional politics.[16]

The Persian Gulf War ended with the expulsion of Iraqi troops from Kuwait, the destruction of much of Saddam's military capacity, and the establishment of an autonomous Kurdish region protected by U.S. air power in northern Iraq. Ten years later, however, a far weaker Saddam Hussein did become a diabolical figure, at least in the rhetoric of the second President Bush and his advisers. Several factors drove the campaign of diabolization, including American desires to control Iraq's oil supplies, pro-Israel fury at Saddam's financial support for the families of Palestinian suicide bombers, and, perhaps, memories of the alleged plot to assassinate the elder President Bush. The new, intolerable Saddam also illustrates a general strategic/rhetorical principle: for those who advocate war, the most convincing way to put troublesome objections to rest is to produce an Evil Enemy. The Evil Enemy is a violent adversary, known for brutality toward his own people, who harbors a constant and implacable intention to harm Americans and violate their cherished values. The fact that he was a former friend or ally of the United States, as Russia's Joseph Stalin and Usama bin Laden's Afghan comrades were, is not a requirement for EE status, but this adds to his apparent treachery.

Are there Evil Enemies? In the absolute sense of one driven by pure malice to destroy the Good, I think not. Even Adolf Hitler was a creature of history, not an avatar of supra-historical Evil. In the relative sense, yes—but they are rarities. The world is full of violent leaders and organizations who have no interest in harming us, and leaders and organizations hostile to our power that are not committed to violence, except, perhaps, in their own defense. If Saddam Hussein had been presented only as a brutal dictator like Robert Mugabe of Zimbabwe, or as a radical nationalist on the order of, say, Venezuela's President Hugo Chávez, it would have been impossible to make the case that his very existence imperiled America. It takes both an evil character and evil intentions to construct an Evil Enemy. A campaign of diabolization thus becomes an early warning sign of war. At the point that we begin to hear about Chávez's or Mugabe's satanic character, intentions, and capacity to harm us, we will know that a campaign to use force against him has begun. Our job, if this should occur, is to avoid being stampeded by allegations of brutality or hostility, either of which may be true, into concluding that both are true, and that an attack against us is therefore imminent or inevitable.

BASIC ATTRIBUTES OF THE DIABOLICAL ENEMY

An enemy who incarnates the spirit of destruction—one who seeks to destroy the Good simply because it is good—is an old theme in American discourse about war.[17] One of the features that makes the devil diabolical is his insatiable lust for power. His ambition is universal; he wants to be God. The very existence of such a foe therefore implies a need for immediate self-defense and makes a case for a preemptive strike. Why wait for an inevitable attack if an attack is truly inevitable? Moreover, a diabolical enemy gives a major boost to virtually every other justification for war, such as the need to rescue his victims from intolerable oppression. Finally, the allegation that an adversary is absolutely evil, not just wrongheaded or overly aggressive, is difficult to refute without seeming to appease the enemy. Critics who argued that Saddam Hussein was merely a brutal tyrant in a world filled with such creatures could not thwart the Bush administration's drive to brand him a clear and present danger to the United States. Distinctions based on relative degrees of wrongdoing were washed away by the assertion that an absolutely malicious force was loose in the world, and that its intended target was America.

Public acceptance of this charge, it seems clear, was conditioned by the horrors of the 9/11 attacks. The face of the devil on that occasion was that of Usama bin Laden, but since the al-Qaeda leader had escaped our vengeance—and since his pronouncements and activities continued to inspire widespread fear—Saddam Hussein could serve as a convenient stand-in. If Satan was among us, his mark might well be found on other depraved and malicious figures, such as the Iraqi dictator. And Saddam, unlike Usama, could be located and destroyed. As in the case of the Vietnam War, public approval of the Iraq War flattened out after the first year and declined steadily thereafter.[18] Nevertheless, since Saddam had clearly been a murderous ruler, many Americans believed that he deserved to be overthrown, and (sliding from relative to absolute evil) that he would *eventually* have secured weapons of mass destruction and used them somehow against the United States.

How, then, are Evil Enemies depicted in America? What convinces us that, while conflicts with some individuals or groups can be resolved by negotiation, deterrent threats, or a limited use of force, conflicts with others require nothing less than their complete destruction? Our history provides us with the basic elements of an Evil Enemy image. Psychologists point out that these elements have a dual character. On the one hand, they represent the "not us"—features directly opposed to those of our positive self-image. We are good; they are bad. On the other, they often reflect unwanted aspects of ourselves that we seek to purge or deny by projecting them onto the "not us."[19] We are not so good; no, we are okay, and *they* are the bad ones. In American culture one recognizes the Evil Enemy by signs such as these:

He is a tyrant.[20] In our civil religion, this is a moral judgment, not merely a political description. Not only does the tyrant have too much power—a wrong in itself, according to liberal theorists like John Locke and Thomas Jefferson—he also misuses it because of his destructive impulses and lack of self-control. The Evil Enemy is *addicted* to power and exercises it to satisfy corrupt desires, including a love of domination, financial greed, depraved personal tastes, and sadistic impulses toward those subject to his will. This is how New England Puritans thought of the English rulers they were escaping, and how many Patriot preachers and politicians portrayed King George III and the British colonialists at the time of the American Revolution.[21] Sermons and speeches of that era thunder against "corruption and backsliding, self-love and self-interest, 'dissipation, extravagance, gaming, idleness and intemperance'"—all seen as both American sins requiring expiation and deep-dyed characteristics of the British enemy.[22] From George III to General Santa Anna, Kaiser Wilhelm II,

Adolf Hitler, and Saddam Hussein, the image of the villainous tyrant combines excessive power with vicious personal habits. And destroying the tyrant is frequently linked with the expectation that violence will purify and transform the nation.[23]

He seeks world domination. Like John Milton's Satan, the Evil Enemy is not content merely to reign in hell; he wants to rule heaven as well. Usama bin Laden's religiosity and apparent self-discipline might seem to exempt him from the usual charges of personal decadence, but we see him, nonetheless, as a megalomaniac fiend aiming at world conquest. One perceptive writer notes that, in popular culture, bin Laden

> is the classic evil genius—a combination of Dr. No, Goldfinger, and all those other larger than life villains who were always bent on world domination. One almost imagines bin Laden monitoring the complex progress of his many agents, tracking them on banks of computers and television screens in his hi-tech Afghan cave, watching his handiwork with a quiet satisfaction, stroking his white cat with a depraved chuckle.[24]

One might respond by pointing out that, unlike fictitious villains, bin Laden is the genuine article: a perpetrator of ghastly crimes with the fanatic's absolute certainty that he speaks and acts for God. To be sure—but is he also a would-be global dictator? The answer to this is more complex. Clearly, a true believer like the Saudi jihadist would like to see Islam sweep the earth, consigning all "false religions" to the dustbin of history. Yet the jihad he preaches is aimed not at converting the world but at converting fellow Muslims to his version of the faith, restoring a pan-Muslim caliphate, and ridding the Islamic world of Western influence. If global power dropped into his lap, Usama would be unlikely to reject it, but the notion that his strategic aim is to rule the West is more a Dr. No fantasy than a judgment based on evidence. Of course, there are reasons to combat terrorists like bin Laden—but supposing that they intend to impose Islam on all of us transforms them from genuine adversaries into nightmare bogeymen. This is not helpful.

He is inhumanly cruel. A fixed aspect of the Evil Enemy is extreme cruelty, which often takes the form of ghastly atrocities, including torture, rape, and mass murder, committed against captured soldiers, political opponents, and vulnerable domestic or colonized populations. Inhuman cruelty is more common and far easier to prove than designs to conquer the world, and atrocity stories have a grim fascination for many people. Some degree of choice seems to be exercised in deciding which stories to attend to and which to believe. "Indian captivity" tales, many with strong sexual undertones, as well as tales of cannibalism and other extreme cruelties, were a literary staple from the seventeenth century on.[25] Before the U.S. Civil War, hundreds of thousands of readers were appalled (and, in some ways, thrilled) by the cruelty of Simon Legree, the fictitious plantation owner whose atrocious behavior toward Uncle Tom and other slaves in *Uncle Tom's Cabin* helped crystallize opposition to the southern slave system. We have already noted how reported German atrocities against the Belgians, exaggerated by U.S. newspapers and magazines, prepared Americans to fight the barbaric "Huns." In part because of disenchantment with these exaggerations, the press greatly understated Hitler's mistreatment of the Jews in the early 1940s and basically missed the story of the Holocaust.[26] The Japanese, on the other hand, were considered the masters of cruelty because of their often sadistic treatment of prisoners and subject populations, and because it was easier for white Americans to picture them as subhuman Oriental monsters.[27]

He is deceitful, clever, and malicious. We know the devil as the Father of Lies. The Evil Enemy is also known for his contempt of truth and willingness to advance his interests by speaking falsely. If he were not so persuasive—if he did not present a simulacrum of sincerity, playing skillfully on our trusting instincts—he would not be so dangerous. But he uses his wits to deceive us and tempts us to

This Is the Enemy, *1942. Racist caricature of evil Japanese assaulting a white woman. The long fingernails recall the image of the oriental movie villain Dr. Fu Manchu. (Source: Anonymous poster probably submitted in "This Is the Enemy" poster contest, 1942.)*

believe him, and when we do so, we fall. The purpose of his behavior is not just to achieve instrumental aims—geopolitical advantages, for example—but also to demonstrate his superiority by tricking and humiliating us. That is to say, he is malicious. Such a characterization of the enemy proves as potent an inducement to war as his megalomania or cruelty, since if we cannot believe what the other party says, especially if we think that his real aim in speaking is to deceive and humiliate us, negotiations of any sort are out of the question. "You can't negotiate with those people" means that the other party will employ nonviolent processes to lay the groundwork for his rise and our fall—and that this behavior is dictated by his very nature.

The first embodiment of this deceitful enemy image, perhaps, was the Native American, whom many white settlers considered demonic and congenitally incapable of keeping his word. (This may be a classic example of the "not us" problem referred to earlier, since settlers, state governments, and the U.S. government were notorious for "reinterpreting" or simply breaking treaties and other agreements with the Indians.) But the modern emphasis on deceptive negotiations by maleficent enemies is a product of the twentieth century, with its focus on the importance of sincerity. For Woodrow Wilson's secretary of state Robert Lansing, the primary German sin was insincerity and breach of faith.[28] A more spectacular example of deceit was Adolf Hitler's breach of the 1938 Munich Pact with Britain, France, and Italy, in which he promised to abandon all other territorial claims if the Western powers would allow him to absorb the Sudetenland region of Czechoslovakia. Virtually every U.S. enemy since Hitler has been tarred with the Munich brush in advance of negotiations; the belief that the adversary is a malicious deceiver makes talking peace seem worse than useless. Occasionally, leaders of our government actually believe that negotiations are fruitless for this reason. More often, the image of the Deceiver is invoked as a way of excusing their own refusal to negotiate or a decision to break off talks. (See chapter 5 for further discussion of this point.)

He is radically unlike us. This attribute of the Evil Enemy is often symbolized or crystallized as a difference in skin color and racial features. From the Indian Wars to the U.S. wars against Filipino insurgents, Japanese, North Koreans, and Arab Muslims, America's enemies have been thought of as inferior, nonwhite Others. Even when physical differences between white Americans and their adversaries were nonexistent or minimal, as in the case of Germans in the two world wars, leftist rebels in Latin America, or Arabs and Persians in the War on Terrorism, cartoons, posters, and other visual representations frequently used racial or ethnic stereotypes to portray the Bad Guys as swarthy villains. The persistence of these images in "post-racist" America has been discussed by a number of insightful scholars.[29] Their moral implications are particularly worth noting here, since images of the Other not only define our self-image by contrast but also serve as its shadow double, reflecting aspects of our own character that we despise.

One common image, for example, pictures the enemy as savage and uncivilized—barbarians lusting for blood. People at war sometimes generate such images deliberately, since they want to be thought of as terrifying; one thinks of al-Qaeda's televised decapitations, for example, or of American GIs displaying "trophy" ears and noses in Vietnam. But how civilized or uncivilized we are has always been a sore point for Americans. In earlier days, Europeans thought of us as savages (noble or otherwise). Many non-Americans still consider us a peculiarly violent people. For our part, we may well suspect, at times, that our devotion to respectability and order masks a tendency to throw off these restraints. For many of us, the gleeful abuse of prisoners by U.S. troops at Abu Ghraib Prison in Iraq was an excruciating glance in the mirror.

Similar questions are raised by a related enemy stereotype: the image of America's adversaries as members of an undifferentiated, de-individualized, unthinking horde. At their nastiest, these images turn the enemy symbolically into bugs, snakes, bats, or other vermin. They assert that the enemy is radically unlike us because we are free individuals who make our own decisions, while they are obedient slaves mindlessly following orders. Looked at as the shadow double, they may remind us that observers from Alexis de Tocqueville onward have described Americans as conformists who tend to follow the leader and have trouble thinking for themselves.[30] The vermin metaphor is peculiarly explosive, since it implicitly justifies war not only against the adversary's regime and armed forces but also against the civilian population—and such images, provoking fear and disgust, have long been associated with campaigns to "exterminate all the brutes." Again, American wartime experiences suggest that we are more likely to identify an entire people as the enemy if they are considered racial Others. In World War II, nuclear weapons were used against the Japanese, not the Germans. On the other hand, the Germans' ethnic similarity to many white Americans did not save the inhabitants of Dresden and Berlin from bombing attacks almost as destructive as those that destroyed Hiroshima and Nagasaki. This may be because, by February 1945, the Battle of the Bulge had occurred, and U.S. military deaths worldwide, although dwarfed by those of Russia, Germany, Japan, and China, were approaching half a million. When the struggle becomes intense enough, people dehumanize their enemies, whatever their race may be.

Studies of American attitudes in wartime suggest that early in a war, people identify the adversary regime and its armed forces as the enemy, but that after much blood has been shed, including our own, the Evil Enemy category broadens to include members of the civilian population.[31] The Vietnam War, which killed more than one million Vietnamese combatants and an estimated two million civilians, is a particularly ghastly example of this dynamic. Current efforts by the U.S. government to avoid having the War on Terrorism become a war against all Arabs or all Muslims are praiseworthy, but one needs to remember that the Roosevelt administration's Office of War Information made the same effort with regard to Germans and Japanese in the early days of World War II.[32] At a certain point, if the war escalates sufficiently, popular images of the enemy as deindividualized fanatics, loathsome, dangerous, and requiring extermination or imprisonment, need little incitement to flourish. Indeed, the single attack on Pearl Harbor was enough to incite Americans to intern more than a hundred thousand Japanese Americans and Japanese in detention camps for the duration of World War II.[33] Should our country be subject to another serious attack by Islamist militants, one can easily imagine a popular demand for retribution against all "potential terrorists" (i.e., Muslims) both at home and abroad. The idea that the United States can "scientifically" control the war so as to prevent this sort of violent spiral from occurring strikes me as a form of hubris incubating a great tragedy. War is simply not the best way to deal with the problem of terrorism.

HUMANITARIAN INTERVENTION:
THE CASE OF THE SPANISH-AMERICAN WAR

Defining one's enemy as evil, at least in a relative sense, is not a bad thing in itself. Why else would one feel justified in taking someone else's life or risking one's own in battle? General Carl von Clausewitz's famous statement that "war is a mere continuation of policy by other means" has never gone down well with people who don't believe in fighting except for morally compelling reasons. As noted earlier, Americans do not ordinarily consent to war in order to secure territory, economic advantages, or what some politicians refer to as national interests. We sometimes talk about securing *the* "national interest," but this term has rightly been called inherently ideological, blurring the boundaries between interest and morality by defining each in terms of the other.[34] When we fight, this is usually because we think that our cause is just and that the adversary's isn't.

The problem, however, is that a war cannot really be considered just unless it fulfills a few elementary conditions. First, it must be fought for good reasons, not for personal or national aggrandizement. Second, war must be the only way to realize these just aims. And third, the violence must not be excessive or incompatible with realizing our goals. These are very difficult conditions to meet.[35] But defining an enemy as *absolutely* evil makes it *seem* as though the conditions for just war have been met, even when they have not. If the enemy is satanic, eliminating him is a just cause by definition—no need to think further about less admirable motives for fighting. If he is unchangeably malicious and aggressive, there can be no way to eliminate him other than by conducting a violent crusade against him. No point in talking about changing our behavior, negotiating with the Bad Guys, or even trying to deter them using threats of violence. If a crusade is justified, furthermore, how can violence short of genocide be considered excessive or counterproductive? A struggle against the devil would be worthwhile even if none of us survived to tell about it.

The immensely popular Spanish-American War throws an un-
settling light on these principles and their implications. The 1898
war was a humanitarian intervention fought to liberate Cuba from
Spanish rule at a time when massive numbers of Cubans were dying
in a desperate struggle for independence. I remarked earlier that the
sinking of the battleship *Maine* in Havana Harbor galvanized public opinion because ordinary Americans deeply admired the heroism
of the Cuban guerrilla fighters and were horrified by the Spanish
response. To suppress the insurgency, the colonial authorities had
handed power over to General Valeriano Weyler Nicolau, aka "Butcher
Weyler," whose army tortured and killed prisoners, destroyed crops,
and forced half a million civilians into "reconcentration camps" where
they could be observed and controlled by the authorities. More than
a hundred thousand of these inmates died of starvation and disease.
The Spanish relieved Weyler of his post in 1897, but so far as American public opinion was concerned, the damage was done. The story
dramatized by mass-circulation newspapers and magazines pictured
the Spanish as cruel, anti-democratic despots, the Cubans as selfless
freedom fighters, and the United States as the disinterested liberator
of oppressed peoples. Alone among the world's nations, America could
be trusted to liberate the victims of oppression without stepping into
the oppressor's shoes. Uncle Sam would free Spain's Cuban, Puerto
Rican, and Philippine subjects without making further claims upon
them.

The image of a satanic enemy correlated with an exalted image of
Uncle Sam as a selfless crusader—a Liberator with no selfish interests of his own. But the image's unacknowledged shadow double
was waiting in the wings for his entry. When the brief war ended
with the rout of Spain's land and naval forces, President William
McKinley and his advisers decided that Madrid's former subjects
were not ready to govern themselves after all. How could benighted
Catholic peasants without any experience of capitalism or democracy observe the rule of law and protect their own liberty or (perhaps more importantly) foreign-owned property? McKinley later

recalled that, late one sleepless night in the White House, he was suddenly inspired to understand that

> there was nothing left for us to do but to take them all, and to edu-
> cate the Filipinos, and uplift and civilize and Christianize them,
> and by God's grace do the very best we could by them, as our fel-
> lowmen for whom Christ also died. And then I went to bed, and
> went to sleep, and slept soundly, and the next morning I sent for
> the chief engineer of the War department (our map-maker), and I
> told him to put the Philippines on the map of the United States,
> and there they are, and there they will stay while I am President.[36]

McKinley soon had his way with Congress. Over the protests of a loud but ineffectual dissenting bloc, the United States swiftly took over the defeated nation's Caribbean and Pacific possessions.

Almost immediately, a massive insurgency led by the popular national hero Emilio Aguinaldo erupted in the Philippines. The U.S. Army crushed it in a brutal three-year war that killed four thousand American soldiers, devastated the country, and took more than two hundred thousand Philippine lives. The American authorities pursued what has since become a familiar "carrot and stick" policy. On the one hand, they made serious attempts to win the Filipinos' loyalty and respect (or, as we might say, their "hearts and minds"). They "introduced aspects of their legal and tax codes to replace the hated Spanish system, established clinics to treat diseases, built schools, and did their best to demonstrate an interest in the welfare of the populace."[37] On the other hand, they considered rebellious Filipinos evil savages who merited the maximum punishment. One American general put it in a nutshell: "It may be necessary to kill half of the Filipinos in order that the remaining half of the popula-tion may be advanced to a higher plane of life than their present semi-barbarous state affords."[38]

When the insurgency spread throughout the islands, command-ing general Arthur MacArthur Jr. (father of the World War II hero) decided that enough was enough. He ordered his troops to execute insurgents, imprison their supporters, destroy rebel property, and force civilians into "protected zones," where, just as in Spanish-occupied Cuba, people starved and died of disease en masse. They also practiced several forms of officially sanctioned torture, including one that will be gruesomely familiar to modern readers. Called the "water cure," it involved holding a prisoner down, thrusting a bamboo pole into his mouth, and pouring "some dirty water, the filthier the better, . . . down his unwilling throat."[39]

In March 1902, the rebel leader Aguinaldo was captured, and by the summer the insurgency had been crushed—except for the Muslim Moro people of Mindanao, who are again in rebellion against the Philippine government and its American backers. Cuban independence was equally short-lived; the island would shortly become a U.S. protectorate and, after that, a neo-colonial dependency. Among many former supporters of the Spanish-American War at home, the sense of betrayal was tangible. "In disregard of our pledge of freedom and sovereignty to Cuba, we are imposing on that island conditions of colonial vassalage," said former Massachusetts governor George Boutwell. "God damn the U.S. for its vile conduct in the Philippine Isles," declared philosopher-psychologist William James.[40] Revolted by our excesses in the Philippines, Mark Twain suggested replacing the American flags flying there with "our usual flag, with the white stripes painted black and the stars replaced by the skull and crossbones."[41]

What was most startling and upsetting for Twain, James, and others was the war's shadow-double effect. Within two years, a noble intervention against an enemy guilty of the mass murder of insurgents and civilians turned into a war of occupation whose injustices precisely mirrored those originally targeted by the crusade. The reasons for this ugly transformation implicated motives for fighting the Spanish that had been repressed or soft-pedaled during the period of "save heroic Cuba" propaganda. Leaders like Teddy Roosevelt talked openly among themselves about the need to secure military bases and coaling stations from the Caribbean to East Asia in order to project American economic and military power across the Pacific. (A U.S.-sponsored coup in Hawaii was bringing that land under American domination during these same years.)[42] The Sugar Trust, the Tobacco Trust, and other agribusiness and banking interests were keenly interested in expanding their operations abroad.[43] The U.S. rulers understood as well as Twain and other members of the American Anti-Imperialist League did that the war to liberate Cuba was also a war to create an American overseas empire.

But McKinley was no hypocrite. He believed that the "message" vouchsafed him in the White House represented the voice of conscience. The same humanitarian ideology that convinced ordinary Americans to support the war persuaded the president to annex the Philippines. The face of the Evil Enemy morphed, in effect, from that of a brutal colonizer to that of a fanatical insurgent. The main goal of the crusade changed from liberty (chastened by order) to order (enlightened by liberty). These changes did not seem that uncomfortable, however, to most people outside the Anti-Imperialist League. One reason for this may be that in American civil religion, the archetypal narrative is the Exodus story, and the archetypal liberator is Moses.[44] The original New England settlers believed that they were the "new Israelites," a chosen people reenacting the flight from slavery to the Promised Land. During the Civil War both African Americans and northern whites compared Abraham Lincoln with Moses—an analogy also applied to McKinley after he, too, was felled by an assassin.[45] Later on, Franklin Roosevelt was deemed an American Moses for leading the nation out of the Depression and then defeating the Axis Powers.

Crucially, the figure of Moses has three defining features: he is a Liberator, rescuing the oppressed from slavery and leading them to freedom. But he is also a Reformer, who leads an internal crusade (the Golden Calf incident) to purge his followers of their sins, and a Lawgiver, bringing reason, order, and justice both to his own people and (postmortem, via Joshua) to the pagans who inhabit the new land. The Moses-figure integrates what otherwise might be considered contradictory aspects of the leader. The hero who helps the oppressed rebel against unjust authority and liberates them is the same person who later disciplines and purifies them, and who finally becomes their legitimate authority and lawful ruler. The Puritan leaders performed all these roles. So did America's Civil War leaders. Why, then, should Uncle Sam, having liberated the Spanish king's savage subjects, not also function as their liberator, purifier, and new ruler?

Liberating the oppressed from a radically inhumane regime thus seemed a just cause for war even if the United States then substituted its own rule for that of the deposed Evil Enemy. In the same way, using extreme violence to secure America's rule was considered justified because of the great evil it averted and the great good it claimed to inaugurate. Killing hundreds of thousands of Filipinos was considered a fair price to pay for saving the islands from lawlessness and chaos, and bringing their inhabitants "the blessings of good and stable government . . . under the free flag of the United States."[46] Finally, the war to liberate Cuba was considered unavoidable—a last resort—because of the unreasonableness of the Spanish and their unwillingness or inability to make peace. In fact, the United States had broken off negotiations with the liberal government in Madrid prior to the start of the conflict and refused to meet with Aguinaldo's representative at its end.[47] But that seemed a mere quibble to participants in what appeared to be a holy war of humanitarian liberation.

Not for the last time would American leaders begin by invoking the example of Moses and end by playing the role of Pharaoh. Nor would Mark Twain be the last critic to complain, "There must be two Americas, one that sets the captive free, and one that takes a once-captive's new freedom away from him, and picks a quarrel with him with nothing to found it on; then kills him to get his land."[48] Does this mean that the United States should never intervene militarily to prevent a humanitarian disaster, as it might have done in

1994 in Rwanda, for example, to help prevent acts of genocide? Not at all—but it does mean that we should intervene rarely, if at all, where we have what lawyers call "an interest in the case." Understanding that we are *not* uniquely virtuous liberators able to free the oppressed and then simply walk away, we can learn to resist appeals that make this arrogant assumption. We can demand that humanitarian interventions be made multilaterally, through international and regional organizations, rather than by parties seeking to profit from others' suffering. Indeed, if the acerbic Mr. Twain were still with us, he would very likely suggest that the reason we did not intervene in Rwanda in 1994 was because there was no profit in it.

Moral Crusades:
From the Good War to the Cold War

Most people still regard World War II—the "Good War"—as a successful effort to liberate the oppressed and secure the blessings of democracy and freedom to people around the world. This characterization is in many ways a fair one. Thanks to the Allied war effort, Nazi Germany and Imperial Japan were defeated, and the peoples that they had terrorized (at least, those who survived) were released from inhuman servitude. The United States assisted its Western allies to recover from the war's massive destruction by instituting the Marshall Plan and other forms of assistance. It helped its former enemies to rebuild economically, democratize their societies, and become prosperous new allies. Only our Soviet allies, who had suffered the worst losses of any combatant—about 21 million dead, 13 million of them soldiers, as opposed to 295,000 American military deaths—were excluded from this largesse. After 1949, when China went Communist, this former ally, with its 11 million war dead, including 10 million civilians, would also be excluded.[49] From 1947 on, we considered the Communist powers Evil Enemies: moral and political successors, as it were, to the defeated Axis Powers.

How did this happen? With little breathing room between conflicts, the crusade against fascism ended and a new global struggle began. Officials called it a Cold War, but its features were hot enough: competitive military alliances; a high-risk nuclear arms race; the subversion and overthrow of "unfriendly" regimes; assassinations and other covert actions; proxy wars in Asia, Africa, and Latin America; and immensely destructive armed conflicts in Korea (1950–53), Indochina (1964–73), and Afghanistan (1979–88). Historians remain divided about the extent to which U.S. activities in this period were primarily responses to the threat of Soviet expansionism or efforts to construct, maintain, and establish the supremacy of an American global empire.[50] Here we focus on what the Cold War story has to teach us about the international and internal implications of violent moral crusades.

The Cold War effectively began on March 12, 1947, when President Harry S. Truman appeared before a joint session of Congress to announce his Truman Doctrine, rightly called "the most significant expansion of American foreign policy since the Monroe Doctrine of 1823."[51] The problem that he wanted Congress to address was an alleged Soviet threat to the independence of Greece and Turkey. With the lessons of World War II in mind, Truman proposed to send millions of dollars in military aid to help these nations remain in the pro-Western camp. "I believe that it must be the policy of the United States to support free peoples who are resisting attempted subjugation by armed minorities or by outside pressure," he said. "If we falter in our leadership we may endanger the peace of the world—and we shall surely endanger the welfare of our own nation." The president was not yet proposing to send American troops to fight Communists; that would come three years later, when he ordered U.S. armed forces into action in Korea under the United Nations banner. But he clearly felt that he was applying the same concept of extended self-defense (or "collective security") that Woodrow Wilson and Franklin Roosevelt had used to persuade Americans to support the two world wars. Like his predecessors, Truman described a world divided between the forces of light and darkness, between "free peoples" and "totalitarian regimes." Financier Bernard Baruch, FDR's old adviser, said that the speech was "tantamount to a declaration of . . . an ideological or religious war."[52]

In some ways, the Communist/fascist analogy was convincing. Like the enemies defeated in World War II, the postwar Soviet regime and its satellites were oppressive bureaucracies that stifled political freedom, murdered or imprisoned vast numbers of opponents, terrorized intellectuals, and treated workers and farmers as disposable servants of the state. "Totalitarian" was not an unfair description of Stalin's USSR.[53] But in other ways, the analogy was highly misleading. The Soviet Union had not been a highly advanced industrial state like Germany and Japan before the war. Like China, it was a desperately poor nation that had partially modernized through pure force of will, using both violent dictatorial techniques and egalitarian social ideas to educate and employ its citizens. After losing tens of millions of people and most of its infrastructure fighting the Germans, it had neither the desire nor the wherewithal to threaten the West.[54] Although Truman was convinced that the Soviets wished to dominate the world, their principal territorial ambition (approved for the most part by Churchill and Roosevelt in postwar conferences) was to maintain control over the lands taken by the Red Army in Eastern Europe. In the long run, of course, they hoped for the worldwide triumph of their ideology. But this was a very long run. For the foreseeable future, Stalin's agenda was dominated by his lifelong obsession: the project of building "socialism in one country"—the USSR.

Obviously, in their relationship to other nations, the Reds were no angels. In 1948, Soviet agents overthrew a popularly elected democratic government in Czechoslovakia, and in 1950, Stalin gave Premier Kim Il Sung of North Korea permission to invade the South. But the brouhaha about alleged Soviet plans for world conquest overlooked the obvious: the United States, which had actually prospered as a result of World War II, was well on the way to establishing its own global supremacy. Already hegemonic in Western Europe, the Pacific, and Japan, as well as in its own hemisphere, the United States was now stepping into British shoes in the oil-rich Middle East, East Asia, and Africa. It would shortly replace the Dutch as the leading Western power in Indonesia and move to replace the French as Indochina's chief patron. Therefore, when the British informed Harry Truman that they were no longer able to fulfill their historic role of supporting Greece and Turkey in order to maintain control over the eastern Mediterranean, the president listened with acute interest. The torch of global leadership was being passed from one English-speaking empire to another, and Harry S. Truman was not the man to let it drop.

The alleged Soviet threats to Greece and Turkey were highly exaggerated. In fact, Stalin had *refused* to back the Greek leftists who, having gained popular support as a result of their anti-Nazi activities during the war, had rebelled against the British-backed king and his conservative supporters.[55] Turkey, where the Soviets were seeking relatively minor concessions, "was slipped into the oven with Greece because that seemed the surest way to cook a tough bird," said one U.S. official.[56] Stalin had also ordered the Communist parties in Western Europe to eschew revolutionary politics and work within the democratic system. As George Kennan, the father of America's "containment" policy, stated, "It was perfectly clear to anyone with even a rudimentary knowledge of the Russia of that day that the Soviet leaders had no intention of advancing their cause by launching military attacks with their own armed forces across frontiers."[57] The unspoken threat, however, was that Greece, Turkey, and other nations might pursue an *independent* line in the postwar world rather than becoming part of the new U.S.-dominated world order. (A bit later, several nations seeking this status would declare themselves "nonaligned.") Under these circumstances, the same fear that surfaced in connection with the First Seminole War—the fear that areas of the world not under firm U.S. control might someday be exploited by a hostile power—was used to justify what was, in effect, a preemptive strike against Soviet influence.

In Korea, of course, Kim Il Sung's Communists launched a real military attack with Soviet consent. Truman's answer (after securing a Security Council condemnation of the invasion while the Soviets were boycotting the council) was the Korean War. Again, the public justification for fighting was the need to defeat an Evil Enemy bent on world conquest. But this rationale was becoming a bit tattered, and after several years of indecisive but bloody warfare, a majority of Americans would demand that Truman's successor, Dwight D. Eisenhower, end the war and bring the troops home.[58] This suggested that many Americans had, in practice, abandoned the Manichean philosophy that drove the Cold War. As in Greece, the forces supported by U.S. intervention were not righteous democrats and libertarians but authoritarian militarists whose sole endearing quality was their anti-Communism. A civil war in South Korea had already taken a hundred thousand lives before the Americans intervened. The right-wing leader, Syngman Rhee, had censored the press, smashed the trade unions, jailed and shot political opponents, and created a virtual military dictatorship in the South and had conducted repeated raids into North Korea prior to the invasion. The equally ruthless North Koreans replied with raids and forays of their own and finally got Stalin's permission to cross the 38th parallel to put an end to the Rhee regime.[59]

The invasion, it seems clear, was a wrongful attempt by North Korea to resolve its conflict with the Rhee regime by force. Since Korea was *not* of great strategic importance to the United States, however, Truman and Dean Acheson declared that the challenge thrown down by Kim Il Sung must be met for another reason: because Joseph Stalin intended it as a general test of America's will to fight. "When the invasion of South Korea occurred," one historian writes, "in their minds Stalin became Hitler, Communists were Nazis, and Korea was Czechoslovakia. Aggression had to be stopped or it would spread and become even more aggressive, like cancer out of control."[60]

Yes—but the event that arguably provoked this new hard-line

stance had occurred the previous year, traumatizing America's leaders and frightening a good many of their followers. It was neither an invasion nor an act of foreign aggression but a popular uprising supported by hundreds of millions of people (and greeted with little enthusiasm by the Soviets): the revolution in China led by Mao Tsetung and his comrades. More than sixty years later, it is easy to forget what a shock it was in the West to see the world's poorest and most populous nation, as well as a former U.S. ally, "go Communist." Cold War ideology expressed deep fears of underhanded Soviet plots, subversion, and surprise attacks, but the Chinese Revolution represented a different sort of nightmare for U.S. leaders. It demonstrated that, with the old empires fading and a passion for decolonization boiling up in Asia, Africa, and the Middle East, people might choose some independent road to modernization rather than accept America's global leadership. The issue was particularly fraught in places like Lebanon, Iraq, Iran, Vietnam, and Indonesia, where the United States was standing in for the old imperialist powers and was allied with conservative local elites. Nevertheless, during the Cold War it became an article of faith to believe that no nation would willingly choose an alternative road. It was assumed that anyone who wasn't with us was being forced to be against us. In that case, we could treat Third World dissenters not as people making their own choices but as victims requiring our humanitarian intervention.

Stalin's regime *was* evil, relatively speaking; we have plentiful evidence of that. But, once again, turning an adversary into a diabolical enemy ("Godless Communism") obscured the emergence of the shadow double: the America that, while treating most of its own citizens decently most of the time, mistreated certain domestic minorities and most foreign rebels with totalitarian gusto. While decrying subversion, the United States overthrew independent governments in Iraq, Iran, Guatemala, Chile, South Vietnam, Grenada, Panama, Nicaragua, and El Salvador and abetted the overthrow of regimes in Brazil, the Congo, Dominican Republic, Indonesia, and many other nations.[61] While fulminating against Communist dictatorships, American leaders supported brutal pro-Western dictatorships in scores of Third World nations. This is sometimes considered hypocrisy, but it really represented a misguided form of sincerity. Backing anti-democratic elites reflected the conviction that if the enemy is wholly evil, one must use "all means necessary" to defeat him, including the methods associated with his evil form of rule.[62]

Violent moral crusades typically produce a cult of moral tough-ness that condemns refusals to use the enemy's own methods against him as weak, squeamish, and disloyal. This raises an obvious but discomfiting question: in order to defeat an Evil Enemy, to what extent must we become *his* shadow double? John Le Carré's brilliant Cold War novels explore how it feels to live on this moral knife's edge.[63] The typical political response, however, actually worsens the dilemma while purporting to solve it: it is to conduct an *internal* crusade to ferret out domestic enemies ("fifth columnists"), purify and unite the population, and establish a clear differentiation be-tween righteous Us and evil Them. It may be useful to look a bit more closely at the relationship between external and internal cru-sades.

Campaigns of National Purification: A New Look at McCarthyism

From the earliest days of the American republic, wars against a devilish enemy were accompanied by intense campaigns of internal purification.[64] World War I generated a fierce mass movement to pro-mote patriotism, intimidate German Americans and other immigrant groups, discover and expose people suspected of disloyalty, and re-dedicate a united nation to traditional norms of "Americanism."[65] World War II, which saw the punitive internment of Japanese Ameri-cans, also spawned a popular campaign to rekindle popular enthusi-asm for democratic ideals.[66] The Cold War movement remembered as "McCarthyism," however, remains the subject of conflicting inter-pretations. Many critics consider it primarily a product of popular hysteria and political opportunism—"the great fear," as historian David Caute calls it—while admirers see it as a response to a genuine threat of Soviet espionage.[67] Both viewpoints have much to recommend them. But McCarthyism may be best understood as a campaign of internal purification structurally related to the global crusade against an Evil Enemy.

McCarthyism neither began nor ended with Senator Joseph McCarthy of Wisconsin.[68] The hunt for disloyal Americans began simultaneously with the start of the Cold War, in 1947, when President Truman instituted a loyalty-security program for federal employees. In the same year, the House Un-American Activities Committee (HUAC) began its investigation into Communist influence in Hollywood, and the Motion Picture Association of America instituted a blacklist of suspected Reds and "fellow travelers." The pace of the campaign accelerated in 1949–50, when headlines were dominated by stories of Communist successes abroad—notably, the USSR's explosion of an atomic bomb and Mao's triumph in China—and subversion at home. There *was* espionage at home; in 1950, Alger Hiss was convicted of perjury, and Julius and Ethel Rosenberg were arrested and charged with atomic espionage. Other Soviet spies were also at work. But an increasingly fearful public imagined links between external reverses and internal disloyalty or corruption even where they did not exist.

The story of the 1950s "Red Scare" is well known: HUAC's Hollywood adventure; the Senate Internal Security Subcommittee's search for a traitor responsible for "losing" China to Communism; Senator McCarthy's famous "list" of 205 names of Communists allegedly working in the State Department; J. Edgar Hoover's FBI vendetta against anyone he suspected of disloyalty; and the firing of thousands of suspected radicals by cooperative employers around the country. This internal crusade, however, was not simply the product of Senator McCarthy's ambition or J. Edgar Hoover's paranoia. In important ways, it was less about national security, in the narrow sense of the phrase, than about spiritual security. From the beginning, the campaign connected the idea of ridding the nation of disloyal or "alien" elements with a confessional ritual in which former Reds or Communist sympathizers proved their personal purity by recanting their former beliefs and accusing other wrongdoers ("naming names").[69] Playwright Arthur Miller explored the inquisitorial aspects of McCarthyism in his allegorical play about the Puritan witch trials, *The Crucible.* But ordinary Americans participated by the millions in other sorts of rituals designed to make them spiritually worthy to fight the war on Communism.

The principal religious voice of the crusade was that of evangelist Billy Graham, who expressed his admiration for Senator McCarthy (retracted years later), and who consistently maintained that the Cold War was a fight to the finish between Christianity and "Godless Communism." "We are dealing with a treacherous and vicious enemy who has the supernatural forces of evil behind him," Graham insisted. "Either communism must die, or Christianity must die, because it is actually a battle between Christ and anti-Christ."[70] Millions attended revivalist "Crusades" at which Graham argued that a movement of national purification was needed to prepare Americans to win the fight against Satan. Like Moses descending upon the worshippers of the Golden Calf, the evangelist told citizens of the wealthiest, most materialistic society on earth that their survival depended upon renouncing the worship of power and pleasure and returning to Jesus Christ. It is interesting to compare this rhetoric with the movement of internal spiritual renewal that accompanied World War II. That movement, represented by figures like Reinhold Niebuhr and Rabbi Stephen Wise in religion, and by films like *The House I Live In* (title song by Frank Sinatra) in popular culture, preached a national rededication to the principles of freedom, social justice, and religious tolerance.[71] But the early Cold War years found Americans in a different frame of mind altogether—uncertain, jumpy, and highly vulnerable to appeals that exploited the moral insecurity generated by their new domestic situation and role in the world.

These prewar to postwar changes were mind-boggling. Military spending had ended the Great Depression, and the postwar economic boom generated wealth on a scale previously unimaginable. A consumer society based on principles of obligatory hedonism undermined the old values of thrift and self-restraint. The economy, and with it American politics and culture, was going global, and the steady advance of U.S. alliances, foreign aid pacts, and military bases around the world was an astonishing new fact of life. A surprising response to this immense increase in U.S. wealth and power was fear. Perhaps recalling past traumas like the stock market crash of 1929 or the Pearl Harbor attack, people felt that their new good fortune could be lost in a moment. There was a significant moral dimension to this worry as well: Did Americans *deserve* these blessings? Or were we becoming the sort of idolaters, lusting after money, pleasure and power, that our parents and grandparents had warned us against? Perhaps America could lose the conflict with the Soviets, despite its vast advantages in wealth, technology, and productive capacity, because the Communists were dedicated to a cause, while we were dedicated only to ourselves. This was exactly the point that Billy Graham made in sermon after sermon. The Red "anti-Christ" was selflessly dedicated to his cause. Could we hold our own against him without becoming equally dedicated to ours?

McCarthyism proper ended in the mid-1950s, when the Wisconsin senator's attack on alleged Communists in the U.S. Army finally alienated President Eisenhower, and his disastrous performance on television in the Army-McCarthy Hearings of 1954 alienated most of the viewing public. He was censured by the U.S. Senate in 1954 and died of alcohol-related disease three years later. Eventually, U.S. Supreme Court decisions reversed many of the worst legal excesses of the era, and in 1984, even Billy Graham abandoned his loathing for the Soviets long enough to preach a series of sermons in the USSR. But the campaign of internal purification, rather than ending, went into abeyance. In some ways, it did not even abate; from 1956 until the early 1970s, for example, the FBI conducted a secret campaign of provocation, sabotage, and disruption against a wide range of dissenting groups under the heading of COINTELPRO: the domestic counterintelligence program.[72] What did abate was popular support for this sort of program, which faded at the end of the Vietnam War. But there remains a strong potential for the revival of a mass-based internal crusade. Why? Because one can't crusade against a diabolical external enemy without at some point reviving the spirit and methods of the internal purification campaign.

The Cold War ended in 1989 with the fall of the Soviet Empire. America's wars in the Muslim world began almost immediately afterward, with the Persian Gulf War of 1990–91 and the imposition of sanctions on postwar Iraq. The War on Terrorism, in many ways a response to these events, began in the mid-1990s and escalated sharply after al-Qaeda's devastating 2001 attacks on targets in New York and Washington. The initial U.S. response was to hunt for Islamist extremists in the United States as well as abroad but to focus primarily on foreign operations such as the war against the Taliban regime in Afghanistan. Meanwhile, a broad spectrum of leaders representing both major political parties counseled Americans to avoid harassing or victimizing American Muslims or attacking Islam per se. Denunciations of Islam as a violent religion and calls for an American religious revival to combat it were limited, for the most part, to a few far-right spokespeople and fundamentalist groups. But the militants of al-Qaeda and similar groups were immediately branded diabolical enemies who must be killed or captured, and anti-Muslim sentiment simmered just beneath the surface of American cultural life.[73] The USA Patriot Act, which greatly increases the federal government's power to police the population in pursuit of suspected terrorists, sets the stage for possible further curtailment of civil liberties of Muslims and others if the War on Terrorism escalates.

In the event of an escalation, I fear, one can anticipate a new campaign not only to discover and punish internal enemies but also to purify the nation for an all-out struggle against Evil. Despite President Obama's decisions to abjure the use of torture of prisoners and to close the U.S. prison at Guantanamo Bay, the tactics of American forces in Afghanistan, Pakistan, Yemen, and elsewhere still generate discomfiting questions.[74] To what extent has the struggle between terrorists and counterterrorists become a kind of gang war, with each side seeking revenge against the other by "all means necessary"? To what extent do current methods of fighting erase moral distinctions between the United States and its adversaries? The discomfort grows if those rebelling against our authority, despite the gross inhumanity of their methods, are in some ways representative of millions of others who see us as interlopers and want us to withdraw from their part of the world. And it grows even more if the costs of making war—the suffering we impose upon our own armed forces, as well as on large numbers of foreign fighters and civilians—do not seem likely to produce corresponding benefits.

Campaigns of national purification correspond to a felt need to draw a "bright line," morally speaking, between ourselves and our adversaries—to affirm our virtue and their vice, and to put nagging doubts about the justice of our cause to rest. They also aim to take the issue of costs off the table by inspiring the public to sacrifice without reservations or limits for the sake of the Cause itself. We can see why crusades against Evil Enemies so often call internal crusades into being. The question that must concern us now is how to develop practical and ethical alternatives to both.

4

"LOVE IT OR LEAVE IT":

PATRIOTS AND DISSENTERS

If they sang at all, the crowds at American baseball games used to sing "Take Me Out to the Ball Game" during the seventh inning stretch. Now, as if obeying some unspoken command, they also sing "God Bless America." Baseball contests begin with the singing of the national anthem, as do basketball, football, hockey, and soccer games, boxing matches, track meets, and sanctioned automobile races. During the playing of the anthem, federal law requires all those present to stand facing the American flag bareheaded, with hats held in their left hands and their right hands over their hearts. (If there is no flag displayed, they are obliged to stand in the same position, facing the place where the flag would ordinarily fly.) Meanwhile, halftime festivities at pro football's Super Bowl game and other major sports events feature overflights by military aircraft and other patriotic/military rituals. And every morning, in virtually every school in the United States, children and teenagers stand to salute the flag.

Observers around the world wonder at the unusual intensity of American patriotic sentiment. People elsewhere have strong affection for their nations, too, but relatively few experience the fervent, quasi-religious nationalism that makes supporting wars seem a patriotic duty. Theories about this patriotic passion abound, some emphasizing the heritage of New England Puritanism, with its belief in the American colonies' divine mission, others exploring the nation's identification with the spirit of freedom, democracy, or material progress.[1] Such explanations, however, are too abstract and general, too focused on formal ideologies and creeds, and too static to account for the power of patriotic associations and feelings. The questions that most concern us are these: What accounts for the peculiarly militaristic style of American patriotism? How did love of country become a reason to make war? What role does patriotism play at present in sustaining popular support for continuous warfare?

I began this study by taking issue with two common ideas about Americans' willingness to make war—the "innocent dupe" and "frontier killer" hypotheses. In the same way, I want to oppose the notion that Americans are such insensate patriots (and mindless dolts) that they fight simply because some Leader commands them to. Like every other society, we have our share of authoritarian personalities—people who believe in following orders simply because they issue from an authoritative source. Especially when it comes to warmaking, however, we generally do not "snap to" and send our loved ones out to kill or be killed on command. A process that some social psychologists call "moral disengagement" must first take place to convince people that it is okay, even necessary, to act in ways that they were previously taught to regard as wrong. The fact that someone in authority gives an order to fight may facilitate this process, but much more than official authorization is needed to convince most Americans to accept the justice and necessity of war.[2] In fact, the term "moral disengagement" is somewhat misleading, since it is not just a question of quieting people's normal inhibitions against violence but also one of reengaging them morally in some violent cause. Most Americans need reasons to kill.

We have already discussed several key arguments and images

used to make the case for war: the need for self-defense, the existence of Evil Enemies, and the duty to undertake humanitarian interventions or moral crusades. All of these appeals are patriotic, in one sense. They identify the nation with democratic institutions, universal principals of freedom and justice, or civilized moral values and call on citizens to express their commitment to these ideas by representing the nation on the battlefield. Some analysts consider this a healthy form of patriotism, as opposed to unhealthy, knee-jerk nationalism of the "My country, right or wrong" type. According to them, the good patriotism involves a dedication to universal principles by which the United States itself can be judged, while the bad type justifies obeying the government because it is the government, because we are superior to other nations, or because of nationalist groupthink.[3]

In the run-up to war, however, this good/bad distinction tends to break down. Pro-war propaganda generally appeals to universal principles as well as narrow nationalism—and "principled" patriotism is just as likely to be misused as knee-jerk patriotism. The fact that World War II is generally considered a good war throws an aura of righteousness around the universalistic principles (such as the Four Freedoms) used to mobilize popular support for the Allied cause. But the same sort of patriotism was used to promote and justify American participation in World War I, the Vietnam War, and both wars in Iraq. Because it is difficult or impossible to separate patriotism into healthy and unhealthy types, many people have argued that patriotic nationalism of any sort is a trap that leads otherwise decent people to support indecent wars. Our loyalty ought to be to all of humanity rather than to the corner of the world we happen to be born into. This anti-patriotic, "cosmopolitan" perspective merits further consideration, along with the opposing view of analysts who believe that "moderate patriotism" can avoid the ultra-nationalist trap.[4] But that discussion will make more sense after we have briefly sketched the modern history of American patriotism, paying particular attention to an aspect of it that has not attracted much attention: the sense of *community* that it both embodies and attempts to create.

PATRIOTISM AND AMERICAN COMMUNALISM

We are talking here about the nation not as an idea or an embodiment of principles but as a place and a people to which we feel special ties of affection and loyalty. This sort of patriotism is very widespread.

> *Breathes there the man, with soul so dead,*
> *Who never to himself has said,*
> *This is my own, my native land!*[5]

These famous lines by Sir Walter Scott play an important role in Edward Everett Hale's bestselling short story "The Man Without a Country," a tale written during the Civil War but still assigned in many American schools. We can use it as a key to unlock some of the essential features of American patriotic thinking.

The anti-hero of Hale's story, U.S. Army Lieutenant Philip Nolan, is accused by a court-martial of plotting treason with Aaron Burr. When the judge asks him to affirm his loyalty to the country, he curses America: "Damn the United States! I wish I may never hear of the United States again!" Appalled, the military judge grants his wish. He sentences Nolan to life in exile on board U.S. Navy ships, under the condition that nobody must ever speak to him again about the United States or give him one word of news about his homeland.

The punishment is just but savage, and it is carried out to the letter. At length (after hearing the Scott poem recited), Nolan repents and later redeems himself by heroism in battle. In what will turn out to be his final speech, he summarizes the lessons of his experience for the benefit of the story's young narrator. First, he equates the nation with home and family:

"Youngster, let that show you what it is to be without a family, without a home, and without a country. And if you are ever tempted to say a word or to do a thing that shall put a bar between you and your family, your home, and your country, pray God in his mercy to take you that instant home to his own heaven. Stick by your family, boy; forget you have a self, while you do everything for them."

Then he converts the family-feeling he has been describing, which supersedes concern for the "self," into a duty of exclusive loyalty to one's country, including an obligation to fight for it.

"And for your country, boy," and the words rattled in his throat, "and for that flag," and he pointed to the ship, "never dream a dream but of serving her as she bids you, though the service carry you through a thousand hells. No matter what happens to you, no more matter who flatters you or who abuses you, never look at another flag, never let a night pass but you pray God to bless that flag."

Finally, Nolan returns to the theme of family, now identifying the nation as a mystical entity separate from both the government and the people—a Mother to whom ultimate loyalty is due.

"Remember, boy, that behind all these men you have to do with, behind officers, and government, and people even, there is the Country Herself, your Country, and that you belong to Her as you belong to your own mother. Stand by Her, boy, as you would stand by your mother, if those devils there [Portuguese slave traders captured by the Americans] had got hold of her to-day!"[6]

Hale published the story in the *Atlantic Monthly* in December 1863, when the Civil War was at its height. The battles of Gettysburg and Vicksburg had tilted the military balance in favor of the North, but devastating riots against the draft had taken place in New York City, and the death toll both on the battlefields and from disease was appalling.[7] With many more battles to be fought, there was widespread fatigue with the war and great dissatisfaction with President Lincoln.[8] "The Man Without a Country" was a paean to patriotism at a time when, Hale clearly thought, northerners needed this sort of inspiration to continue the war effort. Although the northern war effort by then traded heavily in anti-slavery sentiment, the only mention of slavery in Hale's story is a brief incident in which the ship's captain liberates some slaves on board a Portuguese schooner, and the only mention of the war comes at the end of the story, when the narrator decides to give the dying Nolan some news of his country. "I told him everything I could think of that would show the grandeur of his country and its prosperity," he says, "but I could not make up my mouth to tell him a word about this infernal rebellion!"

There is another reason for the narrator's silence about the Civil War. If the nation is a family, how to interpret the South's attempt to secede? One could portray the Confederates as kinfolk wanting to leave home to establish a new place of their own. But the speech presents southern secession as a frontal attack on the family—in fact, as an attempted violation of the Mother! Ironically, Hale describes the United States as a natural, organic association at the very moment that its constituents are killing each other because, among other things, they cannot agree on whether it is a coherent, unified community or not. In the view of most southerners, the Union was an artificial creature—the product of a compact between sovereign states.[9] The northern view was best expressed by Lincoln in his First Inaugural Address, which he concluded by appealing to the "bonds of affection," common history, sacrifices, and "mystic chords of memory" uniting the two sections. "The Union is much older than the Constitution," he asserted, meaning that the nation was a social and cultural fact, not just a legal construction.

The most serious crisis of identity in American history produced radically different answers, North and South, to a series of fundamental questions—the same sort of questions that make individual identity crises so painful (and politically explosive): Who are we, collectively? Who are kinfolk and who strangers? Whom can we trust?[10] In the end, consensus and compromise having failed, violence was used to answer them.

Communal patriotism was thus born in the fires of communal warfare. The Civil War linked the existence of a culturally coherent national community—a quasi-family—with a duty to fight for one's fictive brothers and sisters whenever they were in danger. The idea of the American nation as an organic community has persisted ever since, notwithstanding that it is what Benedict Anderson calls an "imagined community"—an ideal based partly on real communal relationships and partly on dreams of overcoming deep social divisions. "Regardless of the actual inequality and exploitation that may prevail in each," Anderson writes, "the nation is always conceived as a deep, horizontal comradeship. Ultimately it is this fraternity that makes it possible, over the past two centuries, for so many millions of people, not so much to kill, as willingly to die for such limited imaginings."[11] Between 1860 and 1865, more than six hundred thousand Americans died for an imagined national family. The idea of the nation-as-family may sometimes be used to justify going to war, but it often provides a powerful reason to remain at war, especially if other reasons for fighting turn out to be unconvincing. Even if U.S. forces had no good reason to be in Iraq after the accusations against Saddam Hussein were disproved, "Support the troops" made emotional sense, *if* one conceived of them as family.

Since the Civil War, communal patriotism has reemerged periodically, in each case with new characteristics, in response to repeated crises of national identity. A crucial reemergence took place during World War I, when a new conception—"100 percent Americanism"— was developed to allay the anxiety produced by the one of the largest, most diverse immigrations in world history. Between 1880 and 1920,

some twenty million people, most of them Europeans, came to the
United States. On the eve of the war, almost 15 percent of the population was foreign-born, and perhaps one third of those living in big
cities were first- or second-generation Americans.[12] The largest single
ethnic group (about five million people) was German and the second-
largest Irish, but a huge new wave of arrivals from Italy, Poland, Russia, and Eastern Europe was transforming urban America, altering
the cultural mix, generating competition for jobs and living space,
and dismaying so many people that, after the war, Congress would
reduce further immigration by Poles, Jews, Italians, and other "unde-
sirables" to a trickle.

The decade before America entered the world war was notable for
violent social struggles between "nativists" and immigrants, gangs
representing different immigrant groups, racist groups and African
Americans, and workers and employers.[13] Even before committing
the nation to war, Woodrow Wilson initiated a patriotic revival designed to inspire or intimidate this diverse quarrelsome population
to settle down and embrace familiar (middle-class WASP) cultural
norms. When the war came, the campaign reached a pitch of near-
hysteria. Wilson's vituperative attacks on "hyphenated Americans,"
a nationwide wave of hatred and repression directed against German Americans, and a Red Scare aimed principally at Italian, Eastern European, and Russian immigrants were intended to associate
difference with disloyalty and to unify the nation behind the war
effort as a single imagined ethnic group. "100 percent Americanism"
was not only advised; it was mandatory.

Beliefs in American concepts of freedom and democracy—and
abandonment of "alien" ideas like anarchism and communism—were
certainly part of what many people meant by Americanism. But the
definition meant more than adherence to an American creed. It indicated a cultural unity or super-ethnicity coinciding, more or less,
with what playwright Israel Zangwill had meant by "the Melting-
Pot":

America is God's Crucible, the great Melting-Pot where all the races of Europe are melting and reforming . . . Germans and Frenchmen, Irishmen and Englishmen, Jews and Russians—into the Crucible with you all! God is making the American.[14]

Yes, but what were the characteristics of this new "reformed" creature? He or she would certainly speak English rather than his or her native tongue—but which customs or cultural norms other than language qualified as essentially, mandatorily, American? The idea remained vague, to be filled in according to the observer's own pre-dilections. To some extent, of course, cultural assimilation was a fact-in-progress. The immigrants' children would soon teach their parents about baseball, unchaperoned dating, and electioneering. But cultural transformation constantly challenged previous definitions of Americanism. Some changes involved "reverse assimilation"— accommodation by natives to the immigrants' ethnic tastes and habits. Already, Americans were eating hamburgers and frankfurters without giving a thought to Hamburg or Frankfurt, while multicultural vaudeville altered their tastes in music, dance, and humor. More controversial changes were related to the enormous social upheavals caused by industrial development. In 1912, almost one million Americans voted for Socialist Party candidate (and future war resister) Eugene V. Debs and his German American running mate, Emil Seidel.

During the 1920s, restrictive legislation curtailed the immigrant flood. "Anglo-Saxon" ideals flourished, the Ku Klux Klan enjoyed a nationwide revival, and the ideal of ethnic coherence remained the basis for communal patriotism. When depression rocked the economy, however, a new source of disunity—class conflict—emerged to challenge the idea of America as a unified community. To defend their class interests, workers organized unions and engaged in strikes and slowdowns in workplaces across the country. To defend against this, the owners formed employers' associations, locked out workers, hired "scab" labor, and employed private armies to keep the unions at bay. Simultaneously, the political spectrum expanded to include groups that many considered wildly "un-American." In 1934 alone, a shutdown of the Auto-Lite plant in Toledo, Ohio, was organized by A. J. Muste's American Workers Party, the Minneapolis Teamsters strike (which made the Teamsters Union a national force) was led by Trotskyists, and a West Coast longshoremen's strike led by Communist Party militants shut the waterfront down for eighty-three days and inspired a general strike in San Francisco.[15] The following year, the Roosevelt administration moved to channel and contain this radicalism. Among other actions, it obtained passage of the Wagner Act, which recognized workers' union rights, and blessed the formation of the CIO—the Congress of Industrial Organizations.[16]

Nevertheless, class conflict continued at a high pitch as Roosevelt began to prepare the nation for a new war. To mobilize the country for intervention meant defining patriotism anew, so that Americans could consider themselves members not only of a single cultural group but also of a harmonious socioeconomic community. Images of the United States as a nation of happy, productive workers and farmers were pressed into service by FDR's Office of War Information, which produced patriotic posters showing workers on the assembly line, workers in the mines and on the farms, workers speaking at public meetings, female workers rolling up their sleeves ("Rosie the Riveter")— and virtually never a banker, businessman, or anyone wearing a tie. Hollywood pitched in with war movies picturing the typical American fighting unit as both an ethnic melting pot and a classless amalgam of tough workers and farm boys with a few educated, middle-class types. (A favorite movie hero was the officer who makes the ultimate sacrifice for his men.)[17] The advertising industry, conscripted willingly into war service, produced ads and posters celebrating free enterprise as a "Fifth Freedom" and a boon to American workers.[18] Class conflict was declared unpatriotic even by the Communist Party, which rushed to support the ban on strikes and boycotts agreed to by most labor unions for the duration of the war.[19] As Roosevelt said, "Dr. New Deal" had been replaced by "Dr. Win-the-War."

Don't Let That Shadow Touch Them *poster for U.S. War Bonds.*
The swastika shadow over the children plays on the righteous
motivations of World War II. Painted by Lawrence Beall Smith,
1942. Made for the U.S. Treasury. (Source: University of
North Texas Digital Library, Posters Collection.)

Communal patriotism now imagined American society as a coherent whole, socially as well as ethnically integrated. The coming of
the Cold War sealed the fusion of patriotism with social conservatism; in the 1950s, any talk of serious social or economic divisions
was considered Communist-inspired, and the image of gangster-ridden

labor unions purveyed by films like *On the Waterfront* was perva-
sive. By the end of the decade, everyone except the very poor was
being called "middle class," and racial discrimination, the American
caste system's most shameful product, was beginning to be viewed
as un-American. But the myth of social unity was about to be challenged again. In the early 1960s, the black-led civil rights movement
spilled over into direct, nonviolent action, provoking a violent southern response that riveted viewers across the nation to their TV screens.
From 1964 through 1968, serious riots erupted in black inner-city
communities from Los Angeles to Washington, D.C., shattering the
assumption of social consensus in the North as well. At the same
time, an angry movement of protest against the war in Vietnam took
to the streets, strikes and demonstrations shut down colleges and
universities across the country, and a youthful cultural rebellion challenged long-accepted norms of sexual, social, and political conduct.[20]
Although most dissenting groups had burned out or demobilized
by the late 1970s, what some called "the Vietnam syndrome"—an
unwillingness to commit U.S. military forces to action abroad—
remained a factor in America politics well into the 1980s.

The Persian Gulf War of 1990–91, America's first large-scale military campaign since the withdrawal from Vietnam, was seen by the
president, among others, as a way to change all that. When George
H. W. Bush decided to use force to expel Saddam Hussein's army
from Kuwait, he conceived of the expedition as a way to move beyond the Vietnam syndrome to a new patriotism that would reestab-
lish war as a viable option for U.S. policymakers. As analyst David
Bailey insightfully notes, Bush set out to redeem the nation from the
"sins" of Vietnam, which, in his view, included going to war without
clear goals, using insufficient force, permitting deep internal political
divisions to escalate, and disrespecting returning veterans. After winning the Gulf War in little more than a week of devastating air and
ground attacks, he immediately declared, "By God, we've kicked the
Vietnam syndrome once and for all." "There is something noble and
majestic about patriotism in this country now," he added a bit later,

and the next day he said, "The specter of Vietnam has been buried forever in the desert sands of the Arabian Peninsula."[21]

Bush clearly intended to revive a communal patriotism that would permit the use of military force, when needed, to defend America's New World Order—but the surge of national pride and unity generated by a quick, relatively painless win in Kuwait might not last very long. The question that remained unanswered was how to imagine and project a new basis for unity that would truly bury the divisions of the Vietnam era.

This reformulation was announced indirectly in 1993, when Harvard political scientist and national security consultant Samuel P. Huntington, a former Vietnam hawk, declared that previous patterns of ideological, economic, and political competition were giving way to a new form of global conflict: a violent "clash of civilizations" in which religious and cultural differences would play the central role.[22] Huntington sometimes used "civilization" as a synonym for culture, but his work emphasized the religious or moral values that seemed to give each civilization its unique identity.[23] The West in general, and America in particular, were now to be thought of as civilizations unified by popular commitment to a common set of spiritual and ethical values, as well as by older forms of ethnic, political, and economic communalism. As conflict between civilizations escalated, Huntington maintained, Americans needed to recognize that their culture, so defined, was increasingly exposed to attack by multiple enemies ("the West against the Rest"). While they could not impose their own values on others, they would have to prepare to defend American civilization, if necessary, by force of arms.

The ideal of a patriotism based on spiritual community was first promoted during the Cold War, when preachers like Billy Graham declared "Godless Communism" to be America's mortal enemy, and the words "under God" were added to the Pledge of Allegiance. But the cultural rebellions of the Vietnam era made it clear that conservative Protestant Christianity, as Graham and others presented it, could not serve as a basis for national solidarity. On the contrary, religiously inspired protests organized by clerics like Martin Luther King Jr., Ralph Abernathy, William Sloane Coffin, and Fathers Daniel and Philip Berrigan were central to both the civil rights and anti-war protest movements. What revived interest in the link between religion and patriotism in the post-Vietnam period was the growing challenge to U.S. power and prestige by Islamist militants, starting with the seizure of hostages at the American embassy in Tehran by young Iranian revolutionaries in 1979–81. The violence continued with bomb attacks on the U.S. Marine barracks in Beirut (1983), the World Trade Center in New York (1993), the Khobar Towers housing complex in Saudi Arabia (1996), and the American embassies in Tanzania and Kenya (1998), the seaborne assault on the USS *Cole* in Aden harbor (2000), and, of course, the use of hijacked airplanes against the World Trade Center and the Pentagon in 2001.

To many observers, the rise of a violently anti-American Islamism seemed to prove that the clash of civilizations predicted by Huntington was taking place, and that Americans had better unite to defend their own spiritual and moral values against assault. The problem was how to define this new form of communal patriotism. Given America's religious diversity and the intensity of people's commitments to their particular traditions and organizations, how could religion or morality serve as the basis for a new nationalist ideology? One answer might be to move away from the fundamentalist, "Moral Majority" definition of American religion toward a broader conception based on the values most clearly challenged by extreme Islamism. This would mean framing certain "progressive" civic values—for example, our dedication to women's rights, religious pluralism, and freedom of artistic expression—as core ethical and spiritual principles of American civilization, and emphasizing the contrast between our enlightened values and the Islamists' benighted ones. In Huntington's terms, it would mean making America the avatar of "Western values." America might then picture herself once again as leader of the Free World—with "Free," in this case, denoting America's liberation from pre-Enlightenment notions of virtue and moral responsibility.

In evaluating this nascent philosophy, it may help to recognize that communal patriotism is akin to what psychologists call a "reaction formation": a way of dealing with unacceptable emotions or situations by asserting their opposite. (For example, I deny, disguise, and unwittingly preserve my negative feelings for someone by displaying great affection for him and convincing myself that these feelings are sincere.) Just as the familial national unity preached by northern patriots like Lincoln was a reaction to (and denial of) profound disunity, Wilson's "Americanism" drive was a reaction to unprecedented ethnic diversity, and Roosevelt's vision of class harmony a reaction to persistent class conflict. For this reason, those preaching a new brand of communal patriotism generally try to broaden its appeal and disguise serious differences by avoiding narrow sectarianism, framing principles broadly, and appealing to other forms of patriotism (for example, dedication to American political and social principles).

Moral/spiritual patriotism, it seems to me, is in large part a reaction formation to deep moral and religious differences in our society (what some people have called our "culture wars").[24] Note, however, that this formulation has two effects. First, it covers up or blurs profound cultural differences among us. (Do women's rights include the right to abortion? Does religious pluralism mean no prayers in schools?) Second—and more important—since millions of conservative Muslims, not just a few extremists, hold attitudes about women, art, and religion obnoxious to many people in the West, this sort of patriotism creates the basis for a war against Islam, not just against al-Qaeda and the Taliban. That is to say, it does not reflect so much as *create* a clash of civilizations. We respect women; they don't. We separate church and state and practice religious pluralism; they don't. We allow artistic freedom; they don't. We respect human life; they don't. Judaism and Christianity are religions of peace; Islam is a religion of violence. We defend; they attack. And so forth.

One can see how easily a communal patriotism based on spiritual values tends to assume our values' superiority and their values' (menacing) inferiority. But, if that is what the conflict is really about, America's War on Terrorism becomes a Holy War, and another of Usama bin Laden's fantasies is realized: the Crusaders are once again visibly on the march. Or, to put this slightly differently, we return to the paradigm of the Evil Enemy and the global moral crusade, with one dangerous difference: rather than promoting the values of liberal democracy, Anglo-Saxon ethnicity, or New Deal–style capitalism, we define the nation as a "big tent" religion. This definition has particularly frightening implications for our domestic life, for communal patriotism, no matter how broadly expressed, always involves an imagined vision of the community that many people reject. For this reason, patriotic ideology requires intense propagation and, for those who refuse to accept it, coercive *enforcement* through the application of social and legal sanctions. If our new crusade is to be founded on religious/moral patriotism, an internal movement to discover and punish domestic heretics is highly likely. The illiberal Patriot Act provisions that now worry some Americans may then seem a trivial foreshadowing of the new Inquisition.

The history of communal patriotism in America raises an interesting and important question: How effective are patriotic appeals in generating national political unity, particularly where decisions about war and peace are concerned? To what extent do successive versions of the imagined community re-create our national identity? Looking at the Wilson administration's campaign for "100 percent Americanism" or Franklin D. Roosevelt's vision of a socially harmonious America, it seems that these ideas can be quite effective in promoting national unity, but only so long as they are in sync with actual currents of social change. For example, if immigrants to the United States arrive during a period of unprecedented economic growth, get regular jobs, send their kids to school, and are integrated into American society in one or two generations, "Americanism" moves from the level of a pious hope to that of an emergent cultural reality. If an even greater industrial boom enriches most workers, creates a thriving middle class, and lessens the social distance between rich and poor, the New Deal's vision of class harmony becomes, if not a reality, at least an apparently credible possibility.

But what of the unity based on common moral and spiritual commitments preached by the latest crop of communal patriots? It seems to me that this vision is more likely to inflame social conflict than to generate consensus, since it is *not* reinforced by current trends in American society. On the contrary, a growing polarization between traditionalists and modernists in religion, culture, and politics seems to be on our social agenda for the foreseeable future. This polarization reflects the breakdown of previous imagined communities, as cultural diversity, fed by an enormous wave of immigration, challenges older ideas of Americans as a single cultural group, and economic inequality, inflamed by a deep structural crisis of the economy, fails to provide a basis for genuine social unity. One reason that governments of both major U.S. political parties have found it so difficult to generate strong support for foreign wars is this crisis of communal patriotism—a situation in which real social conflicts make patriotic appeals more divisive than unifying. As we will shortly see, the first symptoms of this crisis appeared some forty years ago, when large numbers of Americans rejected patriotic appeals and refused to support the Vietnam War.

DISSENTERS AND PARIAHS:
ANTI-WAR MOVEMENTS BEFORE VIETNAM

The issue of national unity leads directly to an inquiry crucial to the analysis of why Americans choose war: Why *don't* some of us choose war? What happens to those who dissent? What effects do opposition movements have on the body politic and the war effort? Such questions may seem a bit off base, since America's wars, most of them victorious, play such a central role in our historical consciousness. Just walk into the American History section of almost any bookstore and count the number of books on wars and warfare! Because of this veritable military fixation, the size and significance of anti-war movements in the United States are seldom registered, and the history of no-war—that is, instances in which military action might have been expected but wasn't taken—remains almost entirely unwritten.

No-wars take place for all sorts of reasons, but one of them, surely, is that policymakers know that substantial elements of the public will be intensely opposed to military action. This prospect, if serious, raises the disturbing possibility that massive opposition may hinder the military effort or even cause serious internal disorders. Opting for war ordinarily involves a judgment by pro-war forces that the opponents can be won over or marginalized politically, and that if they refuse to "go quietly," they can be intimidated, jailed, or interned without sparking a general revolt. Ordinarily, these judgments prove accurate. Most organized movements opposing American wars have been politically defeated or criminalized. Because of this, there is a tendency (especially among those who write "winners' history") to treat them cursorily. But we need to explore some of the main reasons for their political weakness, as well as inquiring into the surprising strength of the movement against the Vietnam War. This will give us a basis for evaluating the low public approval rates of recent conflicts in Iraq and Afghanistan and the likelihood of new anti-war mobilizations in America.

Before the Vietnam War, the activities of American anti-war groups seem to fall into two broad patterns, neither of which is obsolete even today. The first, characterizing much of the opposition to the War of 1812, the Mexican-American War, and the Spanish-American War, we can label "Whig." Whig dissenters criticized the excessive costs of wars and their tendency to increase federal executive power. In the case of the War of 1812, they also considered the conflict ruinous to business and trade. But the main Whig critique branded all three conflicts vulgar, unnecessary power grabs meant to enrich a few special interests at the expense of innocent foreigners and vulnerable U.S. fighting men. The supporters of Whig anti-war movements tended to be middle- and upper-class farmers, businessmen, and intellectuals. Pacifism played no great role in any of their organizations. What motivated them most strongly was a conviction that the war being proposed or fought was partisan, unnecessary, and unjust.[25]

The largest and most serious mobilization of this sort was the Federalist Party's campaign against the War of 1812. The New England–based Federalists considered "Mr. Madison's War" unnecessary, driven by base motives (the "war hawks'" desire to conquer Canada), and dangerously helpful to Napoleon's campaign to conquer Europe. Even though the conflict was fairly popular in the South and West to begin with, one historian calls it "the most unpopular war that the United States ever waged, not even excepting the Vietnam conflict."[26] Enthusiasm for the fight waned when U.S. attempts to conquer Canada were rebuffed, and when Washington, D.C., was occupied and burned by the Redcoats. Federalist dissenters meeting in Hartford, Connecticut, in the winter of 1814–15 made thinly veiled threats of secession, as well as proposing constitutional amendments to limit Congress's warmaking powers. Like the rest of the country, the anti-warriors were unaware that Britain had just signed a fairly equitable peace treaty with the Americans. Andrew Jackson's January 1815 victory at the Battle of New Orleans created an instant national hero, and when the proceedings of the Hartford Convention were made public shortly after that, the Federalists were accused of selfish, unpatriotic behavior. The party entered a sharp descent that ended with its expiration in 1820.

One generation later, leading members of the Whig Party, including Henry Clay, John Quincy Adams, and young Abraham Lincoln, objected bitterly to the Mexican-American War, which they considered a conspiracy by southern slaveholders to acquire vast new territories at Mexico's expense. Votes on President Polk's declaration of war in Congress were fairly close initially, but a majority of Whigs, sensing the war's general popularity, ended by supporting it. According to historian Daniel Walker Howe, they "remembered all too well how the Federalist Party had opposed the War of 1812 and been

AN AVAILABLE CANDIDATE.
THE ONE QUALIFICATION FOR A WHIG PRESIDENT.

*An Available Candidate, 1848. This anti-war cartoon shows
General Zachary Taylor, candidate for president in 1848,
sitting atop a pile of skulls after the Mexican-American War
in which he led the U.S. Army. (Source: University of
North Texas Digital Library, Posters Collection.)*

rewarded with permanent oblivion. They resolved not to repeat that
mistake."[27] Nevertheless, a group of "Conscience Whigs" formed a
faction that was later instrumental in helping to create the Republican Party. Henry David Thoreau refused to pay taxes to support the
war and went to jail, an experience that inspired him to write his
famous essay "Civil Disobedience." The experience also produced a

confrontation that has become a folktale. Visiting Thoreau in jail, Ralph Waldo Emerson reportedly asked, "Henry, what are you doing in jail?" Thoreau is said to have replied, "Waldo, what are you doing *out* of jail?" Again, pacifism was not an issue; many of the Conscience Whigs would later be among those calling for a war to prevent southern secession and end the slave system.

A similar social basis and moral tone flavored the opposition to the Spanish-America War. In its first (Cuban) phase, the business community split, with some commercial interests ("old money," for the most part) condemning President McKinley's policies and Teddy Roosevelt's blustery imperialism, while others favored the projection of U.S. power abroad.[28] Many leading Democrats also opposed the war, although most were silenced by the sinking of the *Maine* and the newspaper campaign to whip up support for intervention. The opponents, including figures like steel baron Andrew Carnegie, Mark Twain, former president Grover Cleveland, psychologist William James, social philosopher John Dewey, Wall Street magnate Edward Atkinson, social reformer Jane Addams, and union leader Samuel Gompers, formed an Anti-Imperialist League dedicated to the idea that the United States must not become a world empire, lest it lose its character as a free republic. After the victory in Cuba, when Washington prevented Cuban leaders from obtaining real independence, and, even more, when the United States fought a vicious three-year war against the Philippine insurgents, the league fulminated against government hypocrisy and military brutality, as well as mourning the small but growing number of American casualties.

To no avail. Again, the social orientation of the Anti-Imperialist League was overwhelmingly middle and upper class, and the high moral tone taken by the organization's leaders and intellectuals did not resonate widely in American society. In fact, one of the most persuasive arguments made by the senators opposing McKinley's annexation of the Philippines (most of them southern Democrats) was that it would bring too many "colored people" under Uncle Sam's protection.[29] As destructive as the Philippine counterinsurgency turned out to be, it soon became a minor item in the newspapers, and most Americans lost interest in it or accepted the view of McKinley and his openly racist successor, Theodore Roosevelt, that the United States had a Christian duty to civilize the Filipino "savages."

There was, however, another form of anti-war protest that had greater capacity to involve large numbers of people and to obstruct war plans or wars in progress. We can label it "Democrat/Socialist," since, in contrast to the Whig style of organization, its popular base was among poorer farmers, workers, and immigrant groups, as well as some sectors of the intelligentsia. Its first appearance was in connection with the Civil War, when the quick, glorious victory expected by both sides failed to materialize, battlefield casualties reached terrifying proportions, and both sides turned to conscription to supply the troops they needed. The conscription system adopted by both parties (but later repealed in the South) provided that people with the means to do so could pay substitutes to serve in their places, so the fighting was done mainly by the poor, many of whom had no interest in ending slavery and even less in getting themselves killed or wounded in the unprecedented battlefield carnage.[30]

For this and other reasons, anti-war activity in the North was widespread and serious.[31] At one point, Lincoln despaired of winning reelection because of the "Peace Democrats'" popularity among midwesterners, as well as among the urban poor and immigrant communities. In 1863, some Irish immigrants torched whole neighborhoods in New York City, lynched scores of African Americans, and looted stores, all in enraged protest against the president's class-biased conscription policies and their own fear of further black migration to the North.[32] In the Midwest, opposition was less riotous, but Democratic newspapers blasted Lincoln's "dictatorship," fulminated against the Negro threat, and advocated draft resistance. Federal authorities broke up a few activist cells planning direct action against the war, and a military court convicted "Copperhead" Congressman Clement L. Vallandingham of Ohio of sedition and sentenced him to prison. (Lincoln freed him but exiled him to the Confederate States.) The Democrats' chances in 1864 were compromised, perhaps fatally, when former commanding general George McClellan, their nominee for president, repudiated the party's peace platform and alienated at least part of his base. Even so, Lincoln had to rely on the "soldiers' vote" (almost 80 percent voted for him) to assure his reelection.

For the first time since the War of 1812, anti-war forces were accused of disloyalty and subjected to social ostracism and legal sanctions. Since the South was in rebellion and the survival of the Union was at stake, one can see why the reaction against dissenters was strong and even appreciate Lincoln's relative restraint in dealing with them. But the development of communal patriotism raised new questions that would henceforth be asked even where the war was fought against a foreign enemy. Did dissent in wartime, implying a lack of patriotism, have the effect of excluding dissenters from the community? Were they, in effect, siding with the enemy, and did this make them fair game for social pressure and legal coercion? The issue would become particularly acute when anti-war agitation was not limited to a few critics who could be ignored but influenced a number of people large enough (and strategically enough located) to pose a potential threat to the war effort.

World War I vividly illustrates this situation. The Wilson administration succeeded in whipping up a wave of patriotic fervor in 1917–18 that obscured the significance of the opposition to that war. Scholars still debate the true size of World War I resistance, but historian Howard Zinn was clearly right in maintaining that "the government had to work hard to create its consensus. That there was no spontaneous urge to fight is suggested by the strong measures taken: a draft of young men, an elaborate propaganda campaign throughout the country, and harsh punishment for those who refused to get in line."[33]

Those who opposed U.S. entry into the war, a clear majority in 1916, were still numerous and vociferous enough a year later to provoke the Wilson administration to pass a series of draconian laws against them and to jail more than one thousand dissenters. Resistance was especially strong among those who believed that the war was primarily for the benefit of Wall Street and the weapons companies, and who refused to accept the demonization of Germany. These included socialist workers (a substantial group in those days), Irish and other anti-British ethnic groups, members of peace churches, rural populists, isolationists, and intellectuals.

To eliminate this resistance (which might have jeopardized the all-important conscription effort, as well as sales of war bonds and other support activities), the government resorted to extraordinary measures of persuasion and coercion. The Committee for Public Information dispatched seventy-five thousand "Four-Minute Men" to five thousand cities and small towns around the country, where they gave short pro-war speeches in movie theaters and at workplaces, town halls, and sports events. The administration sponsored an American Protective League to search out cases of suspected "disloyalty" (estimated by the APL in the millions), frightened the large German American community into silence, and was still forced to classify more than 330,000 men as draft evaders.[34] Even so, the campaign had the overall desired effect. Many labor leaders (including the American Federation of Labor's Samuel Gompers) supported the war, and Socialist leader Eugene V. Debs was jailed for sedition without triggering any major social unrest. Whether a lengthy war might have generated more violent opposition cannot be known. As it was, most soldiers came back from "Over There" within a year of leaving home. Even so, more than one hundred thousand were killed and two hundred thousand wounded in the slaughterhouse of the Western Front.

In the postwar period, anti-war sentiment reached its highest level in American history. The war's ghastly toll in lives and injuries, the victors' failure to solve major international problems, and lurid revelations about military incompetence and war profiteering created an atmosphere of profound disillusionment with military intervention on both the left and the right. The anti-war film *All Quiet on the Western Front* was a blockbuster hit and winner of two Academy Awards (for Best Picture and Best Director) in 1930.[35] Over the course of the 1930s, however, as Germany and Japan began their campaigns of military expansion, the Roosevelt administration moved by stages toward an alliance with Britain and France, and the antiwar consensus began to fray. Opposition to U.S. entry into World War II was organized by the America First Committee, which probably had several hundred thousand members at its height. Led by the heroic aviator Charles A. Lindbergh, the AFC was initially a left-right alliance formed in order to resist FDR's interventionist policies, but it soon began to resemble the Whig pattern of upper-class dissent. Roosevelt considered Lindbergh a dupe of the Nazis and said so in thinly veiled words. Lindbergh did not exonerate himself from these charges by delivering a speech in Des Moines, Iowa, attacking Roosevelt, the British, and the Jews for leading the nation toward war. Even so, the AFC commanded a substantial following until the Japanese attack on Pearl Harbor mooted the debate.[36]

World War II united the nation as no other war had done, limiting opposition activity to a small number of pacifists and a few groups on the far left and right. This virtual unanimity is particularly worth noting in view of the commonly held presupposition that conscription—drafting young people into the armed forces—was the major factor draining public support from unpopular conflicts like the later war in Vietnam. More than sixteen million Americans served in World War II, about ten million of them draftees, yet there was virtually no draft resistance. Relatively few men registered as conscientious objectors, and the rate of draft evasion was considerably lower than in World War I.[37] This suggests that strong and widespread belief in the justice of a war can overcome people's natural tendency to resist compulsory military service.

In fact, even where wars are unpopular for other reasons, it seems that organized opposition will be limited if the cause is considered just. Consider the Korean War, a vastly destructive conflict that killed some 2 million Koreans, 400,000 Chinese, and 36,500 American

soldiers and was the first American war since 1812 to end in a stalemate. Despite the fact that conscription would be needed to fight
that war, President Truman's decision to intervene in order to drive
the North Korean invaders out of South Korea garnered almost universal support. But when the Americans, South Koreans, and other
UN forces drove across the 38th parallel into North Korea, the Chinese came to the aid of their ally, and brutal fighting dragged on for
three more years without a victory. The war became so unpopular
that "by November 1951 a Gallup poll found 51 percent of a frustrated public ready to embrace the dropping of atomic bombs on
'military targets.'"[38] General Douglas MacArthur also flirted with
the use of atomic weapons, but after Truman fired him as commander, unleashing a storm of criticism, Dwight Eisenhower won
the presidency promising to end the war on terms fair to all parties.
(His Democratic opponent, Adlai Stevenson, made the same promise.) Throughout all this political tumult, there was virtually no
draft resistance and little organized anti-war activity other than
criticism of Truman's conduct of the conflict by Republicans in
Congress. It appears that the moral capital accumulated by the U.S.
government in World War II had not yet been exhausted.

The "Movement" and Its Consequences

The next war found this moral account seriously depleted. The Vietnam War, as we know, spawned a movement of opposition larger,
more passionate, and more influential than any previous anti-war mobilization in American history. While polls showed popular support
for the war sinking steadily from 1966 through 1971, activities by organizations opposed to it on political and moral grounds moved from
small protests, teach-ins, and the symbolic burning of draft cards to
large, often tumultuous demonstrations, significant draft resistance
(including the flight of several thousand draft evaders to Canada),
student strikes, a wide range of acts of civil disobedience, and, finally,

the bombing of government and corporate offices by a small group of militants calling themselves the Weather Underground.

In the course of this development, hundreds of thousands of demonstrators descended upon Washington, D.C., and marched in New York City, San Francisco, and other cities. Colleges and universities became foci of dissent and activism. In a sermon at New York's Riverside Church in 1967, Martin Luther King committed the civil rights movement to the support of the anti-war cause. The following year, a large anti-war demonstration in Chicago was violently assaulted by Chicago police—a fracas that disrupted the Democratic Convention and contributed to Hubert Humphrey's defeat by Richard Nixon in that year's presidential election. In 1970, National Guardsmen at Kent State University fired into a crowd of student protestors, killing four students and wounding nine. Two students at Jackson State College were shot and killed under similar circumstances, and a protest strike shut down 450 American colleges and universities. Several hundred thousand demonstrators disrupted Washington, D.C., on May Day 1971, and mass arrests (most later dismissed as illegal) filled the jails. That same year, the *New York Times* and *Washington Post* published the revealing and embarrassing "Pentagon Papers" procured by scholar/activist Daniel Ellsberg. While protesting war veterans threw their medals over the White House fence, anti-war agitation spread to the war zone itself, where "an army, made up increasingly of poor and working-class draftees, was threatening to come apart."[39]

At home, most anti-war protests and demonstrations were peaceful, unless they were disrupted by the police. Acts of civil disobedience like those undertaken by anti-war priests Philip and Daniel Berrigan were scrupulously nonviolent. Yet the protests emitted a violent "vibe" that frightened the government, polarized the country, and made many Americans anticipate increasing furor and instability. In part, this was a result of the movement's aggressive, rebellious style; as journalist Tom Engelhardt writes, the young protestors challenged

America's "victory culture," using images like the "V for victory" sign
of World War II to mean their opposite: V for peace—or, if necessary,
defeat. "In those years when a president feared calling up the reserves
or letting the term mobilize pass his lips," says Engelhardt, "it was
young radicals who joined an umbrella organization called the Mobe,
created a home front, and called out the reserves."[40] One commenta-
tor believes that negative public reactions to the movement's more
radical manifestations actually prolonged the war by helping to elect
Richard Nixon president.[41] But this speculation ignores the dissenters'
role in keeping controversy about the war boiling, with the result that
many people came to believe that ending the conflict abroad was the
quickest way to restore peace at home.

The anti-war movement did not end the Vietnam War, of course;
events on the battlefield were primarily responsible for that. But it
represented the eruption of something new in American politics: an
opposition that combined elements of two older models to produce
a synthesis more potent than either one. Like the Whigs, the movement appealed strongly to well-educated, middle-class Americans.
The universities were its main organizational base, and its weight
among intellectuals generated a large volume of scholarly literature,
artwork, journalism, films, and other products supporting its critiques of the war. But, like the Democrats and Socialists, it garnered
substantial support among workers, urban minorities, and less privi-
leged sectors of the society, particularly older people, who were more
apt to embrace an anti-war position than the young.[42] Public opinion studies convincingly refute the notion that opposition was limited to the affluent and the young. In fact, the group most supportive
of the war was the white middle class, while workers' attitudes reflected those of the country as a whole.[43]

Still, there was something about the anti–Vietnam War activists
that gave them a collective identity separate from that of even their
sympathizers. Unlike previous anti-war groupings, they constituted
a capital-M Movement: a bonded collectivity with its own cultural
(not just political or economic) sense of solidarity. To use one of

Girls Say Yes to Boys Who
Say No, *1968. Anti–Vietnam
War poster advocating draft
resistance. The woman on
the left is singer Joan Baez;
the other two women are
her sisters.*

their own metaphors, they were as much a "tribe" as a political movement. In a nation whose politics had long been influenced by the
play of ethnic, national, and religious communities, they were, in effect, another oppressed minority group making its own claim for
dignity and power.

The Movement's loosely organized, often contentious leadership
constituted an alphabet soup of political organizations and "tenden-
cies." Many older people were involved in its decision making. But
its primary identity was generational, and most young activists were
motivated less by sectarian ideologies than by more general commitments to the values of peace, friendship, race and gender equality,
economic justice, anti-bureaucratism, sexual freedom, and personal
authenticity.[44] These commitments were thought of as leftist, especially in comparison to traditional conservative beliefs. They represented a challenge, to be sure, to older conceptions of patriotic duty,

familial obligation, and self-restraint. But the "hippie" aspects of the Movement—the devotion of many of its members to personal spontaneity, taboo smashing, self-development, and an almost gnostic pursuit of pleasure/wisdom—were the despair of more orthodox leftists, who hoped to win American workers en masse to the socialist cause. There were many attempts to square this circle, including the insistence by some militants that youth itself was a "revolutionary vanguard." But most working people, while opposing the war, resisted calls to transform the socioeconomic system, and the Movement remained, above all, a radical identity group.

What brought this new social formation into existence was a series of unexpected developments in American society that created simultaneous interlinked conflicts. A twenty-year-long economic boom altered the social landscape, generating a vast increase in the number of college students, including working-class and lower-middle-class students.[45] An era of rising expectations and televised communication saw the emergence of a distinctive youth culture, as well as the birth of vibrant, volatile movements for racial equality, women's liberation, economic justice, and gay people's rights. Racial strife moved from South to North (and would become a worrisome source of conflict within the U.S. Army during the war). When President Johnson, elected in 1964 as a "peace candidate," sent hundreds of thousands of U.S. troops to Vietnam, a wave of moral indignation split the clergy of many faiths into pro- and anti-war factions, and disparate popular movements found a common cause. Conscription, which had been accepted as a kind of fate at the time of the Korean War, now struck many of the new generation as an avoidable outrage. In effect, their soaring expectations, moral as well as material, had shifted the burden of proving the war's justice to the government. "Show us that this violence is justified. Otherwise, we won't go." (Lyndon Johnson's "domino theory" was *not* a satisfactory response.)

We have seen that communal patriotism typically threatens dissenters in time of war with exclusion from the community. Clearly, this was one strategy pursued by pro-war forces in the Vietnam era.

Richard Nixon and Henry Kissinger, in particular, blamed anti-war protestors for aiding the enemy and prolonging the war. (Vice President Dick Cheney would resort to the same rhetorical tactics at the time of the Iraq War.) Other critics went further, characterizing the Movement as anti-American, anti-God, and part of the worldwide Communist conspiracy. In response, some activists engaged in dramatically symbolic anti-patriotic acts, like burning American flags. Most believed that they were redefining patriotism, for example, by invoking the ideals of the American Revolution and Civil War and by displaying flags bearing peace symbols. In either case, however, the dissenters insisted that *they* were a community—"Volunteers of America," as the song by Jefferson Airplane declared—which others were invited to join. This self-definition, even while alienating cultural traditionalists, allayed the usual fears of ostracism and repression. In fact, being on the receiving end of police violence or conservative obloquy was considered a badge of honor.

At the same time, the Movement's cultural identity provided numerous links back to the broader society. To take an example that may seem trivial (but isn't), the musical *Hair*, subtitled "The American Tribal Love-Rock Musical," opened on Broadway in 1968 and ran for four years, spreading the gospel of peace, love, self-expression, rock music, racial equality, and anti-war dissent across the land. While political revolutionaries bandaged their wounds and retreated, vowing to fight another day, the "counterculture" influenced American cultural tastes, sexual mores, family relationships, social attitudes, and religious practices across a wide range of social and demographic groups. On the one hand, one could call this a recipe for political extinction, since when the cultural flame burned out, or when its styles were co-opted by consumer industries, that would be the end of the Movement. It is certainly true that, a generation later, those opposing the Iraq War would find themselves without an existing movement to join or a cultural milieu to lean on for support. On the other hand, one could see it as another case of "reverse assimilation." Vast numbers of Americans—especially the young—were participating to some extent

United We Win, *1943. Photograph*
by Alexander Liberman for the
War Manpower Commission.

in the counterculture. This was not merely a matter of hair length and
clothing styles but implicated political and moral values as well. In
later decades, the changes in popular thinking initiated during the
Vietnam era would prove far more than trivial, although less than
revolutionary.

Take conscription, for example. Even before the war ended, the
Nixon administration recognized that draft resistance would no
longer be considered unpatriotic or disloyal if many people considered a war unjust. To counter this, the government adopted an all-
volunteer military model that is still in force. Proposals to revive the
draft are now made by anti-war members of Congress who believe
that this would force a reconsideration of U.S. military efforts in
countries like Iraq and Afghanistan.[46] Similarly, because of the
American public's demonstrated tendency to think more independently about questions of war and peace, U.S. regimes made strong
efforts to prevent Vietnam-style news coverage of subsequent conflicts. During the Persian Gulf War, the first Bush administration
imposed the most rigid restrictions on the press in American history, while Bush II (responding, in part, to press complaints about

the Gulf War) "embedded" journalists with U.S. forces during the Iraq War. "Embedding" clearly presented that conflict from the point of view of the invading U.S. troops, but the advent of new, Internet-driven media, as well as the availability of non-American news sources like the Al-Jazeera television network, has to some extent broadened the coverage of Uncle Sam's continuing wars.

The public mood, in general, remains ambivalent. Disapproving of the war in Afghanistan but unwilling to mobilize strongly against it, many Americans are currently experiencing what might be called "passive discontent." Several reasons have been offered to account for this relative quiet among the citizenry. Some analysts emphasize the post-Vietnam developments that have created professionalized, technologically sophisticated armed forces that do not depend upon conscription to fill their ranks and that offer jobs to large numbers of people who would otherwise be unemployed or underemployed. Others note that the "new militarism" bred in American culture since the 1990s produces an uncritical attitude toward military adventures, and that the centrality of war-related industries to the U.S. economy makes an unending series of interventions seem not only feasible but also economically essential. These explanations are facile, since they beg the question, citing this new militarism as its own explanation. Given a sufficient level of outrage over current wars and interventions, Americans *would* create a new anti-war movement suited to twenty-first-century conditions. We might ask what prevents or inhibits the development of this outrage now.

Three factors seem particularly important:

Fear. This seems crucial to understanding current American attitudes toward war and peace. Many of us are afraid of another 9/11-type terrorist attack. When frightened, people often seek the apparent security of superior military force and strong governmental authority. They do not feel empowered to challenge the status quo.

Co-optation. The election of a new president with liberal credentials, a figure strongly supported by anti-war forces in his campaign for office, clearly had a pacifying effect on potential war protestors.

People do not join serious movements of dissent if they trust a "dissenter in office."

Recession. Economic insecurity focuses many people on survival issues and often inhibits them from taking political chances. The Movement emerged on the heels of an unprecedented economic boom. The U.S. economy remains in precarious shape, and young people, in particular, are worried about surviving a lengthy recession.

The very act of naming these factors, however, suggests conditions that might eliminate them. To take them in reverse order, one can imagine an economic recovery that would radically alter the social atmosphere by raising people's expectations and encouraging them to demand, for example, that military expenditures be lowered significantly to meet unsatisfied civilian needs. As to co-optation, one can envision two possibilities: President Obama either discovers new methods of dealing with the problem of Islamist terrorism or he does not. If he does, this obviates the need for an independent antiwar movement. If he does not, the war escalates, and Obama unwittingly produces one of the prime conditions for the formation of a militant opposition: the moral outrage generated by a Great Betrayal. One can hardly imagine the emergence of the anti–Vietnam War Movement without Lyndon Johnson's betrayal of his liberal followers. By contrast, even though George W. Bush was discovered to have misled the American people about Iraqi weapons of mass destruction, his followers had not identified him as a peacemaker and were not enraged by his warmaking.

Finally, consider what might mitigate the current fear of terrorist attack or demonstrate the ineffectiveness of war as a method of achieving national security. The happy scenario is that Americans (like many Europeans and others) learn to live with the threat of terrorism while pursuing nonviolent methods of eliminating its causes. As I argue in the next chapter, this shift would mean abandoning existing militarist paradigms in order to develop creative new approaches to resolving our conflicts with Islamists and other rebels against U.S. authority around the globe. The unhappy scenario—*extremely* unhappy—is that another terrorist attack takes place, saddening and enraging us, but also demonstrating that, to paraphrase the Prophet Isaiah, there is no real security in weapons and wars of revenge. We can hope and pray to be spared the horror of another attack. But we can only advance toward real security by learning to think about conflict in new ways.

5

WAR AS A LAST RESORT?
PEACE PROCESSES AND NATIONAL HONOR

The noonday train
will bring Frank Miller.
If I'm a man
I must be brave.
And I must face that
deadly killer,
or lie a coward,
a craven coward,
or lie a coward
in my grave.[1]

MANLY WAR AND EFFEMINATE NEGOTIATION

It was 1953 when I first saw Gary Cooper as Marshal Will Kane in Fred Zinnemann's great neo-Western *High Noon*, a tightly constructed black-and-white film dominated by its haunting theme song ("Do Not Forsake Me, O My Darling") and the inexorable movements of the town clock's giant hands. Cooper's conflicted, over-the-hill lawman was a different sort of American hero. Fatigued with violence and ready to retire, he decides to face down a

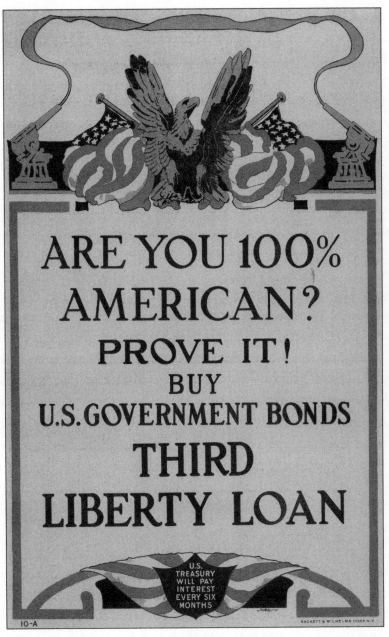

Are You 100% American? Prove It! *1918. World War I poster soliciting people to buy war bonds, using the concept of 100 percent Americanism promoted by the Wilson administration to create an imagined cultural unity. (Source: University of North Texas Digital Library, Posters Collection.)*

sociopathic killer—the former Big Man of the town—despite the disapproval of his Quaker bride (Grace Kelly) and the refusal of the timorous, self-indulgent townspeople to join him in the fight against evil. The marshal's real battle is internal, although its final act is played out in classic style on a dusty street. But this makes him even more quintessentially heroic: not just a brave gunfighter but also a moral champion. "Torn twixt love and duty," he faces down the feminine temptations of tenderness and domesticity and makes the honorable (masculine, heroic) choice.

In an age of serious American "message" movies, *High Noon*'s messages were tantalizingly abstract and ambiguous. Some critics considered the film a liberal condemnation of communal cowardice and passivity in the face of the McCarthyite witch hunts of the early 1950s. The *High Noon* screenplay was written by the former Red and soon to be blacklisted writer-director Carl Foreman. No less a patriot than actor John Wayne branded the movie un-American. Others, however, noting that the murderous Frank Miller had been released from jail by soft-headed judicial liberals, detected more than a trace of law-and-order conservatism. In retrospect, it seems clear that both schools were right, but for reasons not well appreciated at the time. The movie reflected the shared values that, cutting across customary lines of liberal/conservative conflict, helped to unify both camps in the Age of the Cold War.

I was fourteen years old when *High Noon* was released; the Cold War was barely five. The movie was made during a hot phase of the conflict—the bloody, finally stalemated Korean War, which ended shortly after the film's release with the newly elected President Eisenhower fulfilling his campaign pledge to go to Korea to put an end to the carnage. There was a glaring contrast, in fact, between the "no-win/no-lose" negotiated conclusion of that punishing war and the stark alternatives presented by the movie: honorable violence or cowardly passivity. Marshal Kane did not negotiate an agreement with Frank Miller to withdraw to opposite sides of a demilitarized zone. He did what the United States didn't: he finished the job.

Might there be some sort of relationship between the compromises imposed on a dissatisfied nation by the complex dangers of the Nuclear Age and *High Noon*'s affirmation of a simpler ethic of courage and honor? Was Will Kane, tired of violence but forced to fight again, an avatar of post–World War II America? Mass consciousness in the United States mirrored the division between either/or ideals and blurry realities. In 1951, when General Douglas MacArthur, who wished to extend the war in Korea to bombing China, was relieved by President Truman of his post as commander of the U.S./UN forces in Korea, New Yorkers gave him the most enthusiastic ticker-tape parade since the end of World War II, and Congress greeted him as a wronged hero. Yet the same Americans spurned him as a political contender and elected the more "responsible" and compromising Eisenhower, who promised not to win the war but to end it.

At the time, of course, I did not have a thought about all this. But I clearly remember how uncomfortable I felt, sitting in one of the well-worn seats of the Central Theater in Cedarhurst, Long Island, to watch Coop, his usual strong-and-silent certitude replaced by anxious doubt, prepare to face down a really scary villain and his villainous gang. "Love or duty": what a choice! Love was Grace Kelly in her first significant acting role, wearing white, white, white, and promoting pacifist ethics (naïve, naïve, naïve). Duty was the obligatory confrontation with the evil Miller, whose eighty-five-minute approach to the town, innovatively filmed in real time, was measured by omnipresent ticking clocks. What would I do in such a situation, I asked myself (along with every other teenaged boy in the house)? Give up the Virgin Kelly to "step outside" with the local bully? Duck the bully but get the girl? In the film, the marshal's choices are even more constrained, since the screenplay makes it clear that Frank Miller intends to hunt Will Kane down wherever he may go. Miller's appetite, like that of all pathological aggressors, is only whetted by appeasement. I remember thinking that there ought to be some alternative other than appease or fight, but when I mentioned that doubt to my father, he reacted quite sternly, like the good Truman Democrat he was: "There are times when you *have* to fight."

The external conflict—Marshal Kane vs. Frank Miller—mirrored and was mirrored by this internal struggle: Courageous Me, able to renounce softie love, step out alone, and face the bully, vs. Cowardly Me, as much afraid of dealing out violence as of receiving it, and in love with all the Grace Kellys of the sophomore class. What made the struggle particularly acute was that it was not just a matter of the Cowardly Lion needing his bottle of Courage, but also of love conceived of as a selfish domestic comfort, the diametric opposite of "Duty, honor, country!" A real man would leave his home and family, just as the heroes of World War II and Korea did, and go off alone to face the foe. That was the essence of honor, wasn't it? "I could not love thee, dear, so much, loved I not honor more." It was something that women, even Grace Kelly—especially Grace Kelly—simply couldn't understand.

High Noon endures as a poetic version of how many Americans still feel about national honor. Although gendering these distinctions is no longer acceptable, we range weakness, passivity, naïveté, cowardice, and *talk* on one side of the divide, and strength, energy, wisdom, bravery, and *action*—violent action—on the other. In some ways, this seems a throwback to frontier days, when men defended their honor (meaning their reputation for virile courage) by fighting duels against those who insulted them or threatened the people under their protection. But there are more modern causes for our tendency to equate negotiation with weakness.

True, one gets a strong whiff of cowboy machismo when public officials assert that we must not withdraw from some military position or offer to talk with adversaries because that would appear weak. The "rational" defense of this position alleges that peace moves of any sort suggest an unwillingness to fight, thereby inviting new enemy attacks. In most cases, however, this argument falls apart as soon as one looks closely at it. Consider the withdrawal of U.S. forces from Somalia in 1993, after a disastrous and ill-prepared raid in Mogadishu led to the deaths of eighteen Army Rangers and Special Operations soldiers there. It is commonplace to assert that, by demonstrating weakness, this retreat incited Usama bin Laden to mount further attacks on U.S. positions. Yet the evidence suggests that aggressive acts by the United States provoke and embolden terrorists rather than deterring them.

The withdrawal from Somalia, of course, was dictated by military necessity. To put an end to the anarchy and warlordism in that nation would have required a massive, years-long intervention that nobody advocated. The withdrawal was not part of any peace process, and the people in the United States who demanded it most vociferously were hard-headed conservatives in Congress. Of course, bin Laden (who later claimed, without much verification, to have inspired the Somali resistance) was delighted by the Americans' failure to capture General Mohamed Farrah Aideed, the principal warlord. But there is no evidence that increasing the American presence in Somalia would have had any deterrent effect on bin Laden. On the contrary, his plan was always to draw the United States into a wider war. After al-Qaeda bombed American embassies in Kenya and Tanzania five years later, Bill Clinton dispatched cruise missiles to destroy three of their training camps in Afghanistan and a factory in Khartoum. Rather than retreating, the terrorists responded by attempting to bomb the Los Angeles Airport (a plot that was thwarted) and by assaulting the USS *Cole* in Aden harbor. According to a witness cited by the 9/11 Commission, when the United States did not immediately respond to the attack on the *Cole*, bin Laden "complained frequently that the United States had not yet attacked . . . Bin Laden wanted the United States to attack, and if it did not he would launch something bigger."[2]

There may be times when talking peace rather than acting violently does invite aggression. The 1938 negotiations at Munich between Nazi Germany, Britain, France, and Italy, which Hitler used to strengthen his position for the coming world war, is a prime example. That traumatic deception continues to cast its shadow over proposals to negotiate, even where the circumstances are entirely different from those that obtained at Munich. The United States' current power and international role are vastly different from those of England or France at Munich, and the power and role of today's terrorists have little in common with those of Nazi Germany. But when officials or foreign policy specialists assert that we must give proof of our toughness or else make ourselves vulnerable to aggression, they do not ordinarily consider whether the Munich conditions apply, any more than they consider whether al-Qaeda would prefer us to retaliate or hold our fire. As Marshal Kane might put it, "Some people talk or run; a man stands and fights."

This attitude not only recalls frontier ideals of masculine honor but also signals a fear of what talking implicitly means. Any sort of dialogue, even "negotiation from strength," involves some form of recognition of the other party, if only the recognition that the person across the table has followers and some claim to represent them. It also acknowledges that our power, although great, is not limitless, and that we and the enemy, despite our differences, inhabit a common universe, speak a mutually comprehensible language, and share other human characteristics and concerns. In addition, dialogue has the potential to destabilize certain comforting assumptions. For example, we may discover in talking and listening that we bear some share of responsibility (however small) for the conflict, and that there are satisfactory alternatives (however speculative) to continuing to try to destroy each other. That is why, although it would seem that parties in conflict have little to lose by talking, they frequently act as if they are risking a great deal. What one risks in negotiation is usually not a Munich-style deception or a loss of honor but one's *conflict identity*—the sense of the absolute differences separating our side from the enemy. In intense, long-lasting conflicts, people tend to define the other side as a negative of themselves. This way of thinking sometimes verges on solipsism—the idea that only we really exist. Talking with the enemy threatens to deprive us of this splendid (even if destructive) isolation and to bring us into relationship with others whose reality and human needs demand recognition.

I am not sure if Americans tend more toward political solipsism than other peoples, but there are reasons to think that this may be the case. For several centuries, the ex-Europeans who settled North America lived isolated both from their homelands and from "the native people of the woods." As cultural historian Richard Slotkin notes, "All emigrants shared the sense that they had been, willingly or unwillingly, exiled from their true homes in the motherlands of Europe."[3] Americans' consciousness of other peoples was shaped by their long separation from the rest of the world by three oceans: the Atlantic, the Pacific, and the Arctic.[4] But even when geographical barriers became less forbidding, the "American Way of Life"—a unique mix of rich natural resources and economic opportunities, racial and social inequalities, mass culture, adversarial democracy, and religious pluralism—separated us from most other nations. Even now, despite the appearance of the Internet and other forms of global communication, more than two thirds of the American public admit to knowing very little about the world outside the United States, and more than half state that they are not interested in learning more.[5]

This cognitive provincialism has been the subject of much finger wagging, as if it were simply a bad habit or the result of deficient high school curricula. But I suspect that it has something to do with Americans' consciousness that they have long lived a charmed, isolated life, relatively free of many of the problems and hazards that beset other societies, and their anxious recognition, especially since 9/11, that this apparent exemption from the common fate is now in jeopardy. (The debate over global climate change also brings this anxiety to the surface.) In the administration of George W. Bush, the phrase "God bless America," conventionally used to close presidential speeches, became "May God *continue* to bless America"—a covert admission of the possibility that blessings conferred can also be withdrawn. The growing consciousness of their threatened uniqueness presents Americans with two options. We can accept membership in a world community as one nation among many, relinquishing the burden of global leadership in order to play an important but not dominant role. Or we can insist on "global leadership," which is a euphemism for empire-building—that is, for remaking the world in our own image. The outcome remains in doubt. Growing up is an exhilarating but nerve-wracking experience, and so is recognizing one's membership in a larger human community. Little wonder that it feels to many people like losing their freedom and identity.

This returns us to Marshal Will Kane. The myth of the solitary hero, a staple of American culture from colonial days onward, persists even now as a dramatization of the "global leadership" option. The marshal's temperament and actions are those of a lone gunfighter, but his office—his five-pointed star—makes him the community's violent protector. At the time of the Korean War, the Defense Department issued a statement calling the U.S./UN forces intervening in that conflict "the sheriff of the world."[6] Two decades later, in an interview with the journalist Oriana Fallaci, Secretary of State Henry Kissinger compared himself to "the cowboy who leads the wagon train by riding ahead alone on his horse, the cowboy who rides all alone into the town."[7] But we seem to conceive of the entire nation as a solitary hero—a people once chosen by God to create a new-model civil society, and now chosen by circumstances to order the world through military action. Mort Zuckerman, conservative editor in chief of *U.S. News & World Report*, put it in a nutshell when asked on CNN, shortly after the invasion of Iraq in 2003, why there was so little support for that war outside the United States. "It always makes me remember Gary Cooper in 'High Noon,' when he had to defend the town, even when the rest of the town wasn't willing to support him," said Zuckerman. "We are the sheriff in the world, whether we like it or not. We're the only country able to project power as we did in Afghanistan, as we did in Iraq."[8]

Zuckerman did not ask *why* it is that we are the only country able to project such power. Clearly, if we wanted to share our military technology with other nations or international organizations, we could do so, as we have already done to a small extent with NATO and a few other allies. If we wanted to adopt a "defensive defense" posture, abandoning offensive weapons and weapons of mass destruction, as several nations have done, we could do that, too. And if we decided to help create regional and international bodies to regulate the use of violence, that also would be within our power. It will simply not do to develop most of the world's most advanced military technologies, then to prevent other nations from acquiring them, and, finally, to claim that we are obliged by this monopoly of power to "project" it to Iraq and Afghanistan. The unspoken premise of the argument is that *only* Americans can be trusted to wield great power. A second assumption is that this power confers upon us the responsibility to bring law and order to a savage world. As the rest of the world recognizes, however, even if we do not, this is the philosophy and program not of a sheriff but of an emperor.

WAR AS A LAST RESORT, AND OTHER FOLKTALES

The tendency among Americans to equate negotiation or dialogue with weakness creates another sort of problem as well, since to justify a war one must show that the choice of violence is compelled by the situation and that no other honorable and effective course of action is available. "A state may resort to war only if it has exhausted all plausible, peaceful alternatives to resolving the conflict in question, in particular diplomatic negotiation." The idea that war should be a last resort has been one of the key elements of just-war theory ever since the Middle Ages.[9] Yet this is the slipperiest of all the reasons to fight.

Part of the problem is definitional. After engaging in lengthy and fruitless peace talks, for example, how can one conclude that further negotiations might not succeed? But the more serious issues are

political. When policymakers decide to make war, they always argue that we have no choice but to fight, either because our side has
negotiated in good faith while the adversary has refused to act rea-
sonably, or because negotiating under the circumstances would be
useless, wrong, or dangerous. The flimsiness of many of these arguments suggests that pro-war advocates bank on the American distrust
of "mere talk" to help convince the public that nonviolent methods
of resolving the conflict are impossible. More surprisingly, while
American policymakers do sometimes negotiate peace agreements,
they frequently present the results as the products of threats and violence.

Sham negotiations. Like other governments, the U.S. government
sometimes enters into negotiations in order to give the impression
that it wants peace, even though it has already decided to make war
if its demands are not met immediately and in full. In this case,
something advertised as an offer or proposal is really an ultimatum,
and the alleged negotiation is a sham. We have already described a
classic example, the Slidell Mission of 1844–45 to Mexico City whose
predictable failure precipitated the Mexican-American War.[10] A second is the McKinley administration's negotiations with the Spanish
government over Cuba, which the Americans broke off because of
domestic political pressure.[11] What distinguishes genuine negotiations
from this sort of playacting is the requirement of good faith. Good
faith implies a willingness to discuss which issues are negotiable and
which are not and then to work for a compromise, within reasonable
limits, of the negotiable issues. But when diplomatic exchanges take
place in secret, and when lies or misstatements about them are made
public, it is particularly difficult to determine whether a government
is negotiating in good faith. Journalist George Monbiot puts it suc-
cinctly:

> Those who would take us to war must first shut down the public
> imagination. They must convince us that there is no other means
> of preventing invasion, or conquering terrorism, or even defend-

ing human rights. When information is scarce, imagination is easy to control. As intelligence gathering and diplomacy are conducted in secret, we seldom discover—until it is too late—how plausible the alternatives may be.[12]

The most dramatic recent examples of this principle are America's two wars against Iraq, neither of which was a genuine last resort.

Recall that when Saddam Hussein sent his troops into Kuwait at the beginning of August 1990, President George H. W. Bush dispatched half a million troops to Saudi Arabia as part of Operation Desert Shield.[13] As a specialist in conflict resolution, I followed events in the region closely, especially when reports began circulating of efforts by Arab leaders and others to negotiate a peaceful solution to the crisis. As the buildup toward war accelerated, I moderated a panel discussion, broadcast nationally by C-SPAN, on "War in the Gulf: What Are the Alternatives?"[14] The panelists agreed that war could be avoided with honor, since there was growing evidence that Saddam could be negotiated out of Kuwait in exchange for symbolic face-savers, without the United States making any real concessions. What we did not understand was that President Bush, his defense secretary, Dick Cheney, and others in the administration were anxious to avoid any solution to the conflict that stopped short of destroying Iraq's armed forces.

As the military buildup accelerated, Saddam Hussein became increasingly desperate. First, using Arab intermediaries, he offered to withdraw his troops in exchange for significant concessions. Then he dropped these demands and asked only for minor concessions, such as recognition of Iraq's rights in the disputed Rumaillah oil field. Finally, when the United States remained adamant, he agreed to leave Kuwait unconditionally, provided that the Americans give him three weeks to remove his forces and equipment. World leaders ranging from King Hussein of Jordan to François Mitterand of France, Russia's Mikhail Gorbachev, and Pope John Paul II urged the Bush administration to negotiate a peaceful settlement, but U.S. officials rejected all Iraqi offers out of hand. "Although it was clear that the Iraqis were making reasonable offers for negotiation," writes one historian, "it appears in retrospect that the Bush administration wanted war and did everything possible to block a negotiated diplomatic settlement."[15] It finally became clear that America's aims were not simply to liberate Kuwait but also to rid the United States of a menace to its authority in the Gulf region. This could only be done by destroying Iraq's army and air force, degrading its infrastructure, and neutering the region's most modern nation in local and international affairs.[16]

The second Iraq War presented an even more egregious example of bad faith, this time on the part of the second Bush administration. On March 20, 2003, after the devastating American attack on Baghdad had begun, Secretary of Defense Donald Rumsfeld held a press conference in which he stated, "Let me close by saying that war is the last choice; let there be no doubt. The American people can take comfort in knowing that their country has done everything humanly possible to avoid war and to secure Iraq's peaceful disarmament."[17]

In invoking the last-resort doctrine, Rumsfeld was referring to almost two years of intense diplomatic conflict precipitated by U.S. charges that Iraq was in possession of chemical, biological, and possibly nuclear weapons, and that Saddam Hussein was plotting with terrorists to injure the United States. United Nations weapons inspectors found no evidence of such weapons. The American-led Iraq Survey Group concluded that Saddam had abandoned his weapons program in 1991. And no evidence of Iraqi contact with al-Qaeda or similar terrorist groups was ever produced. Nevertheless, insisting that they had reliable intelligence to support these charges, Bush, Cheney, and Rumsfeld obtained an authorization from Congress to use force against Iraq, if needed, to obviate threats to American security.[18] Despite the UN Security Council's refusal to authorize military intervention, the United States moved quickly toward war.

To head off the threatened attack, agents of Saddam Hussein's government approached the CIA's former head of counterterrorism, Vincent Cannistraro, and told him that the Iraqis were prepared to allow American troops to enter the country to search for weapons of mass destruction and would prove to Washington's satisfaction that they had no relationship with al-Qaeda or knowledge of the 9/11 attacks. In addition, Saddam offered to hold internationally monitored elections within two years. "All these offers had at bottom the same thing—that Saddam would stay in power, and that was unacceptable to the administration," Cannistraro said. "There were serious attempts to cut a deal but they were all turned down by the president and vice president."[19]

According to Pulitzer Prize–winning reporter James Risen of the *New York Times*, further offers were made through various diplomatic and private channels, culminating in undertakings to open up the entire country to a weapons search, to turn over a suspect in the 1993 World Trade Center bombing who was being held in Baghdad, to cooperate actively with the United States in the fight against terrorism and in the Middle East peace process, to favor American oil companies, and to make whatever other concessions were necessary, short of "regime change." These offers were made directly to top Bush official Richard Perle through a Lebanese American intermediary. "Mr. Perle said he sought authorization from C.I.A. officials to meet with the Iraqis," Risen reports, "but the officials told him they did not want to pursue this channel, and they indicated they had already engaged in separate contacts with Baghdad. Mr. Perle said, 'The message was, "Tell them that we will see them in Baghdad."' "[20]

The Iraq War was a last resort only if one assumes that regime change in Iraq, without weapons of mass destruction, terrorist contacts, or any evidence of plans to injure the United States, was a justifiable war goal. (But if it was, why did the Bush administration go to such lengths to try to make good its specific accusations against Saddam Hussein?) Donald Rumsfeld's statement to the contrary was therefore a falsehood, plain and simple. Even so, one can see how easy it is to slip from a conviction that one's war aims are justified to an assertion that the war is a last resort because the other side has not proved willing to accept those aims in negotiation. This was the case, more or less, in the diplomatic talks that preceded the Spanish-American War, when the Spanish offered to end their counterinsurgency campaign in Cuba and give the Cubans a degree of autonomy within the Spanish Empire—but not the full independence demanded by rebel leaders and many Americans. President McKinley found himself beset by a public, a congressional opposition, and leaders of his own party, all demanding "Cuban independence or war!"—and in an election year. Although he did not favor Cuba's independence except under tight U.S. control, McKinley declared that the Spanish had failed to negotiate in good faith and turned the matter over to a jingoistic Congress.[21] As soon as the war ended, he and his government immediately took steps to make Cuba an American colony in all but name.[22]

Refusals to negotiate—and to admit negotiating. At the extreme, sham negotiations become refusals to negotiate. The behavior of the two Presidents Bush prior to their wars against Iraq can certainly be described in these terms. But there is also a more general sort of refusal that rejects even the semblance of peace talks on the ground that an evil adversary bent on destruction cannot be trusted to keep his word and will use any negotiating process to feed us false information, collect intelligence, and keep us off balance—to advance his own interests and to damage ours. In this situation, war is both a first and last resort, since negotiation can only worsen the conflict, not resolve it.

There are such cases, of course. Who could trust Hitler as a negotiating partner after he tore up the 1938 Munich Agreement? A far more common situation, however, is that illustrated by American diplomatic behavior during the Cold War, when public refusals to negotiate based on the enemy's alleged malice and untrustworthiness alternated with periods of open bilateral negotiation ("thaws") and, on several occasions, intense rounds of secret diplomacy. In order to achieve the flexibility they sought, U.S. officials gave the public mixed messages about talking with the enemy. If America went to war, as it did in Korea and Vietnam, and, later, in the Persian Gulf, government spokesmen relied on the Hitler analogy, explaining that negotiations would be worse than useless, since the adversary was an Evil Enemy who must be stopped by military force, not "appeased." On the other hand, if the United States decided to negotiate, the same officials would explain that responsible leadership required talking with the adversary to defuse nuclear threats or to gain other advantages, and that the result of these bargains would be to make America stronger and more secure. Thus, after U.S. leaders had refused to recognize mainland China for more than two decades on grounds that the Communists were Evil Enemies, Henry Kissinger made a secret trip to Beijing in 1971 to negotiate a new, collaborative relationship that was confirmed publicly by Richard Nixon in his dramatic visit to China the following year.

In practice, U.S. policies followed three unwritten Cold War rules. Rule 1: Negotiate with your global enemy when you think it would be advantageous to do so. Rule 2: Fight hot wars by proxy or by using your own troops against the global enemy's proxy, but do not fight the global enemy's troops directly. Rule 3: Do not negotiate with your enemy's proxy at the beginning of a hot war, but negotiate to end the war when you consider it necessary to do so. It may seem odd to state the rules so abstractly, but peace researcher Michael Cox surely had it right when he wrote in 1990, "The Cold War was more of a carefully controlled game with commonly agreed rules than a contest where there could be clear winners and losers."[23] This was certainly so after Truman left office and Stalin died. Subsequent rulers of both nations, beginning with Eisenhower and Khrushchev, pursued an increasingly interactive dialogue that culminated in the negotiations that defused the Cuban Missile Crisis of 1962.

Rule 1 is illustrated not only by Nixon's trip to China but also by Ronald Reagan's dramatic turnabout during his second term of office, when he went from denouncing the USSR as an "Evil Empire" and threatening a new arms race to participating in a veritable orgy of negotiation. As Cox notes, "After [Reagan's] second election four summit meetings were held, the INF treaty was signed, bilateral relations expanded and key regional disputes were resolved. Reagan even stopped referring to the USSR as an Evil Empire"[24] These initiatives were hardly irrational on Reagan's part, but they were clearly inconsistent with his previous approach to negotiating with the Soviets. This sort of inconsistency, fluctuating between the poles of "moralism" and "realism," continues to this day in the case of adversaries like the Afghan Taliban. The implicit message to the public, from Cold War days to the present, is "The government will decide when to negotiate and when to fight. Trust us to do what is right."

When it came to dealing with the Evil Empire's proxies, however, the watchword was moralism. As Rule 2 suggests, negotiations were out of the question, at least at the start of hostilities, when the Communist foe tended to be characterized as a Hitler-style aggressor. Thus, American officials framed the U.S. interventions in Korea and in Vietnam as defensive responses to Kim Il Sung's invasion of South Korea and North Vietnamese attacks on U.S. destroyers, all characterized as acts of power-lust. These narratives obscured the fact that America's clients in both nations were also brutal dictators who had committed repeated acts of violence against their enemies at home and in neighboring lands. They also diverted attention from our own government's failure to respond to offers to negotiate prior to taking up arms. In 1950, United Nations efforts to draw the United States into talks with the USSR over the rapidly worsening situation in Korea failed to get the Truman administration's attention.[25] In 1964, efforts by several international parties to find a peaceful solution to the Vietnam conflict were repudiated by the Johnson administration.[26]

In both cases, however—this is Rule 3—as soon as it became clear that the United States would not win a quick victory, the reluctance to negotiate vanished, and peace talks took place on a stop-and-start basis over a period of several years. Oddly, or so it seems now, the Nobel Peace Prize for 1973 was awarded to Henry Kissinger and Le Duc Tho, the American and North Vietnamese negotiators of the Paris Peace Accords, who had spent the previous three years simultaneously discussing peace terms and justifying the killing of millions. (Kissinger accepted his award; Le Duc Tho did not.) The model of negotiation that this suggests, which remains orthodox among many U.S. foreign policy experts, is the reverse of von Clausewitz's famous dictum about war and politics. It is that *negotiation is the continuation of war by other means.* When the Cold War produced America's first peacetime militarization and unleashed a drive to establish and maintain U.S. global military supremacy, the key foreign policy idea, dominating all others, was that force works. Violence and the threat of violence would "contain" the Soviets, avert the threat of nuclear war, and enable the United States to extend its influence and to defend its interests globally. Maintaining this focus in the face of contrary pressures (including people's general dislike of violence, and their insistence on moral justifications for using it) meant denying or minimizing the effectiveness of nonviolent methods of conflict resolution. Therefore, this further oddity: when peaceful negotiations succeeded in avoiding violence or resolving conflicts, officialdom often presented the results as a military victory.

The most dramatic case of this, perhaps, was the Cuban Missile Crisis, which the conventional wisdom paints as a triumph of forceful will by President John F. Kennedy. "We were eyeball to eyeball, and the other fellow just blinked," said Secretary of State Dean Rusk famously. Rusk adverted to the fact that, after discovering that the Soviets had installed intermediate range ballistic missiles in Cuba, Kennedy "faced down" Soviet premier Nikita Khrushchev by threatening a military confrontation that might well have gone nuclear. After demanding that Khrushchev remove the missiles, JFK put the Strategic Air Command on full nuclear alert and declared a "quarantine" of Cuban waters, meaning that the United States would stop and search any ships, including Soviet vessels, trying to deliver goods to Cuba. Meanwhile, he allowed Soviet ambassador Anatoly

Dobrynin to learn that his military advisers were advocating an air attack on the missile sites and a full-scale invasion of Cuba, and suggested that he might not be able to resist the pressure to act. According to the popularly accepted version of the story, these threats of violence, raising the possibility of nuclear war, compelled Khrushchev to remove the missiles in exchange for a few negligible concessions by the U.S. authorities: a public undertaking not to invade Cuba in the future, and a secret agreement to remove American missiles from Turkey and southern Italy.

Other versions, relying on essentially the same facts, tell quite a different story.[27] The Soviets had placed missiles in Cuba to begin with because the Americans had put Jupiter intermediate range ballistic missiles in Turkey, virtually on the Russian border, were supporting Cuban exile attacks on the Castro regime, and were thought to be contemplating an invasion of Cuba to redeem the failed attempt by exiles at the Bay of Pigs. (That same year a proposal by the Joint Chiefs of Staff, code-named Operation Northwoods, suggested committing terrorist acts against Americans and blaming them on Fidel Castro in order to rally public support for an invasion.)[28] Military moves and countermoves during the missile crisis produced a risky stalemate that put President Kennedy as much at risk as Premier Khrushchev. The concessions made by the Americans to avoid a disastrous outcome were not negligible—they freed Castro permanently from the threat of U.S. invasion and continued exile attacks, and they eliminated the Jupiter missiles threatening Russia. Moreover, the switch from military threats to diplomacy set the stage for further negotiations between the two superpowers that produced the Nuclear Test Ban Treaty of 1963. It served the Democratic Party's purposes to picture JFK as a Cold Warrior even tougher than his predecessors, Eisenhower and Truman. So, at Robert Kennedy's insistence, his agreement to remove the missiles from Turkey and Italy was kept secret. The message delivered to the American public once again was "Force works"—*not* "Force didn't work, so we had to negotiate a settlement."

In fact, the practice of mixing war with negotiation—of fighting and talking peace at the same time—effectively abolishes the last-resort doctrine. For if we need to fight in order to set the stage for conflict resolution, it makes no sense to demand that those advocating war show that there is no peaceful alternative to violence. These difficulties are well illustrated by the situation in Afghanistan in 2010, when President Barack Obama ordered a "surge" of thirty thousand additional American troops to fight the Taliban and implement counterinsurgency strategies mapped out by his commanding general, Stanley McChrystal. At the same time, Obama promised to begin withdrawing some of those troops in the summer of 2011. Some U.S. officials described the troop surge as an inducement to the Taliban to negotiate, suggesting that talks with that organization's leaders could take place at any time, perhaps using the Saudis or Pakistanis as intermediaries. Others insisted that the Taliban must be defeated, or at least stalemated, before meaningful negotiations could take place. Still others asserted that talking peace might induce midlevel leaders to defect but could not hope to succeed in persuading the Taliban's central leadership to give up their alliance with al-Qaeda or their hope of ruling all Afghanistan.

Current American policies toward Afghanistan remain as ambiguous and secretive as Richard Nixon's policies toward Vietnam or Ronald Reagan's toward the USSR. We say that we are fighting to force the other side to make peace, but what we are demanding and what we are prepared to concede are equally unknown—not only in the sense of being kept secret but, apparently, of being undecided at the highest level. Such a policy is essentially *experimental*: "Let's fight and see what happens next." Therefore, if some elements of the American public choose to interpret President Obama's promise to withdraw an undefined number of troops from Afghanistan in 2011 as indicating a firm commitment to end the war soon, they are free to do so. And if they prefer to interpret the promise as a meaningless sop to the Democratic Party's liberal supporters, they are free to do that as well. Barack Obama is reputedly a very different sort of political figure than Nixon or Reagan. But the message of his moralist/realist policy is the same: "These decisions are for us, not you, to make. We will decide whether the enemy is incurably evil or trustworthy, whether negotiations are in America's interest or not, whether to talk peace or to fight. Trust your government to do what is right."

Fortunately, however, this is not the only way to think about negotiation or to practice conflict resolution. There is good news to report—news that has the potential to reinvigorate the last-resort doctrine and help Americans participate more actively in decision making about matters of war and peace. We turn to these new developments now.

Beyond Negotiation: Conflict Resolution and Its Implications

The end of the Cold War and the Soviet Union's collapse generated widespread fear that a wave of violent ethnic, nationalist, and religious conflicts would sweep across Eastern Europe and the former Soviet republics, causing great suffering and imperiling the peace of the world. In the 1990s, these fears were realized in the former Yugoslavia, especially in Bosnia, where a vicious communal war took the lives of some sixty thousand soldiers and forty thousand civilians, ending only when NATO intervened and the international community (with active U.S. participation) forced the disputants to make peace. War also raged in the Russian province of Chechnya, whose mostly Muslim inhabitants sought autonomy or independence from the post-Soviet Russian regime. Elsewhere, however, in nation after nation where violence had been expected, the feared bloodbaths did not materialize. In some cases, alienated communities avoided violence but could do no better than to maintain a "cold peace," while in others they moved toward long-term reconciliation. A long list of nations escaped the predicted disaster, and in several cases where violence did occur, it was brought under control by peaceful means.

There were many reasons for this surprising success. Superpowers attempting to maintain their control over dependent nations invariably predict that their withdrawal will cause chaos and bloodshed. This sometimes happens, but more commonly, their former subjects (breathing great sighs of relief) find methods of resolving their differences internally.[29] In post-Soviet Eastern Europe and Central Asia, however, another factor was also at work. Since the 1960s, a growing group of scholars and practitioners had been developing a new set of theories about social conflict and a range of practical methods to help parties in conflict resolve their differences peacefully. They called the new discipline conflict resolution, conflict management, or conflict transformation, but its basic principles were the same regardless of the label. By the time the Cold War ended, they had already been involved in designing and facilitating peace processes of various sorts in Northern Ireland, Spain, Cyprus, the Middle East, Malaysia, Indonesia, Fiji, South Africa, Sudan, the Horn of Africa, Liberia, Mozambique, and elsewhere. In the wake of the Soviet collapse, these conflict resolvers played important roles in helping to prevent or manage serious internal disputes in the Baltic nations, Moldova, Macedonia, Hungary, Armenia/Azerbaijan, Georgia, Ukraine, and Tajikistan, to name a few sites. Conflict specialists acting independently of governments are currently practicing actively in virtually every region of the world where major social conflicts are experienced. Yet their discoveries are just now beginning to work their way into official thinking about foreign policy, war, and peace.[30]

Both in theory and practice, conflict resolution differed from traditional diplomacy in crucial ways. First, and in some ways most important, its focus was analytical, not power-based. The first task that conflict resolvers set themselves was to assist alienated or warring parties to understand the causes or "drivers" of their conflict—especially the systemic causes and conditions—so that they could begin to consider how to change the conditions generating alienation or violence. This did not mean giving the parties their own interpretation of the conflict's causes, which would inevitably reflect the biases of outside "experts," but eliciting the insiders' own views through sensitive, expert facilitation. Second, they worked to help those trapped in serious conflict to think creatively about resolution options—to develop ideas that they might have been prevented from imagining because of the tunnel vision that conflict so often produces. Third, they facilitated discussion of which options were mutually acceptable and politically feasible and which not, and how to gain the community support needed to implement agreed-upon solutions. Finally, they helped the parties build personal relations that would permit them to work together over the long haul to reconcile their divided communities.

At certain points, these tasks resembled conventional diplomacy. For example, diplomats also evaluate the costs and benefits of proposed terms of agreement. But, overall, the conflict resolvers steered away from the sort of threats, promises, and bargaining strategies that often characterize negotiations between diplomats or lawyers. The main problem with diplomacy, as they saw it, was that bargaining on the basis of one's group's or nation's power short-circuits the process of discovering the real problems generating the conflict and truncates the exploration of new options for resolving it. Since power differentials exist, they must be taken into account in later stages of the peace process, for example, in evaluating the practicability of proposals. When it is successful, what some have called "Track Two diplomacy" leads toward the more formal negotiations of "Track One."[31] But conflict settlements dictated by the more powerful party are almost certain to fail, unless they somehow also identify and eliminate the conflict's underlying causes and restore shattered relationships. For the same reason, power-based settlements rarely lead in the direction of the sort of social and cultural rebuilding that is needed to permit bitterly opposed parties to reconcile and move toward "positive peace."

One important implication of this new model of peacemaking is that conflict resolvers generally operate independently of governments or other interested parties. If our own government, say, is either a direct party to a conflict or indirectly committed to one side or the other, it will probably lack the detachment needed to facilitate an analytical, problem-solving process, or to envision solutions that might require significant changes in U.S. policies and behavior. Probably the best-known exception to this rule was President Jimmy Carter's skillful facilitation of the Camp David Accords between Anwar Sadat of Egypt and Menachem Begin of Israel in 1978. But even in that case, the priority of America's relationship with Israel prevented the parties from inviting the Palestinians to participate, and the "cold peace" between Egypt and Israel, although no mean achievement, was dependent upon continued financial and political support for both parties by the United States.[32]

A more typical conflict resolution process was that managed by former senator George J. Mitchell in connection with the Protestant-Catholic struggle in Northern Ireland. Although Mitchell was named a U.S. special envoy for the peace process, he insisted upon acting as an independent facilitator, and this independence had a great deal to do with his successful mediation of that violent, long-lasting dispute.[33] It helped that independent conflict resolvers had been conducting workshops for Catholic and Protestant leaders since the mid-1980s. By the time skilled practitioners began working with the Northern Irish parties, both sides had fielded an assortment of active, well-armed paramilitary groups, and the "Troubles" dating from the late 1960s had taken more than three thousand lives, most of them civilians. Great Britain, acting as protector of the Protestants, had sent troops to keep the peace, but the British troops, accused of favoring the Protestants, became a focus of violence. The Irish Republic demanded that Ireland be unified under its leadership to protect the Catholic minority of the "five counties" from further discrimination and violence, but the Protestants accused Dublin of sheltering and arming terrorist groups. British and Irish attempts to resolve the conflict had repeatedly broken down. Although people were exhausted by twenty years of struggle, there seemed to be no exit from this "intractable" conflict.

All this began to change in the late 1980s, in part because of fatigue with the violence, in part because of the conflict resolvers' efforts.[34] Intensive participation in numerous workshops with skilled, nonpartisan facilitators helped Catholic and Protestant leaders to reconceptualize their problem as well as to know each other better. They recognized that Ireland and Britain, which they had thought of, respectively, as their protectors or saviors, were inflaming the conflict because of their own political concerns and interests. The idea that began to germinate in these dialogues was that of de facto independence: a Northern Ireland ruled, without British or Irish domination, by a government sharing power and guaranteeing the basic needs of both sides. If the Protestants would consider giving up their reliance on British troops, and the Catholics would drop their demand for all-Irish unification, the two parties might find a way to live together in a nation recognized and supported by the new European Union. When George Mitchell arrived in Northern Ireland in 1995, he had three years of hard, often discouraging work ahead of him to secure the agreement of all parties concerned, including Great Britain and Ireland, to this new concept, to convince the Catholics and Protestants to agree to disarm, and to construct a power-sharing agreement. The result was the Good Friday Agreement of 1998. Given the difficult problems still to be solved by the Northern Irish, the agreement cannot yet be accounted an unqualified success—but it has clearly been a giant step toward peace.

Such successes (often incomplete, but successes still) are now becoming part of the modern history of formerly war-torn nations from Sierra Leone and Mozambique to Cambodia and East Timor. A particularly notable success story is that of South Africa, which boasts one of the largest communities of conflict resolution specialists in the world. Conflict resolvers in that country were instrumental in helping to facilitate national and local processes that ended the apartheid system without mass bloodshed. More recently, conflict prevention techniques—a spin-off of the new discipline of particular interest to European conflict resolvers—are being put to work to prevent violent conflicts from erupting across the globe. Postconflict reconciliation or "peacebuilding" has become part of the repertoire of numerous government and nongovernmental agencies in America and abroad, including the U.S. Agency for International Development, which operates an Office of Conflict Management and Mitigation, and the U.S. Department of State, which houses an Office of Reconstruction and Stabilization. The United States Institute of Peace, a government-funded agency designed to link conflict resolution specialists with policymakers, has enjoyed a significant increase in funds and personnel.[35]

An unanswered question, however, is whether conflict resolution concepts and methods can be used to resolve conflicts to which great powers like the United States are a party. If (as I firmly believe) they can, the failure of conventional diplomacy to make peace between the United States and some adversary does not satisfy the last-resort requirement. In order for war to be justified as a last resort, conflict resolution efforts must also have been attempted and have failed.

Let me underline this point. To prove that a war is necessary, it is no longer sufficient to say, "We tried to negotiate, but they wouldn't cooperate." Nor is it acceptable to maintain, "We can't negotiate with them because they are trying to kill us." Conflict resolution processes often take place where the parties are still shooting at each other and where each side considers the other a fanatical terrorist or imperialist. The general rule is "no preconditions for talking." These processes are voluntary. If facilitated discussions move the parties toward peace, so much the better; if they do not, nothing has been lost. What is required, at least for purposes of justifying a war, is a commitment by the government to participate fully in the process, even though some critics will say that this means "recognizing" the enemy, and even though by participating, people run the risk that their thinking may be changed. To insulate the participants from pressure and publicity, conflict resolution workshops or dialogues are generally held under conditions of strict confidentiality. Often, they are most successful when the individuals participating are not the top leaders of each country or group but influential members able to think more freely about the issues and to communicate their new insights to the leadership. Usually, workshops or other dialogues take place at regular intervals over a period of several months or longer, with the participants returning to their home communities between sessions.

The result is an intensive interaction that has the potential to help conflicting parties think new thoughts about their situation and how to improve it. Imagine, for example, that the next time President Obama comes to Congress for funds to continue the war in Afghanistan, congressional representatives, nongovernmental organizations, and members of the public were to say, Hold on! Have you tried to secure the services of independent, trusted, expert facilitators to assist the Afghan government, the Taliban, the Northern Alliance leaders, major ethnic communities, and other parties in that war-torn land to resolve their differences *without* relying on American troops? Why do you think it helps, rather than hurts, to have U.S. forces occupying large parts of the country and trying to dictate peace terms? If your answer is that, without American troops to stop them, the Taliban would otherwise march into Kabul, the same question must be asked: Have you tried to secure the services of competent facilitators to help resolve the U.S. government's conflict with the Taliban? If the answer to this question is no, war is not a last resort, and we cannot support it.

Why not use conflict resolution now? One should not reach the stage of Track One bargaining until confidential Track Two discussions, preferably facilitated, have clarified all the parties' priorities and needs. There is nothing to be lost by engaging in workshops or dialogues with the Taliban immediately, before the military campaign has had maximum effect, since the purpose of the process is not to bargain to an agreement based on the parties' relative power but to discover the deep-rooted sources of the conflict and what can be done to alter them. For example: Is the alliance between the Taliban and al-Qaeda America's most pressing concern, as the president seemed to suggest? If so, what, if anything, would the Taliban be willing to do to address this concern? If the dialogue does not take place and the question is not directly asked and addressed, one begins to suspect that there are other U.S. concerns beneath the surface: concerns about geopolitical influence and economic resources in Central Asia, perhaps, or about national prestige and global authority, or even about the president's political future. Understand: I am *not* alleging that there are such concerns in play. I *am* asserting that unless attempted conflict resolution takes place and such questions are clarified, we have no way of knowing whether this war is necessary to protect our security and freedom, or whether it is merely the latest version of the old Mexican War/Iraq War shell game.

A true story: When war clouds were gathering prior to George W. Bush's 2003 invasion of Iraq, I asked an employee of the United States Institute of Peace to permit me to facilitate a discussion there of alternatives to war in Iraq, bringing together conflict resolution specialists, experts from academia and think tanks, informed journalists, and U.S. government officials. I assured my contact that the discussants would include people strongly in favor of an invasion and "regime charge," as well as those opposed, and that the entire exchange of views would remain off the record. The answer, following a short silence, was "I'll see what I can do." After a few days of waiting and no reply, I called again and asked, "What about the Iraq forum?" The answer: "They told me, 'You've got to be kidding. There is no way the administration will let this happen.'"

Moral: It is not that the government does not know about conflict resolution. Certain federal agencies have adopted some of its concepts and techniques, and the United States Institute of Peace, in particular, has made serious efforts to educate others in Washington about the new discipline's potential. But there is a conflict that may be irresolvable between maintaining one's status as the world's only superpower—an empire in all but name—and participating in conflict resolution processes. Not long after the Iraq War began, for example, it became clear that Iraq's Sunni, Shia, and Kurdish communities, as well as a number of smaller communities, desperately needed the opportunity to make collaborative decisions about a host of questions, including the structure of the future government, the disposition of oil revenues, church-state relations, and relations with Iran and other regional neighbors. America's answer, under the regime of occupation, was to assume that the locals could not possibly reach agreement on such issues on their own (shades of President McKinley and the Philippines), and, therefore, that envoy Jerry Bremer and other U.S. satraps would have to make these decisions for the fractious Iraqis.

Did it not occur to Messrs. Bush and Cheney that there were experienced Islamic facilitators, people expert in traditional as well as modern conflict resolution techniques, who could help the local parties make their own decisions? Was it not clear to them that the allegedly empowering U.S. presence was actually depriving the locals of decision-making power? My own view is that they were not able to consider conflict resolution seriously because of their deep commitment to maintaining and expanding American power in the Gulf region. Using conflict resolution techniques would have meant pulling back—withdrawing, if you like—to an extent sufficient to permit alienated Iraqi communities to explore what changes would be needed to reconstruct their relationships. And this independent process might have threatened America's control over the country and, ultimately, over the region.

The same sort of question is likely to be posed in connection with other parties in other parts of the world. What if Venezuela's Hugo Chávez were to do something that the U.S. government considered threatening to American interests in Latin America or American security at home? American officials might undertake conventional negotiations, if only to convince the public that everything possible had been done to avert a violent confrontation. But, without deeper consideration of the reasons for the alienated U.S.-Venezuela relationship—in fact, without a probing joint analysis of

America's controversial, changing role in Latin America—bilateral negotiations would very likely come to naught. The next step, for an informed, awakened American people, would *not* be to approve the use of force as a last resort but to demand that the government enter in good faith into conflict resolution processes, using an appropriate facilitator.

In short, without an honest attempt at conflict resolution, war is never a last resort.

CONCLUDING NOTE
FIVE WAYS TO THINK MORE
CLEARLY ABOUT WAR

#1: Refuse to Accept the Normality of War

Since the end of the Cold War, American debates about war and peace have taken place in a curious vacuum. Familiar arguments about self-defense, Evil Enemies, the morality of intervention, and the risks of negotiating are trotted out and discussed as if the United States were still a rising young nation expanding its continental frontiers or flexing its muscles abroad, and not the most dominant superpower since Rome, with more than 140 military bases (seven or eight hundred, if one counts bases controlled by the United States) in at least 63 foreign countries.

At the end of the nineteenth century, when the United States first became a global power, the arguments for occupying other nations or bringing them under our control included an American version of Rudyard Kipling's "White Man's burden." As noted earlier, after a long night meditating in the White House, President McKinley decided to take over the Philippines because "there was nothing left to do but to take them all, and educate the Filipinos, and uplift and Christianize them."[1] Indiana senator Albert J. Beveridge added racial fuel to McKinley's religious fire: "We will not renounce our part in the mission of our race," he orated, "trustee, under God, of the civilization of the world."[2] Feelings of racial superiority and religious duty no doubt colored America's early imperial ventures, and are not yet entirely absent from our international outlook. But recent events have spawned an additional rationale for military intervention abroad, one that appeals for mass support on pragmatic, "realistic" grounds rather than preaching a moral crusade.

Recognizing that the United States *is* the world's only superpower, this argument asserts that our military capability and our will to fight are all that stands between a relatively civilized world order and chaos. America left Vietnam vowing not to become the world's policeman. But with regional conflicts multiplying, the United Nations hamstrung, and other nations unable or unwilling to confront local bullies and lawbreakers, the United States proved to be the only power capable of saving Kuwait from Saddam Hussein, Kosovo from the depredations of Slobodan Milosevic, and Afghanistan from Taliban dictatorship. Who else will lead a global struggle against al-Qaeda and its network and fight to rid the world of Islamist extremism? "If this be empire, make the most of it," say many American conservatives; like it or not, the United States must lead the world.

Liberal disagreement, thus far, seems based more on style than on substance. It emphasizes a more judicious use of force coupled with the instrumentalities of "soft power," but does not generally question the need for U.S. global leadership, including maintenance of the world's largest military-industrial complex and deployment of the world's largest, most far-flung military establishment.[3] Whether in liberal or conservative hands, the "new world order" rationale does not attempt to justify specific wars, but rather tries to legitimize the sort of continuous military intervention represented by the War on Terrorism (or what some in the Obama administration now call GCOIN: global counterinsurgency). This has two effects. On the one hand, it reduces publicity about specific conflicts, accustoms people to support undeclared wars, and generates consent to a high level of "normal" military activity. On the other hand, this consent, although widespread, is paper-thin, exposing the current system's advocates to objections both practical (such as America's inability to pay the costs of global policing) and moral (for example, the high rate of civilian deaths in Iraq, Afghanistan, and other war zones).

Furthermore, positioning the United States as a global superhero is clearly an incitement to further violence. Every empire—even the most well-intentioned, like the Persian Empire of King Cyrus or the British Raj in India—breeds resentment and revolt, and provokes the superpower to engage in brutal counterinsurgency campaigns. The technologically advanced empire has all the weapons one can dream of, but its rebellious subjects even the score by combining fanatical determination with the ability to use simple weapons against overly complex systems. One might call this the superpower's "Kryptonite problem." To overcome it requires taking off the hero's costume and asking two Clark Kent–like questions:

First, what about conflict resolution? Those who resort to violence generally do so because of unsolved problems, not just out of sheer fanaticism, malice, or power-lust. By giving up the struggle to maintain our sole superpower status—an addiction all the more powerful for being largely unconscious—we free ourselves to assist conflicting parties to identify those problems and work them out in their own way.

Second, how about international or regional law enforcement? If conflict resolution doesn't work and force is needed, what the world requires is a legitimate source of diplomatic coercion—one whose authority people could accept regardless of their socioeconomic status, political views, or culture. This does not mean the UN Security Council, at least not in its present form. It means new institutions, perhaps associated with regional organizations, that could be designed and brought into existence quickly, if only we abandon our superhero/superpower dream.

#2: THINK CALMLY AND STRATEGICALLY ABOUT SELF-DEFENSE

Almost a decade after the 9/11 attacks, American thinking on self-defense remains fixated on that great trauma. The consciousness that we were subjected to a totally unexpected, bloody assault, and that members of the same organization that attacked us are still at large, has given us the same mind-set that afflicts people who have been in a disastrous and unexpected auto accident. After a car ran a red light and struck my auto amidships, it took me almost a year before I could drive through a controlled intersection without a panicky sense that someone might plunge through the light and hit me again. The al-Qaeda terrorists inspire more fear, of course, since their acts were intentional and they have threatened further attacks, but still, our response has been to consider them "typical drivers"—the quintessence of all terrorists and insurgents—and to attribute *their* desire to harm the United States to all the others. Therefore, if Sunni or Shiite insurgents in Iraq, Taliban fighters in Afghanistan, or even FARC guerillas in Colombia violently resist U.S. forces on missions in their territory, we equate this emotionally with al-Qaeda's assaults on the World Trade Center and the Pentagon. Even where terrorists or insurgents do not attack our forces but only their own governments or members of rival groups, we say that "we" are under attack!

This confusion not only costs American lives and money but also operates as a self-fulfilling prophecy. For if we meddle in conflicts that have little to do with self-defense but much to do with exerting U.S. power abroad, groups that formerly had no interest in attacking us suddenly find us in their crosshairs. Say, for example, that we provide military assistance and advice to Filipino troops fighting against Islamic rebels in Mindanao in the Philippines. (Which we do.) One of the rebel groups, the guerrillas of Abu Sayyaf, is now said to be "linked" with al-Qaeda, and perhaps it is, now that our government has declared it an enemy of the United States. Similarly, the Somali group called al-Shabaab, which currently controls most of southern Somalia, started as a homegrown movement, but was radicalized when Ethiopian troops invaded with U.S. backing in 2006. Even now, although the group is said to be close to al-Qaeda, its interests and ambitions lie exclusively in Somalia. Could conflict resolution processes help the Somalis resolve their internal disputes? Perhaps; but what will *not* help are U.S. attempts to exert imperial control over the nations of East Africa.

Earlier, I proposed four questions that ought to be asked when self-defense is proposed as a justification for war: What are we defending? Against whom are we defending it? Is the chosen method of self-defense rational? How long will it take, and how much will it cost? These questions need to be asked even when, as in the case of al-Qaeda itself, the answers seem obvious. Repeatedly, one hears U.S. government officials saying, "We are at war. Terrorists are trying to kill us. We need to kill them first, not negotiate with them." Common sense, right? No, not necessarily. In violent conflicts, the enemy is always trying to kill you. Even under these conditions, there are times when warring parties decide to settle their conflict peacefully, either through negotiation or conflict resolution. One expert describes the situation in which conflicts are ripe for resolution as a "hurting stalemate," but there are other situations in which nonviolent techniques are more conducive to long-term security than continued fighting.[4] How can we tell whether a given policy constitutes a rational self-defense strategy?

The first step is to understand the adversary. Unfortunately, on the subject of "Islamist extremists," the following comments are typical:

> The struggle against Islamist extremists is unlike any other war we have fought. Osama bin Laden and those like-minded intend to make plain that our government cannot keep us safe, and have sought our retreat from the Islamic world and our relinquishment of the idea that human rather than their version of divine law must control our activities. This movement is not driven by finite grievances or by poverty.[5]

These are the views of a former U.S. attorney general with a reputation for normally good judgment. But one cannot build a rational self-defense strategy on the basis of this sort of gross misunderstanding.

To begin with, the War on Terrorism is *not* entirely unlike other wars we have fought. It is a counterinsurgency struggle similar in many respects to those waged in the Philippines, Vietnam, and Iraq. Furthermore, to speak of "Osama bin Laden and those like-minded" lumps al-Qaeda with other "Islamist extremists," and, in effect, declares war on them all. But a rational self-defense strategy might well dictate trying to *separate* al-Qaeda from other Islamist groups by bringing the others into dialogue and reconstructing our relationship with the Islamic world. It is true, as the author says, that bin Laden has "sought our retreat from the Islamic world"—but what of that? The U.S. role in the Muslim nations is highly controversial, to say the least. Discussing it with our adversaries could provide the basis for serious conflict resolution. To speak of "retreat," as if reconsidering our policies and practices would be dishonorable, is a way of refusing to think about what we are actually doing over there and how change might help us to become more, not less, secure.

As for the Islamists seeking to force us to accept their version of divine law, this fantasy of jihadists at the gates seems designed to induce a frenzy of religious self-defense. To be sure, one can find speeches by fanatical Islamists calling down divine judgment upon the Godless West, just as one can find speeches by fanatical Islamophobes suggesting that the Koran dictates murder and mayhem, but this conflict is not about religious beliefs. It is about who calls the shots in nations inhabited mostly by Muslims. When the author says, "This movement is not driven by finite grievances," he means that it is driven by pure religious intoxication, and that there is therefore nothing to do other than kill the fanatics. It is useful to recall, however, that Rome thought that this was exactly the case in connection with the fanatical sectarians who called themselves Christians, never dreaming that their martyrs would become "the seeds of the Church."

Of course, the early Christians did not resort to terrorist violence, so far as we know, while some Islamists (like the Maccabees of bibli-cal times) consider themselves holy warriors. This leads many people to think that talking with them would be useless. But there is a growing literature on the topic of negotiating with terrorists that suggests conditions under which talking may make very good sense.[6] My own view is that the United States ought not "negotiate"—that is, bargain—with al-Qaeda. We ought to engage in extensive conflict resolution processes with leading figures in the Islamic world, including militant Islamists, and invite al-Qaeda representatives to participate if they wish to do so. Thinking clearly about self-defense means discovering the best methods to provide Americans with long-term security. And long-term security depends ultimately on decent relationships, not on weapons of war. The United States does not have to disarm to begin to resolve conflicts like this, but if it does not begin to resolve them, all the weapons in the world will not provide the safety we seek.

#3: Ask Hard Questions About Evil Enemies and Moral Crusades

There is evil in the world, no doubt. But when government officials ask us to kill other people and risk our own lives to combat some great evil, they tend to diabolize any adversary, and we begin to imagine the enemy leader or even a whole people as transcendentally Evil—malicious, treacherous, power-mad, and cruel. Like the fallen angel, Lucifer, whom we picture as both superhuman and superbad, the Evil Enemy combines inhumanity with power: a frightening specter designed to rouse us to feats of heroic violence. Because this image is such strong medicine, hard questions ought to be asked whenever it reappears. For example:

How is the word "evil" being used? Does it mean that the leader or group is diabolical in the sense of wanting to destroy everything good and decent? Does it refer to unusual ruthlessness or cruelty?

To a desire to dominate a nation, a region, or the world? Or does it mainly indicate strong hostility toward the United States? (Defining evil does not mean giving up the right to use the word.)

Are there reasons, other than evil character, for this person or group to think and act this way? Can reasons be discovered in their own backgrounds or experiences? What about reasons rooted in the current situation, or in the behavior of other people, including Americans? Do these reasons suggest ways of communicating with them or altering their behavior? (Discovering reasons will not excuse their actions.)

What are the possible responses to such a leader or group—and which responses make most sense? Should we avoid talking with alleged enemies out of fear that negotiations or conflict resolution processes will compromise us and embolden them to do more harm? Should we fight them—and, if so, how can we assess the likely results of violent conflict? Is there some trusted third party or facilitator who could help resolve these issues? (Assessing the virtues of alternative responses does not constitute inaction.)

We saw earlier that enemy images often represent a "shadow double" of ourselves—a projection on some alien screen of characteristics we dislike and want to be rid of. Getting rid of these unworthy or shameful traits makes us feel purer and better—the very opposite of the violent, fanatical, self-interested, and power-hungry Other. And so we feel equipped to engage in moral crusades, knowing that we will be able to act as altruists, not hedonists; liberators, not oppressors. What should flash before our eyes when we are invited to undertake military crusades for democracy, freedom, or even world order, are the words of the Roman centurion in the gospel of Matthew (8:8)—"Lord, I am not worthy." As individuals, we may be willing to fight in a foreign land for no purpose other than to help its inhabitants solve some problem, happy to leave forever as soon as the job is done. But the world's sole superpower does not export hundreds of thousands of well-equipped troops at a cost of hundreds of billions of dollars merely out of the goodness of its heart. Good-hearted citizens without great wealth or power may forget that the entity proposing to intervene for humanitarian reasons is an empire whose political rulers and business leaders usually have interests of their own to pursue.

The issue appears in its most poignant form where the subject is intervention to prevent mass murder or genocide. Particularly since the publication of Ted Robert Gurr's pioneering study *Minorities at Risk*, genocide prevention has become a topic of great interest to conflict resolution professionals, scholars, and policymakers across the globe.[7] The United Nations has appointed a special adviser to the secretary-general on genocide prevention. The international journal *Genocide Studies and Prevention* is widely read. A host of nongovernmental organizations have entered the field, and an innovative program called Engaging Governments on Genocide Prevention has brought together international experts on genocide and officials from governments around the world to teach about the early warning signs of genocide and nonviolent methods of preventing it.[8]

If only the United States had intervened in Rwanda in 1994, we often hear, we could have saved hundreds of thousands of innocent lives. Yes, to be sure. But why didn't we? Why do we intervene almost exclusively in places such as Cuba, the Philippines, and Iraq, where, to use the vernacular, there is always something in it for us? Even in 1999, when American forces flew bombing missions under NATO auspices to protect the endangered Kosovars against Serbian troops, the United States emerged from the short, sharp confrontation with the largest military base in Europe, the gigantic Camp Bondsteel in Kosovo, which it apparently plans to own and operate for the foreseeable future. In cases of threatened genocide, as well as in other cases where humanitarian intervention is necessary, suggestions that we intervene unilaterally should prompt us to ask the same two questions mentioned a bit earlier. What about a serious attempt at conflict resolution? If conflict resolution has been tried and has failed, what about international or regional intervention? In the event that genocide is imminent or ongoing and neither option is available, it seems to me that the United States should then intervene—but under the conditions that the intervention be limited to the minimum time and force necessary to prevent a humanitarian crisis, and that we leave when the job is done, rather than maintain military bases or other imperial installations in the country.

The assumption of unique American virtue that has underpinned past interventions has also led us down the road of self-deception and replication of inhumane forms of oppression. To genocide, we should say, "Never again!" And to the slaughter of insurgents and civilians, the very same slogan: "Never again!"

#4: ANALYZE PATRIOTIC APPEALS.
RESIST CAMPAIGNS OF NATIONAL PURIFICATION

Patriotism is not necessarily the last refuge of scoundrels, as Dr. Johnson quipped, but it is the ultimate justification for dubious wars. In its most primitive form, the catechism goes like this: Q: Do you love your country? A: Yes. Q: Are you willing to fight for it (or to send your family and friends to fight for it)? A: Yes.

We Americans are conditioned to slip quickly from the first Q and A to the second. The unspoken connective is: If you love your country, you will fight for it. But that is exactly the connection that needs to be proved in particular cases rather than asserted in general. Loving one's country does *not* mean following its leaders' orders unconditionally. It certainly does not imply killing foreigners or putting American lives at risk on their command. To make that leap requires a different sort of catechism that ought to be administered to anyone advocating war.

Q: What do you mean by "love of country"? This is a multiple-choice question. The answers might include: (a) affection for certain people and places; (b) admiration for certain political, economic, and moral principles; (c) attachment to certain customs, mores, and cultural products; and (d) participation in certain forms of communal life. Some people may consider this list incomplete, on the ground that love of country involves something more general and absolute, like a sense of being part of an ineffable whole: "the mystical body of the Nation." But I have repeated the word "certain" to underline the fact that loving one's country does not mean admiring all of its people, places, principles, cultural products, or forms of communal life. In fact, the more one loves certain aspects of America, the more one very likely detests others.

Furthermore, the list specifies discrete types of patriotism, because self-declared patriots often affirm broad communal definitions that are "imaginary" in that they merge an ideal America with the actual America. These concepts of nationhood describe a unified, coherent community that is supposed to include all of us but that actually denies our real differences and excludes or marginalizes many of us. Patriotic ideologues have described Americans as a family, an ethnic community, a classless society, and, most recently, a moral/spiritual "civilization"—and *that* is the nation we are supposed to love . . . or else. Revivals of communal patriotism almost always generate campaigns of national purification that try to unite us through persuasion, intimidation, or persecution.

Q: *Why, in this particular case, does loving the country require fighting for it?* This question really demands two answers:

First, the justification for war must show a connection between some specific aspect of the nation and a credible threat to it. For example, if people who advocate an escalated War on Terrorism think that Islamists threaten America's religious and moral identity by trying to impose their version of divine law on us, let them prove it and show that the threat is credible. Or, if what requires protection is our system of democratic participation and individual rights, let the war advocates show exactly how that system is jeopardized (other than by our own ultra-nervousness about security). We should not commit mass violence in support of theories that do not clearly identify the "America" in danger and show how it is being threatened.

Second, it requires a demonstration that force is the only way or best way to remove the threat. For example, some Islamists say that the state of Israel, a longtime American ally, is illegitimate, and that its Jewish community should be destroyed. If there is no other way to avert a massacre of Israeli Jews than to use force to protect them, indirect or direct intervention by the United States is justified. But conflict resolution specialists and many other policy analysts believe that there *are* effective, feasible ways to make Israel's Jewish and Palestinian communities secure that do not involve continuing Israel's heavy reliance on violence. Even if these alternatives involve significant changes in current American and Israeli policies, those changes *must* be made in order to justify the use of force in the Middle East.

Answering such questions is difficult, but not impossible, at least when a war is actually justified. War advocates should bear a heavy burden of proof. The problem lies in finding the courage to ask them, when any serious questioning of a proposed military campaign is likely to be branded unpatriotic or cowardly. Our friendly critic Alexis de Tocqueville, whose classic study of America I quoted at the beginning of this book, remarked at length on the irony of the world's freest people finding it so difficult to challenge the tyranny of respectable opinion. Where we can find that courage is in religious and ethical traditions, as well as political ideologies, that make it clear that the nation is a worthwhile human association, not a god demanding human sacrifice. These same traditions insist that human life is infinitely valuable and that no particular nationality's lives are worth more than those of any other. To assert that American lives are inherently more valuable than those of other peoples is not patriotism but a particularly vicious form of idolatry.

Unlike most other political questions, questions of war or peace operate on the plane of absolutes: the worldly absolutes of life and death. In a democracy, we can fix most of our mistakes by throwing the rascals out or changing policies, but we cannot resuscitate the dead or cure those permanently maimed in body or in spirit. Therefore,

we are not only entitled but also *required* to ask whether the sacrifices demanded by war advocates are absolutely necessary in pursuit
of our security and integrity. If a positive answer is not clear and
convincing—as loud and clear as God's voice was to Abraham,
when he lifted his knife over his son, Isaac—we should not shed
blood, either ours or anyone else's.

#5: DEMAND THAT WAR ADVOCATES DISCLOSE THEIR INTERESTS

As development experts know, one-crop economies, even if they
temporarily produce great riches, are ultimately disastrous for a nation's economic and social life. Since the 1950s, the United States has
gone a good part of the way toward developing a one-crop economy
whose principal product is war. Direct military spending by the federal government now accounts for about one fourth of the total U.S.
budget (almost one trillion dollars).[9] Our military expenses are almost equal to those of all other nations of the world combined.
More than half of *Fortune* magazine's Top 100 companies are deeply
involved in defense production, and the extent of our total economy
dependent upon the continued expansion and use of U.S. war capa-
bilities, as well as the international trade in weapons and military
goods, can only be guessed at.[10] To describe fully the American war
system goes beyond the scope of this book, but the moment we are
asked to approve a war, the question of any war advocate's private
interest becomes relevant.

We Americans are fairly hardheaded people, ordinarily. If someone asks us to donate money to help the poor people of a far-off
land, or even to support our local police or firefighters, we want to
know how much of the donation actually goes to the advertised
cause, and how much ends up in other people's pockets. But if we
are asked to give our sons and daughters or our sweethearts to fight
on foreign soil, patriotic sentiment or some other inhibitor often

stops us from asking similarly hard-nosed questions. Who stands to gain from the war? How many military careers, civilian jobs, executive salaries, and stockholder dividends hang in the balance, as we decide whether or not to fight? I am not suggesting that most wars are fought purely for private profit, or that one cannot fight a just war that also makes some people rich. But having an interest in a case affects how one evaluates it, which is why judges and other public servants are expected to disclose such interests. In short, we need to demand that those advocating war tell us what's in it for them, so that we can take that into account when making our own decision.

There is another reason why many people may be reluctant to make that demand. The American economy is now so dependent upon war spending that we ourselves, workers and farmers as well as bankers and military-industrial tycoons, can be said to have an interest in the case. According to some experts, we have been practicing "military Keynesianism" for some time, using enormous military expenditures to supply needed economic demand to a system plagued by congenital overproduction. Can Americans stop fighting what Dexter Filkins calls "the forever war" without jeopardizing their own jobs and the health of their communities?[11] We urgently need to confront this issue openly, since it is putting us in an impossible moral position. Shall we sacrifice people's lives and health in wars of dubious value because this is the only way to keep the economy afloat? Aren't there ways of rethinking and reorganizing the economy that would eliminate this dilemma? The topic of peace-to-war economic conversion has become an important one in discussions around the world, although relatively few Americans are currently studying it.[12] Surely it is worth making the topic a high priority if we are to avoid killing and dying for the sake of livelihood.

The war system's main response to these concerns has been breathtakingly simple: minimize American casualties. At least since the

Vietnam War, it has been clear that while casualty rates alone do not determine public attitudes toward war, they have considerable weight when combined with other factors.[13] Official thinking appears to be that if the number of American battle deaths and serious injuries can be greatly lowered, the public will find much less cause to complain about America's apparently endless wars. To this determination, there are two answers that we ought to keep in mind:

First, U.S. experience since the Persian Gulf War of 1990–91 shows a significant decrease in American deaths produced by the use of high-technology offensive weaponry and improved defensive measures (body armor, for example), but horrifying increases in injuries generated by asymmetric warfare against hostile groups wielding low-tech weapons, such as improvised explosive devices. American veterans' hospitals are jammed with soldiers suffering the effects of severe head injuries, amputations, and post-traumatic stress—and the suicide rate among combat veterans has skyrocketed. Furthermore, we must question official definitions of "high," "low," and "acceptable" casualty rates. Was the Iraq War worth more than forty-three hundred American lives and thirty-two thousand wounded?

The second answer is that even if the number of U.S. casualties could be lowered to zero, that would not secure our consent to the slaughter of foreigners in unjust wars. At least one hundred thousand civilians died in the Iraq War, with some estimates running as high as five hundred thousand. Those who believe that we would easily sacrifice other people's lives in exchange for a guarantee of our own armed forces' safety do not have a very high opinion of Americans' moral character. The major premise of this study, which I want to close by reaffirming, is that we will *not* kill and die without being convinced that the struggle is justified on grounds of legitimate self-defense or moral duty. The current war system, with its pattern of continuous interventions in an ever-expanding zone of conflict, seems designed, consciously or unconsciously, to wean us from the habit of demanding justifications for specific wars. It is an act of faith, perhaps, to assert that this will not work—that Americans will remain unwilling to fight, except for a cause they are convinced is just. Nevertheless, I will keep that faith, and invite you, dear reader, to keep it as well.

ACKNOWLEDGMENTS

In writing this book, I was able once again to rely on the strong and helpful support of the Institute for Conflict Analysis and Resolution of George Mason University, a unique academic institution that encourages creative thinking about conflict and practical work for peace in the world. Special thanks to ICAR's director, Andrea Bartoli, and past director, Sara Cobb, for their encouragement and advice; to colleagues Kevin Avruch, Sandra I. Cheldelin, Christopher R. Mitchell, James R. Price, Dean G. Pruitt, Daniel Rothbart, and Solon Simmons for their critiques and suggestions; to Ekaterina Romanova for her very valuable research assistance; and to the splendid and varied ICAR student body for responding to the ideas presented here with their usual candor and energy.

I owe a particular debt of gratitude to the Rockefeller Foundation, which permitted me to spend a month writing this book at its Study Center in Bellagio, Italy, and to the gracious manager and guiding spirit of the Villa Serbelloni, Ms. Pilar Palacia. It was a special treat to reside in Bellagio with a congenial and stimulating group of scholars and artists, several of whom made important contributions to my work. Mark J. Lacy and David Dunlap were especially helpful, for which I thank them sincerely.

Portions of this book appeared in an earlier version in my article "Why Americans Fight: Justifications for Asymmetric Warfare," in *Dynamics of Asymmetric Conflict*, volume 2, number 1 (October 2009). Thanks to editor Clark McCauley and his colleagues for their useful criticism and suggestions.

I am most grateful for the assistance of my literary agent, Gail

Ross of Gail Ross Associates, and my talented editor, Pete Beatty of Bloomsbury Press.

My immediate family members know how much their loving support means to me. Thank you, Susan, for seeing me through another labor of love. Thank you, Hannah and Shana, for your comradeship and suggestions. And thank you, Matt, for taking the time and effort to read and comment on the manuscript.

SELECTED BIBLIOGRAPHY

Abbott, Philip, ed. 2007. *The Many Faces of Patriotism*. Lanham, Md.: Rowman & Littlefield.

Adamic, Louis. 2008. *Dynamite: The Story of Class Violence in America*. New York: AK Press.

Adamthwaite, Anthony P. 1989. *The Making of the Second World War*. 2nd ed. London: Routledge.

Aiello, Thomas. 2005. "Constructing 'Godless Communism': Religion, Politics, and Popular Culture, 1954–1960." *Americana: The Journal of American Popular Culture* 4:1 (Spring 2005). http://www.american popularculture.com/journal/articles/spring_2005/aiello.htm (consulted January 19, 2009).

Albright, Madeleine K., and William S. Cohen. 2008. *Preventing Genocide: A Blueprint for U.S. Policymakers*. Washington, D.C.: United States Institute of Peace.

Anderson, Benedict. 2006. *Imagined Communities: Reflections on the Origin and Spread of Nationalism*. Rev. ed. New York and London: Verso.

Anderson, Fred, and Andrew Cayton. 2005. *The Dominion of War: Empire and Liberty in North America, 1500–2000*. New York: Viking.

Andrews, Robert. 1993. *Columbia Dictionary of Quotations*. New York: Columbia University Press.

Angrosino, Michael. 2002. "Civil Religion Redux." *Anthropological Quarterly* 75:2 (Spring): 239–67.

Arendt, Hannah. 2004. *The Origins of Totalitarianism*. New York: Schocken Books.

Bacevich, Andrew J. 2005. *The New American Militarism: How Americans Are Seduced by War*. Oxford and New York: Oxford University Press.

Bailey, David. 2008. "Kicking the Vietnam Syndrome: George H. W. Bush, Public Memory, and Incomplete Atonement During Operation

Desert Storm." Paper presented at the annual meeting of the 94th NCA National Convention, TBA, San Diego, Calif., November 20. http://www.allacademic.com/meta/p257011_index.html (consulted October 25, 2009).

Bailey, Thomas A. 1948. *The Man in the Street: The Impact of American Public Opinion on Foreign Policy.* New York: Macmillan.

Bamford, James. 2001. *Body of Secrets: Anatomy of the Ultra-Secret National Security Agency From the Cold War Through the Dawn of a New Century.* New York: Doubleday.

Bandura, Albert. 2004. "The Role of Selective Moral Disengagement in Terrorism and Counterterrorism." In F. M. Mogahaddam and A. J. Marsella, eds., *Understanding Terrorism: Psychological Roots, Consequences, and Interventions.* Washington, D.C.: American Psychological Association Press. http://www.des.emory.edu/mfp/Bandura2004.pdf.

Barnet, Richard J. 1968. *Intervention and Revolution.* New York: World Books.

———. 1972. *Roots of War.* Harmondsworth, U.K.: Penguin.

Basinger, Jeanine. 2003. *The World War II Combat Film: Anatomy of a Genre.* Middletown, Conn.: Wesleyan University Press.

Battle, Joyce, ed. 2003. "Shaking Hands with Saddam Hussein: The U.S. Tilts Toward Iraq, 1980–1984." National Security Archive Electronic Briefing Book No. 82, February 25. http://www.gwu.edu/~nsarchiv/NSAEBB/NSAEBB82/ (consulted August 2, 2009).

Bellah, Robert N. 1967. "Civil Religion in America." *Daedalus* 96:1 (Winter), 1–21.

———. 1975. *The Broken Covenant: American Civil Religion in Time of Trial.* New York: Seabury Press.

Bercovitch, Sacvan. 1978. *The American Jeremiad.* Madison: University of Wisconsin Press.

Berenskoetter, Felix, and Michael J. Williams, eds. 2008. *Power in World Politics.* London: Routledge.

Berg, A. Scott. 1999. *Lindbergh.* New York: Berkley Books.

Berinsky, Adam J. 2001. "Public Opinion During the Vietnam War: A Revised Measure of the Public Will." web.mit.edu/berinsky/www/Vietnam.pdf (consulted December 6, 2009).

————. 2009. *In Time of War: Understanding American Public Opinion from World War II to Iraq*. Chicago: University of Chicago Press.

Bernstein, Iver. 1990. *The New York City Draft Riots: Their Significance for American Society and Politics in the Age of the Civil War*. New York: Oxford University Press.

Blackstock, Nelson. 1988. *COINTELPRO: The FBI's Secret War on Political Freedom*. New York: Pathfinder Press.

Blum, John Morton. 1976. *V Was for Victory: Politics and American Culture During World War II*. New York and London: Harcourt Brace Jovanovich.

Boggs, Carl. 2005. *Imperial Delusions: American Militarism and Endless War*. Lanham, Md.: Rowman & Littlefield.

Bonilla-Silva, Eduardo. 2009. *Racism Without Racists: Color-Blind Racism and Racial Inequality in Contemporary America*. 3rd ed. London and New York: Rowman & Littlefield.

Boot, Max. 2002. *The Savage Wars of Peace: Small Wars and the Rise of American Power*. New York: Basic Books.

Booth, Ken, and Moorhead Wright, eds. 1978. *American Thinking About Peace and War: New Essays on American Thought and Attitudes*. Sussex: Harvester Press; New York: Barnes & Noble.

Brands, H. W. 1992. *Bound to Empire: The United States and the Philippines*. New York: Oxford University Press.

Brewer, Susan A. 2009. *Why America Fights: Patriotism and War Propaganda from the Philippines to Iraq*. New York: Oxford University Press.

Brokaw, Tom. 2008. *Boom! Talking About the Sixties: What Happened, How It Shaped Today, Lessons for Tomorrow*. New York: Random House.

Brown, John. 2006. "'Our Indian Wars Are Not Over Yet': Ten Ways to Interpret the War on Terror as a Frontier Conflict." *American Diplomacy*. http://www.unc.edu/depts/diplomat/item/2006/0103/ca_brow/brown_indian.html (consulted September 1, 2008).

Brunk, Gregory G., D. Secrest, and H. Tamashiro. 1996. *Understanding Attitudes About War: Modeling Moral Judgments*. Pittsburgh: University of Pittsburgh Press.

Bryce, James. 1915. *Report of the Committee on Alleged German Outrages (The Bryce Report)*. http://www.gwpda.org/wwi-www/BryceReport/bryce_r.html (consulted April 24, 2009).

Buchanan, Patrick J. 1999. *A Republic, Not an Empire: Reclaiming America's Destiny*. Washington, D.C.: Regnery.

———. 2008. *Churchill, Hitler, and "The Unnecessary War": How Britain Lost Its Empire and the West Lost the World*. New York: Crown.

Burton, John W., ed. 1990. *Conflict: Basic Human Needs*. New York: St. Martin's Press.

———. 1996. *Conflict Resolution: Its Language and Processes*. Lanham, Md.: Scarecrow Press.

Butler, Michael J. 2003. "U.S. Military Intervention in Crisis, 1945–1994: An Empirical Inquiry of Just War Theory." *Journal of Conflict Resolution* 47:2 (April), 226–48.

Campbell, David. 1992. *Writing Security: United States Foreign Policy and the Politics of Identity*. Minneapolis: University of Minnesota Press.

Campbell, James T., M. P. Guterl, and R. G. Lee, eds. 2007. *Race, Nation, and Empire in American History*. Chapel Hill: University of North Carolina Press.

Cannon, James P. 1975. *The Socialist Workers Party in World War II: Writings and Speeches, 1940–43*. New York: Pathfinder Press.

Caute, David. 1978. *The Great Fear: The Anti-Communist Purge Under Truman and Eisenhower*. New York: Touchstone Books.

Chambers, Whittaker. 1987. *Witness*. New York: Regnery.

Chang, Laurence, and Peter Kornbluh, eds. 1998. *Cuban Missile Crisis, 1962: A National Security Archive Documents Reader*. New York: New Press.

Chatfield, Charles. 1992. *The American Peace Movement: Ideals and Activism*. New York: Twayne Publishers; Toronto: Maxwell Macmillan.

Cheldelin, Sandra, Daniel F. Druckman, and Larissa Fast, eds. 2008. *Conflict: From Analysis to Intervention*. London: Continuum.

Chidester, David. 1988. *Patterns of Power: Religion and Politics in American Culture*. Englewood Cliffs, N.J.: Prentice-Hall.

Chomsky, Noam. 1970. "After Pinkville." *New York Review of Books* 13:12 (January 1). http://www.nybooks.com/articles/11087 (consulted January 22, 2009).

———. 1993. "The Pentagon System." *Z Magazine*. February. http://www.thirdworldtraveler.com/Chomsky/PentagonSystem_Chom.html (consulted February 14, 2010).

———. 2007. *Failed States: The Abuse of Power and the Assault on Democracy*. New York: Henry Holt.

Cole, Wayne S. 1962. *Senator Gerald P. Nye and American Foreign Relations*. Minneapolis: University of Minnesota Press.

———. 1974. *Charles A. Lindbergh and the Battle Against American Intervention in World War II*. New York: Harcourt Brace Jovanovich.

Coles, Roberta L. 1998. "Peaceniks and Warmongers' Framing Fracas on the Home Front: Dominant and Opposition Discourse Interaction During the Persian Gulf Crisis." *Sociological Quarterly* 39:3 (Summer), 369–91.

Collins, Christopher. 2007. *Homeland Mythology: Biblical Narratives in American Culture*. University Park: Pennsylvania State University Press.

Conlin, Joseph R. 1968. *American Anti-War Movements*. Beverly Hills, Calif.: Glencoe Press.

Connolly, William E. 2008. *Capitalism and Christianity, American Style*. Durham, and London: Duke University Press.

Conolly-Smith, Peter. 2008. "Casting Teutonic Types from the Nineteenth Century to World War I: German Ethnic Stereotypes in Print, on Stage, and Screen." *Columbia Journal of American Studies*. http://www.columbia.edu/cu/cjas/conolly-smith-1.html (consulted April 1, 2009).

Conrad, Joseph. 2005. *Heart of Darkness*. 4th ed. New York: Norton.

Cox, Michael. 1990. "From the Truman Doctrine to the Second Superpower Detente: The Rise and Fall of the Cold War." *Journal of Peace Research*, 27:1 (February), 25–41.

Cristi, Marcela. 2001. *From Civil to Political Religion: The Intersection of Culture, Religion and Politics*. Waterloo, Ontario: Wilfrid Laurier University Press.

Cull, Nicholas John. 1997. *Selling War: The British Propaganda Campaign Against American "Neutrality" in World War II*. New York: Oxford University Press.

Cumings, Bruce. 1990. *The Origins of the Korean War, Vol. II: The Roaring of the Cataract, 1947–1950*. Princeton: Princeton University Press.

Daniels, Roger. 2002. *Coming to America: A History of Immigration and Ethnicity in American Life*. 2nd ed. New York: Harper Perennial.

DeBenedetti, Charles. 1984. *The Peace Reform in American History*. Bloomington: University of Indiana Press.

Debrix, François, and Mark J. Lacy, eds. 2009. *The Geopolitics of American Insecurity: Terror, Power and Foreign Policy*. Abingdon, U.K.: Routledge.

Denson, John V., ed. 1999. *The Costs of War: America's Pyrrhic Victories*. New Brunswick and London: Transaction Publishers.

De Tocqueville, Alexis. 1863. *Democracy in America*. Trans. Henry Reeve. Ed. Francis Bowen. Cambridge: Sever and Francis.

Devlin, Patrick. 1975. *Too Proud to Fight: Woodrow Wilson's Neutrality*. New York: Oxford University Press.

Diamond, Louise, and John McDonald. 1996. *Multi-Track Diplomacy: A Systems Approach to Peace*. West Hartford, Conn.: Kumarian Press.

Dobbs, Michael. 2009. *One Minute to Midnight: Kennedy, Khrushchev, and Castro on the Brink of Nuclear War*. New York: Vintage.

Dower, John W. 1987. *War Without Mercy: Race and Power in the Pacific War*. New York: Pantheon.

Doyle, Michael W. 1986. *Empires*. Ithaca: Cornell University Press.

Dumas, Lloyd J. 1995. *The Socio-Economics of Conversion from War to Peace*. Armonk, N.Y.: M. E. Sharpe.

Dunn, Michael. 2006. "The 'Clash of Civilizations' and the 'War on Terror.'" *49th Parallel* 20 (Winter 2006–7). www.49thparallel.bham.ac.uk/back/issue20/Dunn.pdf (consulted January 23, 2010).

Edmonds, Anthony O. 1998. *The War in Vietnam*. Westport, Conn.: Greenwood Press.

Edwords, Frederick. 1987. "The Religious Character of American Patriotism." *Humanist* (November–December), revised at http://www.holysmoke.org/sdhok/hum12.htm (consulted March 29, 2009).

Eichenberg, Richard C. 2005. "Victory Has Many Friends: U.S. Public Opinion and the Use of Force, 1981–2005." *International Security* 30:1 (Summer), 140–77.

Ellsberg, Daniel. 2002. *Secrets: A Memoir of Vietnam and the Pentagon Papers*. New York and London: Penguin.

Elshtain, Jean Bethke. 2003. *Just War Against Terror: The Burden of American Power in a Violent World*. New York: Basic Books.

Engelhardt, Tom. 2007. *The End of Victory Culture: Cold War America and the Disillusioning of a Generation.* Rev. ed. Amherst: University of Massachusetts Press.

Erikson, Erik H. 1994. *Identity: Youth and Crisis.* New York: Norton.

Evans, Harold. 2000. *The American Century.* New York: Knopf.

Faust, Drew Gilpin. 1990. *The Creation of Confederate Nationalism: Ideology and Identity in the Civil War South.* Baton Rouge: Louisiana State University Press.

———. 2008. *The Republic of Suffering: Death and the American Civil War.* New York: Knopf.

Feiler, Bruce. 2009. *America's Prophet: Moses and the American Story.* New York: William Morrow.

Ferguson, Niall. 2000. *The Pity of War: Explaining World War I.* New York: Basic Books.

———. 2004. *Empire: The Rise and Demise of the British World Order and the Lessons for Global Power.* New York: Basic Books.

———. 2005. *Colossus: The Rise and Fall of the American Empire.* London and New York: Penguin.

Fiala, Andrew. 2008. *The Just War Myth: The Moral Illusions of War.* Lanham, Md.: Rowman & Littlefield.

Fiebig–von Hase, Ragnhild and Ursula Lehmkuhl, eds. 1997. *Enemy Images in American History.* Oxford and New York: Berghahn Books.

Filkins, Dexter. 2009. *The Forever War.* New York: Vintage.

Fisher, Ronald J. 2005. *Paving the Way: Contributions of Interactive Conflict Resolution to Peacemaking.* Lanham, Md.: Lexington Books.

Foley, Michael S., and Brendan P. O'Malley, eds. 2008. *Home Fronts: A Wartime America Reader.* New York and London: New Press.

Foner, Eric. 1995. *Free Soil, Free Labor, Free Men: The Ideology of the Republican Party Before the Civil War.* New York: Oxford University Press.

Freeberg, Ernest. 2008. *Democracy's Prisoner: Eugene V. Debs, the Great War, and the Right to Dissent.* Cambridge: Harvard University Press.

Friedel, Frank. 2002. *The Splendid Little War.* Springfield, N.J.: Burford Books.

Fromkin, David. 2005. *Europe's Last Summer: Who Started the Great War in 1914?* New York: Vintage.

Fukuyama, Francis. 2007. *America at the Crossroads: Democracy, Power, and the Neoconservative Legacy.* New Haven: Yale University Press.

Fussell, Paul. 2000. *The Great War and Modern Memory.* New York: Oxford University Press.

Fyne, Robert. 1994. *The Hollywood Propaganda of World War II.* Metuchen, N.J., and London: Scarecrow Press.

Gaddis, John Lewis. 2000. *The United States and the Origins of the Cold War.* New York: Columbia University Press.

———. 2004. *Surprise, Security, and the American Experience.* Cambridge and London: Harvard University Press.

Galtung, Johan. 1987. *U.S. Foreign Policy: As Manifest Theology.* La Jolla: University of California at San Diego, Institute on Global Conflict and Cooperation.

———. 2004. *Transcend and Transform: An Introduction to Conflict Work.* Boulder, Colo.: Paradigm Press.

———. 2009. *The Fall of the US Empire—And Then What?* Oslo: TRANSCEND University Press (Kolofon Forlag).

Gamble, Richard M. 2003. *The War for Righteousness: Progressive Christianity, the Great War, and the Rise of the Messianic Nation.* Wilmington, Del.: ISI Books.

Gardner, Lloyd C., and Ted Gittinger, eds. 2004. *The Search for Peace in Vietnam, 1964–1968.* College Station, Tex.: Tamu Press.

Garfinkle, Adam. 1997. *Telltale Hearts: The Origins and Impact of the Vietnam Antiwar Movement.* New York: Palgrave Macmillan.

Gelpi, Christopher, Peder D. Feaver, and Jason Reifler. 2005. "Success Matters: Casualty Sensitivity and the War in Iraq." *International Security* 30:3 (Winter 2005–6), 7–46.

George, Larry N. 2009. "American Insecurities and the Ontopolitics of US Pharmacotic Wars." In Debrix and Lacy (2009).

Geromylatos, Andre. 2004. *Red Acropolis, Black Terror: The Greek Civil War and the Origins of Soviet-American Rivalry, 1943–1949.* New York: Basic Books.

Gibson, Campbell J., and Emily Lennon. 1999. "Historical Census Statistics on the Foreign-born Population of the United States: 1850–1990." Population Division Working Paper No. 29. Washington, D.C.: U.S. Bureau of the Census. http://www.census.gov/population/www/documentation/twps0029/twps0029.html (consulted January 22, 2009).

Gitlin, Todd. 1993. *The Sixties: Years of Hope, Days of Rage.* New York: Bantam Books.

Glaude, Eddie S., Jr. 2000. *Exodus! Religion, Race, and Nation in Early Nineteenth-Century Black America.* Chicago: University of Chicago Press.

Goodwin, Doris Kearns. 1995. *No Ordinary Time. Franklin and Eleanor Roosevelt: The Home Front in World War II.* New York: Simon & Schuster.

Graham, Billy. 1999. *Just as I Am: The Autobiography of Billy Graham.* New York: HarperOne.

Greenstein, Fred I. 1996. "Ronald Reagan, Mikhail Gorbachev, and the End of the Cold War." In W. C. Wohlforth, ed., *Witnesses to the End of the Cold War.* Baltimore: Johns Hopkins University Press.

Grieder, William. 1999. *Fortress America: The American Military and the Consequences of Peace.* New York: PublicAffairs.

Gupta, Karunakar. 1972. "How Did the Korean War Begin?" *China Quarterly* 52 (October–December), 699–716. http://www.jstor.org/stable/652290 (consulted December 19, 2009).

Gurr, Ted Robert. 1996. *Minorities at Risk: A Global View of Ethnopolitical Conflict.* Washington, D.C.: United States Institute of Peace.

Haass, Richard N. 2009. *War of Necessity, War of Choice: A Memoir of Two Iraq Wars.* New York: Simon & Schuster.

Hackett, R. A., and Y. Zhao. 1994. "Challenging a Master Narrative: Peace Protest and Opinion/Editorial Discourse in the US Press During the Gulf War." *Discourse & Society* 5:4, 509–41.

Halberstam, David. 1972. *The Best and the Brightest.* New York: Random House.

———. 2007. *The Coldest Winter: America and the Korean War.* New York: Hyperion.

Hale, Edward Everett. 1917 (1863). *The Man Without a Country,* Harvard Classics Shelf of Fiction. http://www.bartleby.com/310/6/1.html (consulted January 19, 2009).

Hansen, Jonathan M. 2003. *The Lost Promise of Patriotism: Debating American Identity, 1890–1920.* Chicago: University of Chicago Press.

Hardt, Michael, and Antonio Negri. 2001. *Empire.* Cambridge: Harvard University Press.

Harle, Vilho. 2000. *The Enemy With a Thousand Faces: The Tradition of the Other in Western Political Thought and History*. New York: Praeger.

Harvey, David. 2003. *The New Imperialism*. Oxford: Oxford University Press.

Hedges, Chris. 2003. *War Is a Force That Gives Us Meaning*. New York: Anchor Books.

Heidler, David S. 1993. "The Politics of National Aggression: Congress and the First Seminole War." *Journal of the Early Republic* 13:4 (Winter), 501–30.

Herrmann, Richard K., P. E. Tetlock, and P. S. Visser. 1999. "Mass Public Decisions to Go to War: A Cognitive-Interactionist Framework." *American Political Science Review* 93:3 (September), 553–73.

Herrmann, Richard K., and Vaughn P. Shannon. 2001. "Defending International Norms: The Role of Obligation, Material Interest, and Perception in Decision Making." *International Organization* 55:3 (Summer), 621–54.

Hickey, Donald R. 2006. *Don't Give Up the Ship! Myths of the War of 1812*. Urbana: University of Illinois Press.

Higham, John. 2002. *Strangers in the Land: Patterns of American Nativism, 1860–1925*. New Brunswick: Rutgers University Press.

Hitchcock, Peter. 2008. "The Failed State and the State of Failure." *Mediations* 23:2. http://www.mediationsjournal.org/articles/the-failed-state-and-the-state-of-failure (consulted May 22, 2009).

Hixson, Walter L. 2008. *The Myth of American Diplomacy: National Identity and U.S. Foreign Policy*. New Haven and London: Yale University Press.

Hoey, John B. 2000. "Federalist Opposition to the War of 1812." *Early American Review* (Winter). http://www.earlyamerica.com/review/winter2000/federalist.htm (consulted November 10, 2009).

Hofstadter, Richard. 1989. *The American Political Tradition: And the Men Who Made It*. New York: Vintage.

Horowitz, David. 1969. *Containment and Revolution*. Boston: Beacon Press.

Howe, Daniel Walker. 2007. *What Hath God Wrought: The Transformation of America, 1815–1848*. New York: Oxford University Press.

Howlett, Charles F. 1991. *The American Peace Movement: References and Resources*. New York: G. K. Hall.

Howlett, Charles F., and Robbie Lieberman. 2008. *A History of the American Peace Movement from Colonial Times to the Present.* New York: Edwin Mellen Press.

Hughes, Richard T. 2003. *Myths America Lives By.* Urbana and Chicago: University of Illinois Press.

Hunt, Andrew E. 2006. *David Dellinger: The Life and Times of a Nonviolent Revolutionary.* New York: NYU Press.

Hunt, Michael H. 1987. *Ideology and U.S. Foreign Policy.* New Haven and London: Yale University Press.

Hunter, James Davison. 1992. *Culture Wars: The Struggle to Define America.* New York: Basic Books.

Huntington, Samuel P. 1970. "A Frustrating Task" (with reply by Noam Chomsky). *New York Review of Books* 14:4 (February 26). http://www.nybooks.com/articles/11044 (consulted January 22, 2009).

———. 1998. *The Clash of Civilizations and the Remaking of World Order.* New York: Simon & Schuster.

———. 2005. *Who Are We? The Challenges to America's National Identity.* New York: Simon & Schuster.

Ivie, Robert L. 1998. "Dwight D. Eisenhower's 'Chance for Peace': Quest or Crusade?" *Rhetoric and Public Affairs* 1, 227–43.

———. 2005. "Savagery in Democracy's Empire." *Third World Quarterly* 26:1, 55–65.

———. 2006. *Democracy and America's War on Terror.* Tuscaloosa: University of Alabama Press.

Jarecki, Eugene. 2008. *The American Way of War: Guided Missiles, Misguided Men, and a Republic in Peril.* New York: Free Press.

Jennings, Francis. 1976. *The Invasion of America: Indians, Colonialism, and the Cant of Conquest.* New York and London: Norton.

Jentleson, Bruce W. 1992. "The Pretty Prudent Public: Post Post-Vietnam American Opinion on the Use of Force. *International Studies Quarterly* 36:1 (March), 49–73.

Jentleson, Bruce W., and Rebecca L. Britton. 1998. "Still Pretty Prudent: Post–Cold War American Public Opinion on the Use of Military Force." *Journal of Conflict Resolution* 42:4 (August), 395–417.

Jeong, Ho-Won. 2008. *Understanding Conflict and Conflict Analysis.* Newbury Park, Calif.: Sage Publications.

Johnson, Chalmers. 2004a. *Blowback, Second Edition: The Costs and Consequences of American Empire*. New York: Holt Paperbacks.

———. 2004b. *The Sorrows of Empire: Militarism, Secrecy, and the End of the Republic*. New York: Holt Paperbacks.

———. 2008. *Nemesis: The Last Days of the American Republic*. New York: Holt Paperbacks.

Kagan, Robert. 2003. *Of Paradise and Power: America and Europe in the New World Order*. New York: Knopf.

———. 2006. *Dangerous Nation*. New York: Vintage.

Kagan, Robert, and William Kristol. 2000. *Present Dangers: Crisis and Opportunity in American Foreign and Defense Policy*. New York: Encounter Books.

Kaplan, Amy. 2002. *The Anarchy of Empire in the Making of U.S. Culture*. Cambridge and London: Harvard University Press.

———. 2003. "Homeland Insecurities: Some Reflections on Language and Space." *Radical History Review* 85 (Winter), 82–93.

Kaplan, Amy, and Donald E. Pease, eds. 1993. *Cultures of United States Imperialism*. Durham and London: Duke University Press.

Kaplan, Robert D. 2006. *Imperial Grunts: On the Ground with the American Military, from Mongolia to the Philippines to Iraq and Beyond*. New York: Vintage.

Karnow, Stanley. 1997. *Vietnam: A History*. 2nd ed. New York: Penguin.

Karp, Walter. 2003. *The Politics of War: The Story of Two Wars Which Altered Forever the Political Life of the American Republic, 1890–1920*. Philadelphia: Moyer Bell.

Kellner, Douglas. 1992. *The Persian Gulf TV War*. Boulder, Colo.: Westview Press.

Keniston, Kenneth. 1967. *The Uncommitted: Alienated Youth in American Society*. New York: Dell.

———. 1968. *Young Radicals: Notes on Committed Youth*. New York: Harcourt Brace Jovanovich.

Kinzer, Stephen. 2007. *Overthrow: America's Century of Regime Change from Hawaii to Iraq*. New York: Times Books.

Kohn, Richard H. 2009. "The Danger of Militarization in an Endless 'War' on Terrorism." *Journal of Military History* 73:1 (January), 177–208.

Kolko, Joyce, and Gabriel Kolko. 1972. *The Limits of Power: The World and United States Foreign Policy, 1945–1954*. New York: Harper & Row.

Koppes, Clayton R., and Gregory D. Black. 1990. *Hollywood Goes to War: How Politics, Profits and Propaganda Shaped World War II Movies*. Berkeley: University of California Press.

Koscielski, Frank. 1999. *Divided Loyalties: American Unions and the Vietnam War*. London: Routledge.

Kriesberg, Louis. 2006. *Constructive Conflicts: From Escalation to Resolution*. Lanham, Md.: Rowman & Littlefield.

LaFeber, Walter. 2006. *America, Russia, and the Cold War, 1945–2006*. Columbus, Ohio: McGraw-Hill.

Lansing, Robert, and Louis F. Post. 1917. *A War of Self-Defense*. Committee on Public Information, War Information Series No. 5. Washington, D.C.: U.S. Government Printing Office.

Larson, Eric V., and Bogdan Savych. 2003. *Misfortunes of War: Press and Public Reactions to Civilian Deaths in Wartime*. RAND Corporation. www.rand.org/pubs/monographs/2006/RAND_MG441.sum.pdf (consulted December 21, 2009).

Lebow, Richard Ned, and Janice Gross Stein. 1995. *We All Lost the Cold War*. Princeton: Princeton University Press.

Lederach, John Paul. 1998. *Building Peace: Sustainable Reconciliation in Divided Societies*. Washington, D.C.: United States Institute of Peace.

Lenin, V. I. 1973. *Imperialism: The Highest Stage of Capitalism*. New York: Foreign Language Press.

Liberman, Peter. 2006. "An Eye for an Eye: Public Support for War Against Evildoers." *International Organization* 60:3 (Summer), 687–722.

Lincoln, Bruce. 1989. *Discourse and the Construction of Society: Comparative Studies of Myth, Ritual, and Classification*. New York and Oxford: Oxford University Press.

———. 1999. *Theorizing Myth: Narrative, Ideology, and Scholarship*. Chicago and London: University of Chicago Press.

Linn, Brian McAllister. 2002. *The Philippine War, 1899–1902*. Lawrence: University Press of Kansas.

Lipstadt, Deborah E. 1993. *Beyond Belief: The American Press and the Coming of the Holocaust, 1933–1945*. New York: Free Press.

Lunch, William L., and Peter W. Sperlich. 1979. "American Public Opinion and the War in Vietnam." *Western Political Quarterly* 32:1, 21–44.

Lyons, Terrence, and Gilbert M. Khadiagala. 2008. *Conflict Management and African Politics: Ripeness, Bargaining, and Mediation.* London: Routledge.

MacArthur, John R. 1992. *Second Front: Censorship and Propaganda in the Gulf War.* Berkeley: University of California Press.

Marvin, Carolyn, and David W. Ingle. 1996. "Blood Sacrifice and the Nation: Revisiting Civil Religion." *Journal of the American Academy of Religion* 64:4 (Winter), 767–80. http://www.jstor.org/stable/1465621 (consulted January 14, 2009).

Matlock, Jack F., Jr. 2005. *Reagan and Gorbachev: How the Cold War Ended.* New York: Random House.

Matthews, Shailer. 1917. "Why This Nation Is at War, in Plain Words." *New York Times,* July 1. http://query.nytimes.com/mem/archive-free/pdf?_r=1&res=9F03E2DE133BE03ABC4953DFB166838C609EDE (consulted March 18, 2009).

May, Ernest R., and Philip D. Zelikow, eds. 2002. *The Kennedy Tapes: Inside the White House During the Cuban Missile Crisis.* New York: Norton.

May, Rollo. 1998. *Power and Innocence: A Search for the Sources of Violence.* New York: Norton.

McAlister, Alfred L. 2000. "Moral Disengagement and Opinions on War with Iraq." *International Journal of Public Opinion Research* 12:2, 191–98.

———. 2001. "Moral Disengagement: Measurement and Modification." *Journal of Peace Research* 38:1, 87–99. http://jpr.sagepub.com/cgi/reprint/38/1/87.

McKenna, George. 2007. *The Puritan Origins of American Patriotism.* New Haven: Yale University Press.

McPherson, James M. 1998. *For Cause and Comrades: Why Men Fought in the Civil War.* New York and London: Oxford University Press.

———. 2003. *Battle Cry of Freedom: The Civil War Era.* New York and London: Oxford University Press.

Melman, Seymour. 1970. *Pentagon Capitalism: The Political Economy of War.* New York: McGraw-Hill.

Melville, Herman. 1924 (1886). *Billy Budd.* Charlottesville: University of

Virginia Electronic Library. http://etext.virginia.edu/etcbin/toccer-new2?id=MelBill.sgm&images=images/modeng&data=/texts/english/modeng/parsed&tag=public&part=22&division=div1.

Miller, Perry. 1956. *Errand into the Wilderness.* Cambridge: Belknap Press of Harvard University Press.

Miller, Stuart Creighton. 1984. *Benevolent Assimilation: America's Conquest of the Philippines, 1899–1903.* New Haven: Yale University Press.

Millis, Walter. 1989. *The Martial Spirit.* Chicago: Elephant Paperbacks.

Missall, John, and Mary Lou Missall. 2004. *The Seminole Wars: America's Longest Indian Conflict.* Gainesville: University Press of Florida.

Mitchell, C. R. 1989. *The Structure of International Conflict.* New York: St. Martin's Press.

Mitchell, George J. 2001. *Making Peace.* Berkeley: University of California Press.

Moise, Edwin E. 2004. *The Tonkin Gulf and the Escalation of the Vietnam War.* Raleigh: University of North Carolina Press.

Montville, Joseph V. 1991. *Conflict and Peacemaking in Multiethnic Societies.* Lanham, Md.: Lexington Books.

Moran, Terence P., and Eugene Secunda. 2007. *Selling War to America: From the Spanish-American War to the Global War on Terror.* New York: Praeger.

Muller, Eric L. 2007. *American Inquisition: The Hunt for Japanese American Disloyalty in World War II.* Chapel Hill: University of North Carolina Press.

Murphy, Geraldine. 1989. "The Politics of Reading *Billy Budd.*" *American Literary History* 1:2 (Summer), 361–82.

Nathanson, Stephen. 2003. *Patriotism, Morality, and Peace.* Lanham, Md.: Rowman & Littlefield.

National Advisory Commission on Civil Disorders. 1968. *Report.* Introduction by Tom Wicker. New York: Bantam Books.

National Commission on the Causes and Prevention of Violence. 1970. *To Establish Justice, to Insure Domestic Tranquility (Final Report).* Introduction by James Reston. New York: Bantam Books.

National Commission on Terrorist Attacks upon the United States. 2004. *The 9/11 Report.* New York: St. Martin's Press.

Navasky, Victor S. 2003. *Naming Names.* New York: Hill & Wang.

Neal, Arthur G. 2005. *National Trauma and Collective Memory: Extra-ordinary Events in the American Experience.* 2nd ed. Armonk, N.Y., and London: M. E. Sharpe.

Nugent, Walter. 2008. *Habits of Empire: A History of American Expansion.* New York: Knopf.

Nye, Joseph S., Jr. 2005. *Soft Power: The Means to Success in World Politics.* New York: PublicAffairs.

Offner, John L. 1992. *An Unwanted War: The Diplomacy of the United States and Spain over Cuba, 1895–1898.* Chapel Hill: University of North Carolina Press.

———. 1998. "Why Did the United States Fight Spain in 1898?" *OAH Magazine of History* 12:3 (Spring), 19–23.

Omar, Kaleem. 2005. "Whatever Happened to April Glaspie?" *Third World Traveler.* http://www.thirdworldtraveler.com/Iraq/April_Glaspie.html (consulted October 29, 2009).

Packer, George. 2006. *The Assassins' Gate: America in Iraq.* New York: Farrar, Straus and Giroux.

Pape, Robert A. 1996. *Bombing to Win: Air Power and Coercion in War.* Ithaca: Cornell University Press.

Paul, Ron. 2007. *A Foreign Policy of Freedom: Peace, Commerce, and Honest Friendship.* Lake Jackson, Tex.: Foundation for Rational Economics and Education.

Pearce, Roy Harvey. 2001. *Savagism and Civilization.* Baltimore: Johns Hopkins University Press.

Pérez, Louis A., Jr. 1989. "The Meaning of the *Maine*: Causation and the Historiography of the Spanish-American War." *Pacific Historical Review* 58:3 (August), 293–322.

———. 2008. *Cuba in the American Imagination: Metaphor and the Imperial Ethos.* Chapel Hill: University of North Carolina Press.

Peterson, H. C. 1939. *Propaganda for War: The Campaign Against American Neutrality, 1914–1917.* Norman: University of Oklahoma Press.

Pfeffer, Richard M., ed. 1969. *No More Vietnams? The War and the Future of American Foreign Policy.* New York: Harper & Row.

Polk, William R. 2007. *Violent Politics: A History of Insurgency, Terrorism and Guerrilla War, from the American Revolution to Iraq.* New York: HarperCollins.

Polner, Murray. 1998. *Disarmed and Dangerous: The Radical Life and Times of Daniel and Philip Berrigan, Brothers in Religious Faith and Civil Disobedience.* Boulder, Colo.: Westview Press.

Polner, Murray, and Thomas E. Woods, eds. 2008. *We Who Dared to Say No to War: American Antiwar Writing from 1812 to Now.* New York: Basic Books.

Porter, Kenneth Wiggins. 1951. "Negroes and the Seminole War, 1817–1818." *Journal of Negro History* 36:3 (July), 249–80.

Primoratz, Igor, and Aleksandar Pavković, eds. 2008. *Patriotism: Philosophical and Political Perspectives.* Aldershot, U.K., and Burlington, Vt.: Ashgate.

Pruitt, Dean G. 2005. *Whither Ripeness Theory?* Working Paper No. 25, Institute for Conflict Analysis and Resolution, George Mason University.

———. 2007. "Negotiating with Terrorists." IACM 2007 Meetings Paper. http://ssrn.com/abstract=1031668 (consulted August 13, 2009).

Pruitt, Dean G., and Sung Hee Kim. 2004. *Social Conflict: Escalation, Stalemate, and Settlement.* 3rd ed. New York: McGraw-Hill.

Purdy, Jedediah. 2009. *A Tolerable Anarchy: Rebels, Reactionaries, and the Making of American Freedom.* New York: Knopf.

Quandt, William B. 1986. *Camp David: Peacemaking and Politics.* Washington, D.C.: Brookings Institution.

Quinn, Adam. 2008. "The 'National Interest' as Conceptual Battleground." International Studies Association Convention, San Francisco. http://www.allacademic.com//meta/p_mla_apa_research_citation/2/5/2/9/5/pages252952/p252952-1.php (consulted August 5, 2009).

Quint, Howard H. 1958. "American Socialists and the Spanish-American War." *American Quarterly* 10:2, part 1 (Summer), 131–41.

Ramsbotham, Oliver, Tom Woodhouse, and Hugh Miall. 2005. *Contemporary Conflict Resolution.* 2nd ed. Cambridge, U.K.: Polity.

Rickover, Hyman G. 1995. *How the Battleship* Maine *was Destroyed.* Washington, D.C.: Naval Institute Press.

Risen, James. 2006. *State of War: The Secret History of the CIA and the Bush Administration.* New York: Free Press.

Robinson, Greg. 2009. *A Tragedy of Democracy: Japanese Confinement in North America.* New York: Columbia University Press.

Robinson, Paul, ed. 2003. *Just War in Comparative Perspective.* Aldershot, U.K., and Burlington, Vt.: Ashgate.

Rodin, David. 2002. *War and Self-Defense*. Oxford: Oxford University Press.

Rosen, Stephen Peter. 2009. "Blood Brothers: The Dual Origins of American Bellicosity." *American Interest* 4:6 (July–August), 20–28.

Rothbart, Daniel, and Karinia V. Korostelina, eds. 2006. *Identity, Morality, and Threat: Studies in Violent Conflict*. Plymouth, U.K.: Lexington Books.

Rovere, Richard H. 1996. *Senator Joe McCarthy*. Berkeley: University of California Press.

Rubenstein, Richard E. 1991. "On Taking Sides: Lessons of the Persian Gulf War." Working Paper No. 5, Institute for Conflict Analysis and Resolution, George Mason University. http://icar.gmu.edu/working_papers.html (consulted May 17, 2009).

———. 2006. *Thus Saith the Lord: The Revolutionary Moral Vision of Isaiah and Jeremiah*. New York: Harcourt Books.

Rubenstein, Richard E., and Jarle P. Crocker. 1994. "Challenging Huntington." *Foreign Policy* 96 (Autumn), 113–28.

Salinger, Pierre, and Eric Laurent. 1991. *Secret Dossier*. Harmondsworth, U.K.: Penguin.

Sandole, Dennis J. D. 2005. "The Islamic-Western 'Clash of Civilizations': The Inadvertent Contribution of the Bush Presidency." Paper presented at the annual meeting of the International Studies Association, Hilton Hawaiian Village, Honolulu, March 5. http://www.allacademic.com/meta/p71755_index.html (consulted January 23, 2009).

Sandole, Dennis J. D., Sean Byrne, Ingrid Sandole-Staroste, and Jessica Senehi, eds. 2009. *Handbook of Conflict Analysis and Resolution*. London: Routledge.

Saunders, Harold H. 2001. *A Public Peace Process: Sustained Dialogue to Transform Racial and Ethnic Conflicts*. London and New York: Palgrave Macmillan.

Schmidt, Donald E. 2005. *The Folly of War: American Foreign Policy, 1898–2005*. New York: Algora.

Schrecker, Ellen. 1998. *Many Are the Crimes: McCarthyism in America*. Boston: Little, Brown.

Schuman, Howard, and Cheryl Rieger. 1992. "Historical Analogies, Generational Effects, and Attitudes Toward War." *American Sociological Review* 57:3 (June), 315–26.

Schwalbe, Carol B., B. W. Silcock, and S. Keith. 2008. "Visual Framing of the Early Weeks of the U.S.-Led Invasion of Iraq: Applying the Master War Narrative to Electronic and Print Images." *Journal of Broadcasting & Electronic Media* (September). http://www.entrepreneur.com/tradejournals/article/185385932_1.html.

Scott, Walter. 1805. *The Lay of the Last Minstrel: A Poem in Six Cantos.* http://theotherpages.org/poems/minstrel.html.

Shapiro, Michael J. 1997. *Violent Cartographies: Mapping Cultures of War.* Minneapolis and London: University of Minnesota Press.

Slotkin, Richard. 1998a. *Gunfighter Nation: The Myth of the Frontier in Twentieth-Century America.* Norman: University of Oklahoma Press.

———. 1998b. *The Fatal Environment: The Myth of the Frontier in the Age of Industrialization, 1800–1890.* Norman: University of Oklahoma Press.

———. 2000. *Regeneration Through Violence: The Mythology of the American Frontier, 1600–1860.* Norman: University of Oklahoma Press.

Smith, Sharon. 2006. *Subterranean Fire: A History of Working-Class Radicalism in the United States.* Chicago: Haymarket Books.

Sorabji, Richard, and David Rodin, eds. 2006. *The Ethics of War: Shared Problems in Different Traditions.* Aldershot, U.K., and Burlington, Vt.: Ashgate.

Sternberg, Richard R. 1936. "Jackson's 'Rhea Letter' Hoax." *Journal of Southern History* 2:4 (November), 480–96.

Steuter, Erin, and Deborah Wills. 2008. *At War with Metaphor: Media, Propaganda, and Racism in the War on Terror.* Lanham, Md.: Rowman & Littlefield.

Stevenson, Charles A. 2007. *Congress at War: The Politics of Conflict Since 1789.* Washington, D.C.: National Defense University Press.

Stone, Geoffrey R. 2004. *Perilous Times: Free Speech in Wartime from the Sedition Act of 1798 to the War on Terrorism.* New York: Norton.

Stueck, William. 2004. *Rethinking the Korean War: A New Diplomatic and Strategic History.* Princeton: Princeton University Press.

Suchman, Edward A., R. K. Goldsen, and R. M. Williams Jr. 1953. "Attitudes Toward the Korean War." *Public Opinion Quarterly* 17:2 (Summer), 171–84.

Taylor, A. J. P. 1996. *The Origins of the Second World War.* New York: Simon & Schuster.

Taylor, William R. 1993. *Cavalier and Yankee: The Old South and American National Character.* London and New York: Oxford University Press.

Thoreau, Henry David. 1993 (1850). *The Higher Law: Thoreau on Civil Disobedience and Reform.* Ed. Wendell Glick. Princeton: Princeton University Press.

Trask, David F. 1996. *The War with Spain in 1898.* Omaha: University of Nebraska Press.

Tuchman, Barbara W. 1985. *The Zimmermann Telegram.* New York: Ballantine Books.

———. 2004. *The Guns of August.* New York: Presidio Press.

Twain, Mark. 1901. "To the Person Sitting in Darkness." https://eee.uci.edu/ . . . /Hart%20Reader_pp109_117b_ToPersonSitting.pdf (consulted October 22, 2009).

———. 1963. *The Complete Essays of Mark Twain.* Ed. Charles Neider. Garden City, N.Y.: Doubleday.

Valentine, Douglas. 2000. *The Phoenix Program.* New York: iUniverse.

Virilio, Paul. 1989. *War and Cinema: The Logistics of Perception.* Trans. Patrick Camiller. London and New York: Verso.

Volkan, Vamik. 1998. *Bloodlines: From Ethnic Pride to Ethnic Terrorism.* New York: Basic Books.

———. 2004. *Blind Trust: Large Groups and Their Leaders in Times of Crisis and Terror.* Charlottesville, Va.: Pitchstone Press.

von Clausewitz, Carl. 2008 (1832). *On War.* New York: Wilder.

Wallace, Max. 2004. *The American Axis: Henry Ford, Charles Lindbergh, and the Rise of the Third Reich.* New York: St. Martin's Griffin.

Wallis, Jim. 2006. *God's Politics: Why The Right Gets It Wrong and the Left Doesn't Get It.* San Francisco: HarperSanFrancisco.

Walzer, Michael. 2006a. *Just and Unjust Wars: A Moral Argument with Historical Illustrations.* 4th ed. New York: Basic Books.

———. 2006b. *Arguing About War.* New Haven: Yale University Press.

Weber, Jennifer L. 2008. *Copperheads: The Rise and Fall of Lincoln's Opponents in the North.* New York: Oxford University Press.

Weeks, William Earl. 1992. *John Quincy Adams and American Global Empire.* Lexington: University Press of Kentucky.

Weinberg, Albert K. 1958. *Manifest Destiny: A Study of Nationalist Expansionism in American History.* Gloucester, Mass.: Peter Smith.

Weinstein, Allen, and Alexander Vassiliev. 2000. *The Haunted Wood: Soviet Espionage in America—The Stalin Era*. New York: Modern Library.

Weiss, Peter. 2002. "Terrorism, Counterterrorism and International Law." *Transnational Institute Newsletter*, March 29. http://www.tni.org/detail_page.phtml?page=archives_weiss_terrorism (consulted June 17, 2009).

Welch, David A. 1995. *Justice and the Genesis of War*. New York and Cambridge: Cambridge University Press.

Wells, Robert A. 2005. "Mobilizing Support for War : An Analysis of Public and Private Sources of American Propaganda During World War II." Paper presented at the Annual Meeting of the International Studies Association, Honolulu, March 5. http://www.allacademic.com/meta/p69897_index.html (consulted July 6, 2009).

Western, Jon. 2005. *Selling Intervention and War: The Presidency, the Media, and the American Public*. Baltimore: Johns Hopkins University Press.

Wheelan, Joseph. 2007. *Invading Mexico: America's Continental Dream and the Mexican War, 1846–1848*. New York: PublicAffairs.

Whitaker, Brian. 2001. "Saddam: Serpent in the Garden of Eden." *Guardian*, January 12. http://www.guardian.co.uk/world/2001/jan/12/iraq.worlddispatch (consulted December 13, 2009).

Williams, William Appleman. 1972. *The Tragedy of American Diplomacy*. 2nd rev. ed. New York: Dell.

———. 1988. *The Contours of American History*. New York and London: Norton.

———. 2006. *Empire as a Way of Life: An Essay on the Causes and Character of America's Present Predicament Along with a Few Thoughts About an Alternative*. New York: Ig.

Wilz, John Edward. 1995. "The Making of Mr. Bush's War: A Failure to Learn from History?" *Presidential Studies Quarterly* 25:3 (Summer), 533–54.

Winch, Samuel. 2004. "Constructing an 'Evil Genius': Through the News Frame, Osama bin Laden Looks like Dr. Fu-Manchu." Paper presented at the annual meeting of the International Communication Association, New Orleans Sheraton, New Orleans. http://www.allacademic.com//meta/p_mla_apa_research_citation/1/1/2/8/1/pages112814/p112814-1.php (consulted August 15, 2009).

Woodward, Bob. 1987. *Veil: The Secret Wars of the CIA, 1981–1987.* New York: Simon & Schuster.

———. 2004. *Plan of Attack: The Definitive Account of the Decision to Invade Iraq.* New York: Simon & Schuster.

Wynn, Neil A. 1996. "The 'Good War': The Second World War and Postwar American Society." *Journal of Contemporary History* 31:3 (1996), 463–82.

Xia, Yafeng. 2006. *Negotiating with the Enemy: U.S.-China Talks During the Cold War, 1949–1972.* Bloomington: University of Indiana Press.

Yergin, Daniel. 1978. *Shattered Peace: The Origins of the Cold War and the National Security State.* New York: Houghton Mifflin.

Young, Marilyn B., J. J. Fitzgerald, and A. T. Grunfeld. 2003. *The Vietnam War: A History in Documents.* New York: Oxford University Press.

Zangwill, Israel. 2009 (1908). *The Melting-Pot: A Play in Four Acts.* New York: BiblioLife.

Zartman, I. William. 2008. *Negotiation and Conflict Management: Essays on Theory and Practice.* London: Routledge.

———, ed. 2005. *Negotiating with Terrorists.* Amsterdam: Martinus Nijhoff.

Zinn, Howard. 1973. *Postwar America, 1945–1971.* Indianapolis and New York: Bobbs-Merrill.

———. 2003. *A People's History of the United States, 1492–Present.* New York: HarperCollins.

NOTES

PREFACE

1. See "War in the Gulf: What Are the Alternatives?" C-SPAN Library, August 30, 1990. http://www.c-spanvideo.org/program/17513-1 (consulted May 13, 2009).

CHAPTER 1: WHY WE CHOOSE WAR

1. Alexis de Tocqueville (1865), 327–28.
2. For major U.S. wars and casualties, see Hannah Fischer et al., *American War and Military Operations Casualties: Lists and Statistics,* CRS Report to Congress, May 14, 2008, http://www.fas.org/sgp/crs/nat sec/RL32492.pdf (consulted June 8, 2009). For a complete list of U.S. military operations including Native American wars and foreign military interventions, see "Timeline of United States Military Operations," http://en.wikipedia.org/wiki/List_of_United_States_military _history_events (consulted April 1, 2009). On minor interventions, see Stephen Kinzer (2007). See also Johan Galtung (2009), 34–37, and sources cited therein.
3. Daniel Walker Howe (2007), 762.
4. For a sample of recent liberal/left writing on the American empire and policymakers' motives for war, see Chalmers Johnson (2004a, 2004b), Fred Anderson and Andrew Cayton (2005), Carl Boggs (2005), Stephen Kinzer (2007), Eugene Jarecki (2008), and François

Debrix and Mark J. Lacy (2009). For conservative/right approaches to the same subject, see Patrick J. Buchanan (1999), Jean Belke Elshtain (2003), John Lewis Gaddis (2004), Niall Ferguson (2005), and Robert Kagan (2003, 2006).

5. Empirical studies focusing on popular consent to war include Bruce W. Jentleson (1992), Gregory G. Brunk et al. (1996), Bruce W. Jentleson and Rebecca L. Britton (1998), Richard K. Herrmann et al. (1999), Michael J. Butler (2003), Christopher Gelpi et al. (2005), Peter Liberman (2006), and Adam J. Berinsky (2009).

6. See the discussion in chapter 4.

7. Herman Melville (1924), chapter 22. For commentary, see Geraldine Murphy (1989). See also Rollo May (1998).

8. Terence P. Moran and Eugene Secunda (2007), 1. For other examples of analysis emphasizing the power of propaganda, especially when exploitative of existing American insecurities, see David Campbell (1992), Robert Fyne (1994), R. A. Hackett and Y. Zhao (1994), Andrew Bacevich (2005), Jon Western (2005), Erin Steuter and Deborah Wills (2008), Walter L. Hixson (2008), and Susan A. Brewer (2009).

9. Daniel Walker Howe (2007), 762.

10. "Lincoln introduced eight 'spot resolutions' calling on Polk to answer whether 'the *spot* on which the blood of [American] citizens was shed as in his messages declared was not within the territory of Spain [and then] . . . Mexico,' and related questions." Walter Nugent (2008), 208. The disputed territory between the Nueces and Rio Grande rivers was not part of the Mexican province of Tejas (Texas), and therefore would not have been recognized as part of Texas under international law. The Americans argued that Mexico had recognized the new boundary in the treaty that ended Texas's war for independence, but that treaty was signed by Santa Anna under duress when he was a prisoner of the Texans. See ibid., 194–97.

11. Fred Anderson and Andrew Cayton (2005), 283.

12. Louis A. Pérez Jr. (1989), 294.

13. See John L. Offner (1992), 138: "The Spanish were dumbfounded that the American investigators believed a mine had caused the disaster, and the government realized the grave implications."

14. For the Rickover report, see Hyman G. Rickover (1995), 104 et seq.

The phrase "splendid little war" was that of U.S. Ambassador to Britain John Hay.

15. See H. C. Peterson (1939), 51–70; Ralph Raico, "World War I: The Turning Point," in John V. Denson (1999), 220–24; and Donald E. Schmidt (2005), 87–88. The report of Viscount James Bryce, alleging that the Germans had committed war crimes in Belgium, omitted the most lurid allegations and documented some genuine mistreatment of civilians by the Germans. See Bryce (1915). Controversy about the accuracy of the report continues, in part because the testimony collected by the Bryce Committee mixed eyewitness reports with hearsay, did not require corroboration, and did not provide for cross-examination.

16. See Richard Hofstadter (1989) and Donald E. Schmidt (2005), 77–78.

17. The rhetorical question attributed to Bryan is "Why be shocked by the drowning of a few people, if there is to be no objection to starving a nation?" See Patrick J. Buchanan (1999), 200.

18. Doris Kearns Goodwin (1995), 371.

19. Nicholas John Cull (1997), 170. See also John F. Bratzel and Leslie B. Rout Jr., "FDR and The 'Secret Map,'" *Wilson Quarterly* (Washington, D.C.), New Year's 1985, 167–73; and Francis MacDonnell (1995), 97.

20. Thomas A. Bailey (1948), 13, quoted in Ralph Raico, "Rethinking Churchill," in John V. Denson (1999), 339.

21. Donald E. Schmidt (2005), 263–68, 263 quoted.

22. Ibid., 264.

23. Anthony O. Edmonds (1998), 42.

24. Marilyn B. Young et al. (2003), 77–78.

25. On misstatements used to justify U.S. interventions in Panama, Grenada, and other nations, see Stephen Kinzer (2007), 223–38, passim. On Iraq, the most comprehensive and telling accounts may be those of George Packer (2006) and Bob Woodward (2004).

26. See, e.g., the Pew Research Center survey documenting "the decline in the belief in solid evidence of global warming" (October 22, 2009), http://people-press.org/report/556/global-warming (consulted February 25, 2010).

27. See, e.g., Adam J. Berinsky (2001) and Michael J. Butler (2003).

28. This perspective has been embraced by scholars on the right and left

alike. For "frontier killer" approaches with a conservative slant, see Max Boot (2002), Robert Kagan (2003, 2006), John Lewis Gaddis (2004), and Stephen Peter Rosen (2009). For approaches with a leftist or liberal slant, see Michael J. Shapiro, (1997), Richard Slotkin (1998a, 1998b, 2000), Tom Engelhardt (2007), and John Brown (2006).

29. Robert D. Kaplan (2006), 4.

30. See John Brown (2006). See also Tom Engelhardt (2007), 16–53, for a brilliant description and application of the Settlers vs. Indians scenario.

31. See Bruce Lincoln (1989, 1999).

32. See Michael H. Hunt's (1987) discussion of race as a factor in American foreign policy ideology at 46–91. This is not an exclusively American association; English settlers portrayed the Irish in similar ways, as the Spanish and French did the natives of their colonial territories.

33. See esp. John W. Dower (1987).

34. See Benedict Anderson (2006).

35. Stephen Peter Rosen (2009), 21. *Born Fighting* is the title of James Webb's 2005 book about the Scots-Irish.

36. For pacifist narratives, see Joseph R. Conlin (1968), Murray Polner (1998), and Andrew E. Hunt (2006). For examples of left-wing perspectives, see Todd Gitlin (1993) and Ernest Freeberg (2008). For examples of right-wing/libertarian narratives, see Patrick J. Buchanan (1999) and Ron Paul (2007).

37. For studies of the "new American militarism," see Michael J. Shapiro (1997), Andrew Bacevich (2005), and Eugene Jarecki (2008).

38. This was the case (inter alia) during the first two years of World War I, for most of the period between the world wars, and during the period following the Korean War. See, e.g., Jon Western (2005).

39. For recent sourcebooks on U.S. peace movements, see Charles F. Howlett and Robbie Lieberman (2008) and Murray Polner and Thomas E. Woods (2008). We will discuss anti-war movements more fully in chapter 4.

40. See the empirical studies by Edward Suchman et al. (1953), Christopher Gelpi et al. (2005), and Richard C. Eichenberg (2005).

41. Peter Liberman (2006), 208.

42. Robert Andrews (1993), 471.

43. See Richard E. Rubenstein (1991).

44. For example, the evidence analyzed by Michael J. Butler (2003) suggests that authorities were more likely to authorize U.S. military intervention during the Cold War if military action seemed to vindicate certain just-war principles. See also Gregory G. Brunk et al. (1996) and Richard K. Herrmann and Vaughn P. Shannon (2001).

45. On the United States and Dienbienphu, see Jon Western (2005), 26–61. Lyndon Johnson is quoted in Susan A. Brewer (2009), 195.

46. See Robert N. Bellah (1967). See also Michael V. Angrosino (2002), 259: "Detailed sociological research has tended to confirm Bellah's insight that civil religion is a distinct cultural component within American society that is not captured either by party politics or by denominational religiosity."

47. Michael V. Angrosino (2002), 241. Angrosino believes that three types of American civil religion can be distinguished: civil religion as culture religion, civil religion as religious nationalism, and civil religion as transcendent religion (246).

48. See Robert N. Bellah (1975) and Richard T. Hughes (2003).

49. See Perry Miller (1956), Sacvan Bercovitch (1978), and George McKenna (2007).

50. See Richard M. Gamble (2003).

51. Jim Wallis (2006), 87–208. See also Richard E. Rubenstein (2006).

52. See David Halberstam (1972).

CHAPTER 2: THE TRANSFORMATION OF SELF-DEFENSE

1. This analysis was inspired, in part, by David Rodin's important study *War and Self-Defense* (2002), which insists upon the essentially metaphorical nature of concepts of national defense. For critiques of Rodin's views, see Igor Primoratz and Aleksandar Pavković (2008).

2. The association of a native "enemy within" with a foreign "enemy without" had been a familiar story to Americans since colonial times. "It was a tenet (not entirely without justification) of colonial thought that all Indian raids during and after the Revolution were of English inspiration." David Campbell (1992), 137.

3. Kenneth Wiggins Porter (1951), 253–54.

4. "The Negro Fort was a beacon light to restless slaves for miles around and to it flocked recruits from every quarter." Ibid., 261.

5. The two British subjects in question, Arbuthnot and Ambrister by name, were almost certainly not British agents. They seem to have been lone adventurers, sympathetic to the natives and hoping to make their fortunes by dealing with them. Arbuthnot had long sold the Seminoles weapons, and Ambrister warned them that Jackson and his army were on the way to attack them. A court-martial refused to sentence Ambrister to death, but Jackson insisted on the death penalty for both men, and both were executed.

6. David S. Heidler (1993), 503.

7. William Earl Weeks (1992), 3.

8. See David Campbell (1992), 126–27: "The intensity of the concern and the tenacity of the efforts to draw distinct boundaries between the English and the Indian serve as evidence, not of the natural separateness of each, but of the actual fluidity and porousness of the boundary between their identities . . . The strategy of the early settlers was thus to contain the barbarism within by the constant declaration of civility among themselves in contradistinction to the perceived primitivism without." See also William R. Taylor (1993), Michael J. Shapiro (1997), and Roy Harvey Pearce (2001).

9. Jedediah Purdy (2009), 99–111.

10. John Lewis Gaddis (2004), 17, 21–22.

11. Quoted and discussed in Robert Kagan (2006), 162 et seq.

12. According to John Lewis Gaddis (2004), 19, "By the end of his life [John Quincy Adams] had come to see that whatever continental expansion might do for national security, it could well undermine domestic tranquility by bringing new slave states into the union and thus upsetting the delicate balance that had, so far, prevented civil war."

13. See Richard M. Gamble (2003).

14. See Barbara Tuchman (2004). David Fromkin (2005) disagrees with this view, arguing that the German General Staff converted the crisis of August into a general war. Niall Ferguson (2000) lays equal responsibility on Britain. There is some tendency among historians to confuse the triggering precipitants of the war with its longer-term causes.

15. President Woodrow Wilson's Appeal for Neutrality, Message to the

Senate, August 19, 1914, http://www.sagehistory.net/worldwar1/docs/
WWNeutral1914.htm (consulted September 20, 2009).

16. See Patrick Devlin (1975). What Wilson did not reveal was that the
Lusitania was carrying 1,248 cases of 3-inch shells, almost 5 million
rifle cartridges, and 2,000 cases of small arms ammunition, and that
her captain had been ordered to ram any submarine that surfaced
nearby. See Howard Zinn (2003), 362. German submarines had previously surfaced in order to permit some targeted ships to lower life-
boats and attempt to save their passengers. The new ramming orders
made this impractical.

17. H. C. Peterson (1939), 83. See also Patrick Devlin (1975), 193.

18. See Barbara Tuchman (1985).

19. "Our object . . . is to vindicate the principles of peace and justice in
the life of the world as against selfish and autocratic power and to set
up amongst the really free and self-governed peoples of the world
such a concert of purpose and of action as will henceforth ensure the
observance of those principles." Wilson's War Message to Congress,
April 2, 1917, http://wwi.lib.byu.edu/index.php/Wilson%27s_War_Mes
sage_to_Congress (consulted October 20, 2009).

20. Robert F. Lansing and Louis F. Post (1917), 6. See also Donald E.
Schmidt (2005), 63–68.

21. Franklin Delano Roosevelt, Fireside Chat 16, December 29, 1940,
http://www.mhric.org/fdr/chat16.html (consulted December 8, 2009).

22. Franklin Delano Roosevelt, Fireside Chat 17, May 27, 1941, http://
www.mhric.org/fdr/chat17.html (consulted December 8, 2009).

23. Patrick J. Buchanan (2008). A. J. P. Taylor (1996) made a similar argument about Hitler's ambitions. He did not maintain, as Buchanan
does, that the British could have avoided war with Germany simply
by refusing to guarantee Poland's independence prior to the German
invasion of 1939.

24. See Susan A. Brewer (2009), 104 et seq.

25. Henry Luce was the publisher of *Life*, *Time*, and *Fortune* magazines.
See, e.g., Harold Evans (2000), xiv.

26. The War on Terrorism, known as the Global War on Terror
(GWOT) during the administration of George W. Bush, was renamed
Global Counterinsurgency (GCOIN) by members of the Obama

administration. I use the term War on Terrorism for its simplicity and general acceptance.

27. The State Department list of terrorist organizations may be found at http://www.state.gov/s/ct/rls/other/des/123085.htm (periodically updated; consulted January 5, 2010). Organizations acting violently against U.S. citizens or installations include three al-Qaeda groups and a few others formerly involved in anti-U.S. activities (e.g., Hizballah, New People's Army, al-Shabaab).

28. See Michael W. Doyle (1986), David Harvey (2003), Robert Kagan (2003), Chalmers Johnson (2004a, 2004b), and William Appleman Williams (2006). Niall Ferguson, a conservative scholar, believes that the United States is "an empire . . . that dare not speak its name" (2004, 317; see also 2006). Michael Hardt and Antonio Negri (2001) contend that a globalized "Empire" has outgrown domination by any nation.

29. Authorization for Use of Military Force Against Terrorists, Pub. L. 107-40, 115 Stat. 224. The one "nay" vote in the House was cast by Representative Barbara Lee (D-Calif.).

30. George W. Bush, Speech before joint session of Congress, September 20, 2001, http://archives.cnn.com/2001/US/09/20/gen.bush.transcript/ (consulted June 17, 2009).

31. George W. Bush, Speech on board the carrier USS *Abraham Lincoln*, May 1, 2003, http://www.cnn.com/2003/US/05/01/bush.transcript/ (consulted June 17, 2009).

32. "On September 20, 2001, the Taliban offered to hand Osama bin Laden to a neutral Islamic country for trial if the US presented them with evidence that he was responsible for the attacks on New York and Washington. The US rejected the offer. On October 1, six days before the bombing began, they repeated it, and their representative in Pakistan told reporters: 'We are ready for negotiations. It is up to the other side to agree or not. Only negotiation will solve our problems.' Bush was asked about this offer at a press conference the following day. He replied: 'There's no negotiations. There's no calendar. We'll act on [sic] our time.'" George Monbiot, "Dreamers and Idiots," *Guardian*, November 11, 2003, http://www.guardian.co.uk/politics/2003/nov/11/afghanistan.iraq (consulted July 16, 2009). See also "Diplomats Met with Taliban on Bin Laden: Some Contend U.S. Missed Its Chance," *Washington Post*,

NOTES FOR PAGES 54–61

October 29, 2001, quoted in and linked to http://www.accuracy.org/ newsrelease.php?articleId=2136 (consulted September 12, 2009).

33. On international law regarding sanctuary, see Peter Weiss (2002). The United Nations refused to authorize the U.S./British invasion of Afghanistan in October 2001.

34. Quoted in Peter Baker, "Obama's War over Terror," *New York Times Magazine*, January 17, 2010, 37.

35. See, e.g., CNN/Opinion Research Poll, January 22–24, 2010, http:// www.pollingreport.com/afghan.htm (consulted February 28, 2010).

36. David Rodin (2002), 175.

37. See, e.g., Nic Robertson, "Sources: Taliban Split with al Qaeda, Seek Peace," CNN.com/Asia, http://edition.cnn.com/2008/WORLD/ asiapcf/10/06/afghan.saudi.talks/?iref=mpstoryview (consulted February 28, 2010).

38. "Remarks by the President at the Acceptance of the Nobel Peace Prize," December 10, 2009, http://www.whitehouse.gov/the-press -office/remarks-president-acceptance-nobel-peace-prize (consulted February 26, 2010).

39. On negotiating with terrorists, see I. William Zartman (2005) and Dean G. Pruitt (2007). And compare George J. Mitchell (2001) on negotiating with Catholic and Protestant paramilitary groups in Northern Ireland. See also Ronald J. Fisher (2005).

40. Tom Engelhardt (2007), 212–15. Engelhardt notes, with regard to the vast number of casualties caused by the Phoenix Program and other forms of mass killing, "It was a Vietnamese unwillingness to surrender in the face of a slaughter that only gained in statistical intensity that transformed the war story into a series of embarrassingly un-American-looking atrocities" (214–15). See also Douglas Valentine (2000).

41. Joseph Conrad (1899), chapter 2, p. 7.

CHAPTER 3: BEAT THE DEVIL:
HUMANITARIAN INTERVENTIONS AND MORAL CRUSADES

1. Cheney speech to the Veterans of Foreign Wars National Convention, August 26, 2002. Rumsfeld testimony before the House Armed Services Committee, September 10, 2002.

2. "Rice: Saddam is an 'Evil Man,'" *USA Today,* August 15, 2002, http://www.usatoday.com/news/world/2002-08-15-rice-saddam_x.htm (consulted August 17, 2009).

3. Clinton dispatched twenty-three U.S. Navy cruise missiles to destroy the Iraqi building. David Von Drehle and R. Jeffrey Smith, "U.S. Strikes Iraq for Plot to Kill Bush." *Washington Post,* June 27, 1993.

4. Max Boot, "Colonise Wayward Nations," *Australian,* October 15, 2001, 13. See also commentary by Nick Beams, "Behind the 'Anti-terrorism' Mask," World Socialist Web Site, http://www.wsws.org/articles/2001/oct2001/imp-o18.shtml (consulted August 17, 2009).

5. Richard Lowry, "End Iraq," *National Review,* October 15, 2001.

6. Zell Miller quoted in Walter Woods, "Miller Defends . . . Comment," *Atlanta Business Chronicle,* January 14, 2002.

7. Glenn Kessler, "Rice Lays Out Case for War in Iraq," *Washington Post,* August 16, 2002.

8. See David Morgan, "Ex-U.S. Official Says CIA Aided Baathists," Reuters, April 20, 2003, http://www.commondreams.org/headlines03/0420-05.htm (consulted July 12, 2009).

9. See Joyce Battle (2003) and the documents collected by the National Security Archive.

10. See "Iran-Contra Report; Arms, Hostages and Contras: How a Secret Foreign Policy Unraveled," *New York Times,* November 19, 1987.

11. Richard N. Haass (2009), 56.

12. See Kaleem Omar (2005) for a description of Glaspie's conversation about this with two British journalists.

13. Richard N. Haass (2009), 55. See also his statement that one fairly likely option was that Saddam would "grab a piece of Kuwait to trade for financial help" (57).

14. Roberta L. Coles (1998), 376. The "baby incubator" hoax was produced by the Washington, D.C., public relations firm Hill & Knowlton, which coached the daughter of a Kuwaiti emir to tell the story before a congressional subcommittee. See John R. MacArthur (1992), 54 et seq.

15. As the discussion in chapter 5, shows, I do not accept President Bush's expressed rationale for the Persian Gulf War. See also Roberta L. Coles (1998).

16. See Richard E. Rubenstein (1991).

17. Evil so defined represents a Protestant adaptation of Augustinian ethics. For the seventeenth-century Puritan leader Cotton Mather, New England's wars against the Indians were "one phase of the continuing war between Satan and Christ." Richard Slotkin (2000), 130.

18. Adam J. Berinsky (2009), 31.

19. See Kurt R. Spillman and Kati Spillman, "Some Sociobiological and Psychological Aspects of 'Images of the Enemy,'" in Ragnhild Fiebig–von Hase and Ursula Lehmkuhl (1997), 43–63. See also Vamik Volkan (1998).

20. I use the masculine pronoun because most of those depicted as Evil Enemies have been male. This is not to say that, under certain circumstances, they might not be female. The Spanish considered Queen Elizabeth I of England diabolical, the British demonized Joan of Arc, and World War II gave us villains such as the Japanese propagandist "Tokyo Rose" and Ilse Koch, the "Bitch of Buchenwald."

21. See Jürgen Heideking, "The Image of an English Enemy During the American Revolution," in Ragnhild Fiebig–von Hase and Ursula Lehmkuhl (1997), 95–100. See also the figure of the villainous Colonel William Tavington in Roland Emmerich's 2000 film *The Patriot*, starring Mel Gibson.

22. Sacvan Bercovitch (1978), 119.

23. On redemptive violence in the Civil War, see James M. McPherson (1998, 2003). On the same theme in World War I, see Richard M. Gamble (2003), 182 et seq. On World War II, see Susan A. Brewer (2009), 87–88, pointing out that the promises of national redemption made in that war were somewhat more moderate than those made in World War I, in part because of the disillusionment that followed the latter.

24. Samuel Winch (2004), 18.

25. Richard Slotkin (2000), 94–115, passim.

26. See Deborah E. Lipstadt (1993).

27. See John W. Dower (1987).

28. Robert F. Lansing and Louis F. Post (1917). Lansing lamented "that the promises to refrain from brutal submarine warfare, which Germany had made to the United States, were never intended to be kept,

that they were only made in order to gain time in which to build more submarines, and that when the time came to act the German promises were unhesitatingly torn to pieces like other 'scraps of paper.'" This breach of faith revealed the evil character of the German government, "which is the underlying cause of our entry into the war" (4). (The reference to "scraps of paper" was a passing shot at Kaiser Wilhelm II, who was said to have called Germany's treaty of peace with Belgium a mere scrap of paper.)

29. See Michael H. Hunt (1987), 46–91, including cartoons picturing Cubans and Filipinos as stereotypical Negroes. On anti-Japanese stereotypes in the Pacific War, see John W. Dower's invaluable 1987 study. On the persistence of "color-blind" racism in American culture, see Eduardo Bonilla-Silva (2009).

30. "I know of no country in which there is so little independence of mind and real freedom of discussion as in America." Alexis de Tocqueville (1863), book 1, chapter 15.

31. See, e.g., Susan A. Brewer (2009), 106–7: "Up to the spring of 1944, 65 percent of Americans continued to believe that the German people wanted to be free of their leaders; only 13 percent thought the Japanese wanted to be free of theirs. American attitudes about the Germans as victims of Nazi rule changed when German soldiers killed tens of thousands of GIs following the D-Day invasion of France in June 1944."

32. John Morton Blum (1976), 52 et seq.

33. See Greg Robinson (2009).

34. Adam Quinn (2008), 22. Quinn concludes, "The 'national interest' is not, and cannot be, a decisive or objective factor in determining policy. Rather it is a conceptual battleground on which divergent ideologies meet to dispute their irreconcilable normative and empirical claims."

35. There is a large literature on just-war doctrine. Andrew Fiala (2008) concludes that the possibilities of a war being just under present-day conditions are minimal. Michael Walzer (2006a, 2006b) disagrees. On the considerable impact of just-war theory on U.S. military interventions, see Michael J. Butler (2003).

36. Quoted in Donald E. Schmidt (2005), 40–41.

37. Fred Anderson and Andrew Cayton (2005), 335.

38. Ibid., 336.

39. Ibid., 338. See also Joseph R. Stromberg, "The Spanish-American War as Trial Run, or Empire as Its Own Justification," in John V. Denson (1999), 189. As in the case of Vietnam, there is continuing debate about the justification for this war and its methods. Compare Stuart Creighton Miller's critical view (1984) with Brian McAllister Linn's more pro-U.S. account (2002).

40. Howard Zinn (2003), 511, 515.

41. Mark Twain (1901), 117b.

42. Stephen Kinzer (2007), 9–30.

43. See Howard H. Quint (1958).

44. This idea was inspired by Christopher Collins's excellent *Homeland Mythology: Biblical Narratives in American Culture* (2007), which discusses the importance of the Exodus story (among other biblical stories) in modern American thinking. See also Richard T. Hughes (2003), 19–34; George McKenna (2007), 16–43; and Bruce Feiler (2009). On the importance of the Exodus story to African American thought and northern Civil War ideology, see Eddie S. Glaude Jr. (2000).

45. See the funeral oration by Rev. George James Jones delivered September 19, 1901, at C. M. Church in Oak Hill, Ohio, http://mckinleydeath .com/documents/magazines/Cambrian21-10a.htm (consulted January 5, 2010).

46. "Can we leave these people, who, by the fortunes of war and our own acts, are helpless and without government, to chaos and anarchy, after we have destroyed the only government they have had?" asked McKinley rhetorically. Quoted in Susan A. Brewer (2009), 28–30.

47. John L. Offner (1992), 150–58; H. W. Brands (1992), 48.

48. Mark Twain (1901), 115.

49. Donald E. Schmidt (2005), 206.

50. Compare, for example, the views of William Appleman Williams (1972) and Joyce and Gabriel Kolko (1972) with those of Daniel Yergin (1978) and John Lewis Gaddis (2000).

51. Eugene Jarecki (2008), 77.

52. Quoted in Susan A. Brewer (2009), 146.

53. See Hannah Arendt (2004).

54. "There were 17 million military deaths in the European war; 16 million of those deaths were in the Eastern Front. Of those 17 million deaths, 13 million were Russian. Slightly more than one million deaths on both sides occurred in all other fronts—Africa, Italy, and France." Donald E. Schmidt (2005), 228.

55. Andre Geromylatos (2004). The Greek rebels obtained limited support from Marshal Tito's Yugoslav regime, but that soon ended as well.

56. Walter LaFeber (2006), 53–54.

57. David Horowitz (1969), 11.

58. Tom Engelhardt (2007), 54–65, believes that popular disenchantment over Korea marked the beginning of the end of "American victory culture."

59. They may have been encouraged in this decision by a controversial speech by Secretary of State Dean Acheson, in which he excluded South Korea from the U.S. "defense perimeter" in Asia. See Bruce Cumings (1990). See also David Halberstam (2007), 48 et seq.

60. Donald E. Schmidt (2005), 247.

61. See, e.g., Stephen Kinzer (2007) and Richard J. Barnet (1968).

62. This view was defended by Whittaker Chambers in his memoir, *Witness* (1987).

63. See esp. *The Spy Who Came in from the Cold* (1963), *The Looking Glass War* (1965), *A Small Town in Germany* (1968), *The Honourable Schoolboy* (1977), and *The Perfect Spy* (1986).

64. For the colonial and Revolutionary periods, see Perry Miller (1956) and Sacvan Bercovitch (1978). On the Civil War as a Holy War, see George McKenna (2007), 128–63.

65. See Richard M. Gamble (2003), Jonathan M. Hansen (2003), Walter Karp (2003), and Michael S. Foley and Brendan P. O'Malley (2008), 81–118.

66. See Eric L. Muller (2007) and Susan A. Brewer (2009), 104–22.

67. See David Caute (1978) and Ellen Schrecker (1998) for comprehensive critical views of the phenomenon considered primarily as a "Red Scare." For a perspective stressing the extent of Soviet espionage, see Allen Weinstein and Alexander Vassiliev (2000), whose study is largely based on the Venona papers.

68. In 1919–1920, Woodrow Wilson's attorney general A. Mitchell Palmer supervised the first American "Red Scare," resulting in the arrest and

deportation of more than four thousand radical aliens. See, e.g., Howard Zinn (2003), 375–76.

69. See Victor S. Navasky (2003).

70. "We are dealing," Billy Graham (1999), 382; "Either communism must die" (1954), Graham quoted in Thomas Aiello (2005).

71. "The House I Live In" was a 1945 short film written by Albert Maltz, produced by Frank Ross, and starring Frank Sinatra. Sinatra sings the title song, opposing anti-Semitism and racial prejudice, to a group of boys who were about to beat up a kid because "we don't like his religion." The film received a special Academy Award in 1946. Maltz and composer Earl Robinson were blacklisted during the Red Scare. See http://www.archive.org/details/THE_HOUSE_I_LIVE_IN (consulted March 3, 2010).

72. See Nelson Blackstock (1988).

73. A *Washington Post*–ABC News poll of 2006 found that "a growing proportion of Americans are expressing unfavorable views of Islam, and a majority now say that Muslims are disproportionately prone to violence . . . The poll found that nearly half of Americans—46 percent—have a negative view of Islam, seven percentage points higher than in the tense months after the Sept. 11, 2001, attacks on the World Trade Center and the Pentagon, when Muslims were often targeted for violence." Claudia Deane and Darryl Fears, "Negative Perception of Islam Increasing," *Washington Post*, March 9, 2006.

74. As this volume went to press, the U.S. was continuing the "rendition" of accused terrorists to allied nations that practice torture.

CHAPTER 4: "LOVE IT OR LEAVE IT": PATRIOTS AND DISSENTERS

1. Thoughtful analyses of American patriotism include Robert N. Bellah (1975), Frederick Edwords (1987), Jonathan M. Hansen (2003), Richard T. Hughes (2003), Stephen Nathanson (2003), George McKenna (2007), and William E. Connolly (2008).

2. The theory of moral disengagement is especially associated with the social learning theory of Albert Bandura. See Bandura (2004) and Alfred L. McAlister (2000, 2001).

3. On good and bad patriotism, see Robert N. Bellah (1967, 1975). Michael Angrosino's interesting survey (2002) discusses three types of civil religion: "cultural," "nationalist," and "universal," each with its own form of patriotism. The "My country . . ." quotation is from a toast made in 1805 by Captain Stephen Decatur: "In matters of foreign affairs, my country may she ever be right, but right or wrong, my country, my country." John Davis Collins explains that the toast was offered in response to Thomas Jefferson's concluding a peace treaty with Tripoli that many people considered dishonorable. See "My Country, My Country," http://www.angelfire.com/bc/RPPS/revolu tion_movies/decatur.htm (consulted January 18, 2009).

4. See Stephen Nathanson (2003). See also Igor Primoratz and Aleksandar Pavković (2008), an important edited volume containing essays by Nathanson and others.

5. Walter Scott (1805).

6. Edward Everett Hale (1917/1863).

7. Drew Gilpin Faust (2008), xvi–xvii, discusses the impact of war photographs on the nation's consciousness. See also her study of casualty lists and other sources of war news at 14–17, passim.

8. In 1864, Lincoln won reelection against the Democratic candidate, former commanding general George B. McClellan, by a large electoral majority, but by only four hundred thousand votes out of four million cast, with the southern states not voting, and Union soldiers given leave to return home to vote.

9. See Drew Gilpin Faust (1990) and William R. Taylor (1993).

10. For discussion of the personal/political identity crisis, see Erik H. Erikson (1994).

11. Benedict Anderson (2006), 6–7.

12. Campbell J. Gibson and Emily Lennon (1999). See the full analysis of immigration numbers and trends in Roger Daniels (2002), 123 et seq. On the impact of immigration on American thought in the era of World War I, see John Higham (2002), 194–263.

13. Many of these struggles are described by John Higham in his classic Strangers in the Land (2002). For labor struggles, see Louis Adamic (2008).

14. Israel Zangwill (2009/1908).

15. See Sharon Smith (2006).

16. See, e.g., Barton J. Bernstein (1968).

17. See, e.g., Clayton R. Koppes and Gregory D. Black (1990), 222 et seq.

18. See Robert A. Wells (2005).

19. When a group of Trotskyist leaders insisted on agitating for strikes and advocating a workers' state, they—not American Nazis—became the first people prosecuted and jailed for subversion under the Smith Act. See James P. Cannon (1975).

20. On the racial, political, and cultural movements of the era, see National Advisory Commission on Civil Disorders (1968), National Commission on the Causes and Prevention of Violence (1970), Todd Gitlin (1993), and Kenneth Keniston (1967, 1968).

21. David Bailey (2008). Bailey also notes that the redemption was "incomplete," as evidenced by Bush's unwillingness to run the risks of another Vietnam-style conflict in Iraq.

22. Samuel P. Huntington (1998). For debate about Huntington's advocacy of the U.S. strategy to depopulate the Vietnamese countryside, see Noam Chomsky (1970) and Samuel P. Huntington (1970). See also remarks of Huntington and Eqbal Ahmad in Richard M. Pfeffer (1969).

23. Huntington labeled Russia and the Balkan nations "Orthodox," India "Buddhist," China "Confucianist," and so on. (In his 1998 book, he also used the more neutral word "Sinic" to describe Chinese civilization.) For critical discussion of this and other aspects of the theory, see Richard E. Rubenstein and Jarle P. Crocker (1994).

24. See James Davison Hunter (1992).

25. An interesting current Web site often reflecting "Whig" views is http://www.antiwar.com.

26. John B. Hoey (2000). See also Donald R. Hickey (2006), 255.

27. Daniel Walker Howe (2007), 743.

28. Michael H. Hunt (1987), 38–41; Michael S. Foley and Brendan P. O'Malley (2008), 18–38.

29. The treaty of annexation passed by just one vote more than the necessary two thirds. Michael H. Hunt (1987), 81–90.

30. See James M. McPherson (2003).

31. See Jennifer L. Weber (2008).

32. See Iver Bernstein (1990).

33. Howard Zinn (2003), 364. See also 365–76.

34. On the CPI and APL, see Susan A. Brewer (2009), 55–77.

35. The movie, directed by Lewis Milestone, was based on Erich Maria Remarque's bestselling novel of the same title, published in 1929.

36. For leftist elements in the 1930s anti-war movement, see Charles Chatfield (1992), 62–73. Discussion of the AFC and Roosevelt's attacks on it have again become heated since the publication of Patrick J. Buchanan's book *Churchill, Hitler, and "the Unnecessary War"* (2008), in which Buchanan repeats Lindbergh's contention (made in Des Moines as a prediction) that America's entry into the war condemned the Jews of Europe to die in the Holocaust. For a more measured but pro-AFC perspective, see Wayne S. Cole (1974). Lindbergh's pro-Nazi and anti-Semitic leanings are discussed at length in Max Wallace (2004). See also A. Scott Berg (1999) and Philip Roth's extraordinary historical fantasy *The Plot Against America* (Vintage, 2005).

37. Howard Zinn (2003), 407, 418.

38. Tom Engelhardt (2007), 64. See also 64–65: "By February 1951, eight months into the conflict, only 39 percent of Americans polled supported the war effort—and the figure kept dropping."

39. Ibid., 247–48: "Drug taking was rampant (by 1971, up to 60 percent of returning soldiers admitted to some sort of use); desertions stood at seventy per thousand, a modern high; small-scale mutinies or 'combat refusals' were at critical, if untabulated, levels; incidents of racial conflict had soared, and strife between officers ('lifers') and men was at unprecedented levels."

40. Ibid., 244.

41. See Adam Garfinkle (1997).

42. William L. Lunch and Peter W. Sperlich (1979), 32–34.

43. Ibid., 39 et seq. Lunch and Sperlich identify "middle-class" Americans as being more pro-war than "lower-class," but it is not clear where in this classification blue-collar workers belong. See also Frank Koscielski (1999).

44. See, e.g., Todd Gitlin (1993) and Kenneth Keniston (1967, 1968).

45. According to the U.S. Department of Education's Digest of Education Statisics, the college population quadrupled between 1950 and 1970 and sextupled between 1950 and 1980. "How Educated Are We:

Data Presentation," http://social.jrank.org/pages/1024/How-Educated -are-We-Data-Presentation.html (consulted January 30, 2010).

46. Congressman Charles Rangel (D-N.Y.) introduced a bill to restore the draft on February 14, 2006. "Rangel Reintroduces Draft Bill," http://www.house.gov/list/press/ny15_rangel/CBRStatementon Draft02142006.html (consulted February 2, 2010).

CHAPTER 5: WAR AS A LAST RESORT? PEACE PROCESSES AND NATIONAL HONOR

1. "The Ballad of High Noon" (1952), music by Dimitri Tiomkin, lyrics by Ned Washington, sung in the film by Tex Ritter.

2. National Commission on Terrorist Attacks upon the United States (2004), 239.

3. Richard Slotkin (2000), 18.

4. See the discussion in John Lewis Gaddis (2004), 7 et seq.

5. Harris Poll #81, August 15, 2007, http://www.harrisinteractive.com/ harris_poll/index.asp?PID=797 (consulted February 6, 2009).

6. Quoted in Susan A. Brewer (2009), 152. Brewer notes that "the role of the United States was identified rather modestly as 'a strong member of the U.N. sheriff's posse.'"

7. Kissinger later termed this interview "the single most disastrous conversation I have ever had with any member of the press." See Adam Bernstein, Oriana Fallaci obituary, *Washington Post*, September 16, 2006, http://www.washingtonpost.com/wp-dyn/content/article/2006/ 09/15/AR2006091501145_pf.html (consulted February 2, 2009).

8. Zuckerman on *Lou Dobbs Tonight*, September 11, 2003, CNN Transcripts. http://transcripts.cnn.com/TRANSCRIPTS/0309/11/ldt.00 .html (consulted February 5, 2010).

9. "War," in *Stanford Encyclopedia of Philosophy*, http://plato.stanford.edu/ entries/war/ (consulted October 26, 2009). See also Rob van den Toorn, "Just War and the Perspective of Ethics of Care," in Robinson (2003), 222–25.

10. A leading historian remarks on the differences between Polk's approach to negotiating with the British for purchase of the Oregon Territory and his dealings with the Mexicans. "On Oregon, he wished

to appear uncompromising but achieve a compromise. Regarding the issues with Mexico, however, he wished to seem reasonable and open to discussion while pressing uncompromising demands that would probably lead to war." Daniel Walker Howe (2007), 735; and see 734–38 for further discussion.

11. These negotiations are discussed at length in John L. Offner (1992). The author's overall conclusion that a negotiated solution was impossible should be read in light of the evidence that he presents that McKinley could not have reached agreement with the Spanish and also won reelection.

12. George Monbiot, "Dreamers and Idiots," *Guardian*, November 11, 2003. http://www.monbiot.com/archives/2003/11/11/dreamers-and -idiots/ (consulted December 3, 2009).

13. See the discussion on pages 64–66.

14. The panelists were Eugene Carroll, Muhammad Faour, Abdeen Jabara, and Harold H. Saunders. http://www.c-spanvideo.org/program/ 17513-1 (consulted October 30, 2009).

15. Douglas Kellner (1992). See also Robert A. Pape (1996), 217, and William O. Beeman (2005).

16. This message comes through loud and clear in Richard Haass's recent book about the two wars against Iraq, *War of Necessity, War of Choice* (2009). Haass, who helped manage the Persian Gulf War, states that the Saudis insisted on "destroying enough of Saddam's war-making machine so that they wouldn't have to continue to live in fear and in Saddam's shadow" (79). He notes that Israel had the identical concern (86) and admits that members of the administration were worried about what would happen "if Saddam actually complied with what was being demanded of him" (84). Haass also states that the administration had "no interest" in any compromise that King Hussein ("a major disappointment throughout this crisis") had to propose, since the United States would accept nothing other than immediate Iraqi withdrawal from Kuwait. He recalls sending a cable to Secretary of State James Baker before his meeting with Saddam Hussein emphasizing "that Saddam should not be given rewards or face-savers in exchange for complying with Security Council demands" (108). He does not mention other peacemaking efforts or discuss the last-ditch Iraqi offers to withdraw at all.

17. Department of Defense News Briefing, Donald Rumsfeld, March 20, 2003, http://www.defense.gov/transcripts/transcript.aspx?transcriptid =2072 (consulted February 8, 2009).

18. The bill passed in the House by a vote of 296–133 and passed the Senate by a vote of 77–23. It was signed into law as Pub.L. 107–243 by President Bush on October 16, 2002. See also the discussion in George Packer (2006).

19. Julian Borger, Brian Whitaker, and Vikram Dodd, "Saddam's Desperate Offers to Stave Off War," *Guardian*, November 7, 2003, http://www .guardian.co.uk/world/2003/nov/07/iraq.brianwhitaker (consulted January 7, 2010).

20. James Risen, "Iraq Said to Have Tried to Reach Last-Minute Deal to Avert War," *New York Times*, November 6, 2003, http://www.nytimes .com/2003/11/06/politics/06INTE.html?pagewanted=1 (consulted January 7, 2010).

21. See the detailed discussion of these negotiations in John L. Offner (1992), esp. at 143–93 and 225–36.

22. In 1899, U.S. military officials refused to let the Cuban liberation army participate in "independence" celebrations. When military occupation ended, Congress passed the Platt Amendment (1901), which deprived Cuba of control over its own territory, foreign policy, and finances. See Stephen Kinzer (2007), 35–44.

23. Michael Cox (1990), 31. Cox's basic point is that maintenance of the Cold War "system" served the interests of elites on both sides.

24. Ibid., 35. For an insider account of Reagan's relationship with Mikhail Gorbachev, see Jack F. Matlock Jr. (2005).

25. See Bruce Cumings (1990), 557–59.

26. See the essays collected in Lloyd C. Gardner and Ted Gittinger (2004), esp. David Kaiser's "Discussions, Not Negotiations: The Johnson Administration's Diplomacy at the Outset of the Vietnam War," 45–58.

27. There is a large literature on the Cuban Missile Crisis. It is worth contrasting the more conventional approach to the crisis (e.g., Michael Dobbs [2009]) with approaches emphasizing the importance of conflict management techniques (e.g., Richard Ned Lebow and Janice Gross Stein [1995]). See also Laurence Chang and Peter Kornbluh (1998) and Ernest R. May and Philip D. Zelikow (2002).

28. See James Bamford (2001), chapter 4.

29. Several examples are discussed in William R. Polk (2007).

30. For histories of conflict resolution efforts and introductions to the field, see John W. Burton (1990, 1996), Johan Galtung (2004), Ho-Won Jeong (2008), Louis Kriesberg (2006), John Paul Lederach (1998), Terrence Lyons and Gilbert M. Khadiagala (2008), Dean G. Pruitt and Sung Hee Kim (2004), Oliver Ramsbotham et al. (2005), and Harold H. Saunders (2001). See also Sandra Cheldelin et al. (2008) and Dennis J. D. Sandole et al. (2009).

31. See Joseph V. Montville (1991). Louise Diamond and Ambassador John McDonald (1996) have identified fourteen "tracks" or methods of peacemaking in addition to formal diplomacy.

32. See William B. Quandt (1986).

33. Mitchell describes his experience at length in George J. Mitchell (2001).

34. See the discussion of the Northern Ireland and South African workshops in Ronald J. Fisher (2005).

35. For the Office of Conflict Management and Mitigation, see http://www.usaid.gov/our_work/cross-cutting_programs/conflict/ (consulted February 11, 2010). For the Office of the Coordinator for Reconstruction and Stabilization, see http://www.state.gov/s/crs/ (consulted February 11, 2010). For the United States Institute of Peace, see http://www.usip.org/ (consulted February 11, 2010).

Concluding Note: Five Ways to Think More Clearly About War

1. Quoted in Donald E. Schmidt (2005), 40–41; discussed on pages 76–77.

2. U.S. Congress. *Congressional Record.* 56th Cong., 1st sess., 1900. Vol. 33, 711.

3. See Joseph S. Nye (2005) and further discussion of "soft power" issues in Felix Berenskoetter and Michael J. Williams (2008).

4. See I. William Zartman (2008), 232 et seq., and compare Dean G. Pruitt (2005).

5. Michael B. Mukasey, "Where the U.S. Went Wrong on Abdulmutallab," *Washington Post*, February 12, 2010.

6. See, for example, I. William Zartman (2005) and Dean G. Pruitt (2007).

7. Ted Robert Gurr (1996).

8. See the description at http://www.dynamicsofconflict.iccc.edu.pl/index.php?page=engaging-governments-on-genocide-prevention-eggp (consulted February 13, 2010).

9. The War Resisters League points out that if expenses of past wars (veterans' benefits, interest on the national debt attributable to wars, etc.) are included, the percentage of the total budget devoted to war goes over 50 percent. http://www.warresisters.org/pages/piechart.htm (consulted February 14, 2010).

10. For studies of the U.S. "military-industrial complex" and its effects, see Seymour Melman (1970), William Grieder (1999), Chalmers Johnson (2008), and Eugene Jarecki (2008).

11. Dexter Filkins (2009). On military Keynesianism, see Noam Chomsky (1993).

12. But see Lloyd J. Dumas (1995).

13. See, e.g., Christopher Gelpi et al. (2005). Compare the critique of the "casualty hypothesis" in Adam J. Berinsky (2009).

INDEX

Page numbers in *italics* denote illustrations or captions.

Germany
  atrocities in Belgium, 7–8, 70,
    201n15
  bombings of, 50, 74
  Nazi, 8–10, 40, 46, 48–49, 74,
    81, 83, 117, 133–34, 210n31
  sinking of *Lusitania*, 41, 42,
    205n16
  World War I, 7, 8, 30, 40, 43,
    44, 45, 46
  See also Hitler, Adolf
Girls Say Yes to Boys Who Say No
  (poster), *121*
Glaspie, April, 64
Global Counterinsurgency
  (GCOIN), 159, 205n26.
    See also War on Terrorism
global economy, 90
global empire, U.S.
  Adams-Onis treaty as first step
    toward, 35
  and Cold War, 82, 83–84, 145
  as conflict resolution obstacle,
    155–56
  designation as, 2, 53–54, 206n28
  and moral crusades, 165–66
  as self-defense obstacle, 161–62
  and self-defense transformation,
    52, 53–54
  and superpower status, 136,
    158–60
Gompers, Samuel, 113, 116
Good Friday Agreement, 152
Gorbachev, Mikhail, 139
Graham, Billy, 89, 90, 105, 213n70
Grant, Ulysses S., 6

Great Britain
  arming of Native Americans, 32,
    203n2, 204n5
  blockade of civilian goods, 41,
    43, 44
  Munich Pact, 22, 72, 133–34
  Northern Ireland struggle,
    151–52
  Scots-Irish frontier heritage, 15
  subjects executed, 34, 35, 204n5
  War of 1812, 1, 111
  World War I, 8, 30, 40, 42, 43,
    44, 46
  World War II, 47, 117
Great Depression, 46, 79, 90, 101
Greece, 84, 85, 212n55
Guantanamo Bay, 92
Gulf War. *See* Persian Gulf War
Gurr, Ted Robert, 166

Haass, Richard, 64, 208n13, 218n16
Hair, 123
Hale, Edward Everett, 96–98
Hardt, Michael, 206n28
hatred of United States, xii
Heart of Darkness (Conrad), 58–59
High Noon, 128–32, 136
Hiroshima and Nagasaki, destruc-
  tion in, 50, 74
Hiss, Alger, 88
Hitler, Adolf
  ambitions of, 48, 205n23
  as Evil Enemy, 66, 69, 85
  and Holocaust, 70
  and Munich Pact, 22, 72,
    133–34, 142–43